A Modest Proposal
and Other Satires

A Modest Proposal and Other Satires

Jonathan Swift

With an Introduction by George R. Levine

LITERARY CLASSICS

Prometheus Books

59 John Glenn Drive
Amherst, New York 14228-2197

Published 1995 by Prometheus Books
59 John Glenn Drive, Amherst, New York 14228–2197.
VOICE: 716–691–0133, ext. 207. FAX: 716–564–2711.
WWW.PROMETHEUSBOOKS.COM

Library of Congress Cataloging-in-Publication Data

Swift, Jonathan, 1667–1745.
    A modest proposal, and other satires / Jonathan Swift ; with an
introduction by George R. Levine.
        p.   cm. — (Literary classics)
    Includes bibliographical references.
    ISBN 0–87975–919–4 (paper : acid-free paper)
    1. Ireland—Politics and government—18th century—Humor.
2. Religious satire, English. 3. Political satire, English. I. Levine,
George R. II. Title. III. Series.
PR3722   1994
828'.507—dc20   94–24670
                                                            CIP

Printed in the United States of America on acid-free paper

Literary Classics Series

Contents

Introduction

SWIFT'S WORLD

Jonathan Swift, Doctor of Divinity, Dean of St. Patrick's Cathedral, Dublin, was anything but a cloistered cleric, content to quietly count his beads and say his prayers. Quite the contrary. Here was a man immersed in the secular world of men and women, of politics and political intrigue, of wars, of coffee-houses and practical jokes. Here was a man who was as devoted a friend to those he loved as he was a fearless and implacable enemy toward those he disliked.

Swift's world—England and Ireland in the first half of the eighteenth century—resembled our modern twentieth-century world in many respects. It saw the growth of the mercantile middle classes and the emergence of cities as large commercial centers. There were fierce religious antagonisms and there was grinding poverty among those eking out an existence at the very lowest level of the social scale; profligacy and extravagance among those fortunate enough to find themselves at the top. People won and lost on the stock market. There was even a stock market scandal (the South-Sea Bubble, as it was called) which ruined thousands of greedy investors and almost brought down the government in 1720. Among all levels of society, alcoholism, gambling, and violence were serious problems that ate away at the foundations of society. There were occasional riots by the poor, the homeless and the dispossessed for whom looting was simply an opportunity to put off the pangs of hunger and material deprivation. In an attempt to limit this potential for mob violence, strict laws were passed by a frightened government. But there were also people who tried to cope with social problems by other means—through philanthropy or religion or changes in the legal system.

In these and other ways, Swift's world would have looked familiar to us today, but there were also significant differences. To fully understand Swift's work, it is important to see what some of those differences were and how they helped shape the various pieces contained in this collection.

In the early eighteenth century, literature was a vehicle for public, not private, discourse. As such, it was expected to conform to the conventions of public behavior, the most important of which was the need to keep the public self distinct from the private. Obviously, Swift and his contemporaries found occasion to write also about personal matters, but not usually for publication or broad circulation. Personal expression was generally confined to letters or journals, sometimes sent in installments to friends. Swift's famous *Journal to Stella*, for example, was in effect a diary of Swift's London experiences between 1710 and 1713, sent as letters to Esther Johnson and Rebecca Dingley and published by others only after his death.

Modern readers may sometimes find it difficult to adjust to the impersonality of eighteenth-century literature, perhaps because our expectations are still under the influence of Romantic preconceptions about the nature of literature. Romantic writing tended to be introspective, highly personal. The reader of such lines as Shelley's dramatic "I fall upon the thorns of life, I die, I bleed" becomes, at the most intimate of moments, almost an eavesdropper. It was Lady Mary Wortley Montagu who epitomized the eighteenth-century aesthetic by observing that "fig-leaves are as necessary for our minds as our bodies."[1]

---

1. Cited in Ian Watt, *The Rise of the Novel* (Berkeley and Los Angeles: University of California Press, 1962), p. 272.

Swift's prose was also shaped by other factors. Its rhetorical emphasis was in part a reflection of the growth of periodicals and the appetite among the reading public for the kinds of literature that flourished in periodicals—everything from the brief essay on a topic of general interest to short pieces of fiction to poems to book reviews to light satirical pieces, such as the essay on the art of political lying that Swift contributed to the *London Examiner* in 1710. The first two decades of the eighteenth century saw the emergence of a number of newspapers, led by Richard Steele's *The Tatler* and then Joseph Addison's and Steele's *The Spectator*. Coffee houses in London and elsewhere quickly learned that they could attract patrons by subscribing to these periodicals, and this helped stimulate the popularity of periodical literature in the early eighteenth century.

As periodicals multiplied, so did the demand for writers who could write for them. It is not coincidental that some of the best writers of the age were, like Swift, skilled journalists. Swift contributed to *The Tatler* and *The Spectator* and wrote all of *The Examiner* papers. Alexander Pope contributed to *The Spectator* as did Lady Mary Wortley Montagu, and Pope and John Gay of *Beggar's Opera* fame wrote essays for *The Guardian*.

This proliferation of journals and talented journalists coincided with the emergence of political journalism, especially during that brief period of Tory ascendancy between 1710 and 1714. With some notable exceptions, the best writers of the age, like Swift, were in the employ of the new Tory government. It was at this time that journalism came into its own as a political tool. Shrewd politicians, like Tories Robert Harley, Earl of Oxford, and Henry St. John, Viscount Bolingbroke, and even their Whig successor, Sir Robert Walpole, recognized early on that with the growth and popularity of periodicals, more people could be reached and influenced than ever before. During this time, Swift learned about the power of the press and honed his skills as a political journalist. His later great polemics against English exploitation of Ireland undoubtedly owed much to those days as a London journalist.

There was, however, more to this relationship between Swift and the London periodicals than the journalistic opportunity it gave him. It was really a reciprocal relationship in which Swift contributed as much as he received. When Steele began *The Tatler* in 1709, for example, he took as a pseudonym, Isaac Bickerstaff, Esq., one that Swift himself had made famous in a series of satirical pamphlets he published in 1708–09 ridiculing an astrological quack who had assumed the name of John Partridge. So popular had Swift's pamphlets become that the mere appearance of Isaac Bickerstaff on the masthead of *The Tatler* was a guarantee that the new journal would attract attention and subscribers.

Although literary historians may disagree over how best to define this age, there is one thing that should be obvious to anyone looking at the best literature that Swift and his contemporaries produced—the dominance of satire as a literary form.

Understandably, it is satire that creates the most difficulty for a modern reader. Apart from the political cartoon and the rare presence of a political satirist like Mort Sahl of the 1960s or Mark Russell today, satire has all but disappeared from contemporary discourse. Eighteenth-century satire is also somewhat alien because we are no longer familiar with the historical particulars that gave impetus to the original satire. Even when we are provided with explanatory notes, it is difficult to recapture today the pleasure Swift's ridicule brought to his audience. This is, of course, the problem that all satire faces—the risk of ephemerality.

Yet, as we know, many satires have survived through the centuries, especially Swift's. *Gulliver's Travels, A Tale of a Tub,* and *A Modest Proposal* have become the very touchstones for great satire. What enables such satires to rise above the merely topical? Why do they touch us even when we are ignorant of the historical particulars that prompted them? Perhaps it is because we respond to these works primarily as great literature, quite apart from the satire. What continues to draw us is the power of Swift's vision, the sophistication of his prose, the universality of his comic portraits, the precision of his language—especially his mastery of irony—and his skill in creating and sustaining the personalities of his narrative spokesmen. At the same time, it is essential to recognize that these factors are not always easily separated from his satire. Satire has always had its own unique—some have said, magical—appeal.

In speaking of the universal appeal of Swift's best satires, I am not, of course, suggesting that we limit our responses simply to what is recognizable today. While some readers may not wish to go beyond that, others may find their understanding enhanced by learning more about what Swift and his contemporaries had in mind when those satires first appeared.

Swift's satire is especially difficult for a modern reader because it is not always easy to distinguish Swift's own voice from that of the narrator. The two voices don't always coincide. This difficulty doesn't exist in *Gulliver's Travels* because Swift creates as his narrator a man who is a dramatic character in his own right. But a work like *An Argument Against Abolishing Christianity* can be confusing because of Swift's love of toying with the reader by engaging in deliberate misdirection. To the careless reader, the *Argument* can *appear* to be a plea for little more than token adherence to the superficial forms of Christianity. To the careful reader, Swift is saying nothing of the sort; but to dig out his real meaning takes work. Understanding Swift's satire—or any satire, for that matter—requires more than a passive reading.

Finally, it is important that we try to understand what satire meant to Swift and those of his age who practiced the art—John Dryden, Alexander Pope, John Gay, and Henry Fielding among others. To these men, satire was more than simply attack, ridicule, a convenient tool for heaping scorn upon those whom one disliked. Satire was not simply negative—although it did have an element of negation in it. To a Dryden, a Pope, or a Swift, the satirist's was a noble calling. He was someone who attempted to respond constructively to the follies and vices of a fallible world. He was someone whose views were sometimes even visionary. As Fielding noted, "the satirist is to be regarded as our physician, not our enemy." George Bernard Shaw went beyond Fielding in insisting that upon the satirist depends "the salvation of the world." Swift, I suspect, would have winced at Shaw's hyperbolic association of the satirist and salvation, but he nevertheless would have sympathized with Shaw's intentions. In a periodical essay in *The Intelligencer* in 1728, Swift characterized satire and satire in this way:

> There are two ends that men propose in writing satire; one of them less noble than the other, as regarding nothing farther than the private satisfaction and pleasure of the writer; but without any view toward personal malice; the other is a public spirit, prompting men of genius and virtue to mend the world so far as they are able. As both of these ends are innocent, so the latter is highly commendable.[1]

SWIFT THE MAN

Jonathan Swift was surely one of the most fascinating and enigmatic figures of the early eighteenth century. He numbered among his close friends some of the most distinguished and powerful men of the age. He became the government's chief propagandist between 1710 and 1714. Yet he spent the major part of his life in what he himself characterized as exile in Ireland, away from those friends and away from the stimulation of London. For thirty years, he was a Church of England cleric—ultimately Dean of St. Patrick's Cathedral, Dublin, but he never considered the church a refuge from life. Until he was almost seventy and seriously ill, Swift remained totally immersed in the political, philosophical, and religious issues of his day.

---

1. Number III, in *The Prose Works of Jonathan Swift*, ed. Herbert Davis et al. (Oxford: Basil Blackwell, 1939-68), XII, 34.

Although he was of English heritage, he became the great champion of the Irish against the oppressive control of the English and a hero to the Irish even today.

We know little about Swift's early years other than the fact that he was born in Dublin in 1667 of English parents and educated at Kilkenny Grammar School and at Trinity College, Dublin. Of far greater influence on Swift than those school years was the time spent in England (1689–99) as secretary and assistant to Sir William Temple at Moor Park, Surrey. Here Swift had access to a magnificent library which enabled him to read widely and to cultivate more worldly interests than those that Dublin had offered. Moor Park was a place of great sophistication and culture, and Temple was a man of refined tastes and broad acquaintance among the Whig aristocracy. Some of Swift's closest friendships date to the Moor Park days, among them his relationship with Esther Johnson, whom he called Stella in a series of birthday poems and in the famous *Journal*. It was probably at Moor Park, under the benign influence of Temple, that Swift developed that distrust of pedantry that was so prominent a motif in his first major literary endeavor, *A Tale of a Tub* (1704).

In 1694, during an interval in his stay at Moor Park, Swift decided to enter the Anglican clergy. His decision was not the result of a sudden religious awakening but rather an understandable consequence of his education, intellectual aspirations, and long-standing family tradition. It was not uncommon in the eighteenth century for a young man in Swift's circumstances to choose the church as a way of life. Following his ordination as a priest in 1695, Swift was assigned a small parish in northern Ireland. According to one biographer, Swift's experience during this period with neighboring Presbyterian clergy may well have been the basis for his antipathy toward nonconformist Presbyterians and the religious fanaticism that was reflected in *A Tale of a Tub*.[1]

---

1. Louis Landa, ed., Introduction to *Jonathan Swift, Gulliver's Travels and Other Writings* (Boston: Houghton-Mifflin, 1960), p. xiv.

At any rate, in six months he was back at Moor Park, responding to an invitation from Temple to reclaim his former position.

In the ten years that followed Temple's death in 1699, Swift held a variety of clerical posts, including that of chaplain and secretary to Lord Berkeley, Lord Justice of Ireland. A trip to London in 1701 coincided with the publication of his first political pamphlet, *A Discourse of the Contests and Dissensions in Athens and Rome.* This brought Swift to the attention of the leading Whigs in government, many of whom he had met at Moor Park. These men, like Lord Somers, to whom he dedicated *A Tale of a Tub* in 1704, recognized quickly the value of the young cleric's mind, his incisive wit and his polemic skills. This period became Swift's introduction to politics as well as his initiation into the complexities and uncertainties of English political life. There also seems little doubt that the seeds of Swift's cynicism about politics and politicians were planted during this time, as he found himself alternately encouraged and then disillusioned by the machinations of some of the Whigs he supported.

Swift's religious pamphlets of these and later years cannot really be separated from his political activities, since eighteenth-century politics was inseparable from religious issues. He vehemently defended the prerogatives of the Anglican church in the strongly ironic *Argument Against Abolishing Christianity* (written in 1708) and *Sentiments of a Church of England Man* (1708), which dealt with the relations of church and state. In these and other pamphlets, Swift strongly opposed all those whom he saw as a threat to the stability of the Church of England, particularly Dissenters, Deists, and those Whig politicians who, out of their desire to gather political support from all elements of society, were eager to repeal the Test Act, which excluded all except Anglicans from holding public office. In *A Letter Concerning the Sacramental Test* (1708) and *A Letter to a Member of Parliament in Ireland* (1709), it is clear that Swift was becoming disenchanted with the Whigs and their willingness to compromise on what he felt were matters of principle, especially on such religious issues as the Test Act.

There were lighter moments, however, that offset the frustration of coping with the deviousness of politicians. There was Swift's friendship with Addison and Steele and Pope, and the pleasure of contributing to Steele's new journal, *The Tatler*. And there was the great fun of the Bickerstaff papers (1708–09) in which Swift, under the pseudonym of Isaac Bickerstaff, predicted and eventually described the death of Partridge, who took the bait and proceeded to assure the world that he was still very much alive. Part of the pleasure of the joke was the opportunity it gave Swift of collaborating in some of the Bickerstaff papers with Addison, Steele, William Congreve, the poet Matthew Prior, and the physician-writer John Arbuthnot.

The major literary work of this period was *A Tale of a Tub*, published in London in 1704 (although written earlier). The *Tale* was an extended satire on a variety of subjects—literary and scientific pedantry, the zealotry of religious dissenters (i.e., those who rejected the Church of England and Anglican doctrine), the vacuity of language, and what Swift considered the distorted perspectives with which many modern philosophers viewed the world. In the most powerful section of the *Tale*, Swift focuses on madness as a universal malady that lies behind modern man's willingness to live in a state of perpetual delusion.

Swift's break with the Whigs in 1710 came about in part as a result of his refusal to support Whig attempts to repeal the Test Act. When the Tories came to power that year, Harley and St. John, Queen Anne's chief ministers, recognized Swift's talents as a political journalist, and enlisted his assistance in supporting Tory policy. Swift became their principal political propagandist, editing the *Examiner* for two years (1710–11), and playing a major role in Tory politics until 1714. His pamphlet *The Conduct of the Allies* (1712) was central in helping swing popular sentiment toward terminating the War of the Spanish Succession which had been dragging on for nine years. Swift became an intimate of those in the highest reaches of power and a trusted advisor to Harley and St. John.

This four-year period—probably the happiest in Swift's life—also provided a great stimulus to his literary interests. With some notable expectations, the best writers of the age were enlisted in the Tory cause. They met frequently to discuss literature as well as politics, the arts, the state of English culture. Together with Pope, Arbuthnot, Gay, and the poet Thomas Parnell, Swift founded the Scriblerus Club, a literary group that met regularly to discuss what they considered the deteriorating state of the literary arts and to plan a collective work—or series of works—that would expose dullness, pedantry, and pretentiousness. Their mock hero was to be a numbskull, Martinus Scriblerus or Martin the Scribbler. In all likelihood, three of the most famous satires of the century had their genesis during Scriblerus Club discussions—Gay's *A Beggar's Opera* (1728), Pope's *Dunciad* (the first version of which appeared in 1728), and Swift's most enduring work, *Gulliver's Travels* (1726).

Thanks to the *Journal to Stella* (published posthumously in 1765), we have a much more detailed sense of Swift's life during this time than for any other period of his life. In this series of letters, Swift describes day by day his activities in London between 1710 and 1713. He talks, for example, about the effect of politics on his literary relationships, his estrangement from Addison and Steele, his anxieties, his physical afflictions, court intrigues, essays he was writing, and the attempted assassination of Harley by a disgruntled French émigré whom Harley, St. John, and others had just confronted with evidence of spying for the French. The *Journal*, together with Swift's correspondence with close friends, provides us with an invaluable glimpse of a side of Swift not at all evident in his published pieces—his playfulness, his devotion to his friends, his kindness, his charismatic charm.

This happy period in Swift's life came to an end in 1714 with the death of Queen Anne and the collapse of the Tory government. To Swift's great chagrin, the Tories were only slightly more generous to Swift than the Whigs had been. Instead of a Bishopric in England, which would have enabled

Swift to remain close to London and his dearest friends, he was offered the Deanship of St. Patrick's Cathedral in Dublin. In the absence of alternatives, he accepted. With the exception of two brief visits to England in 1726 and 1727, Swift remained in Dublin for the next thirty years of his life, in "exile," as he himself described it.

But exile or not, Ireland was not a place where Swift was to languish. He kept in touch with his large circle of friends in England through a voluminous correspondence. His mind and imagination remained as fertile as ever. In the two decades following his arrival at the St. Patrick's deanery, Swift devoted considerable effort to defending a debilitated Anglican Church in Ireland against the Irish Presbyterians, and in particular the struggles of an impoverished Ireland against an exploitative England. This was the period of the great Irish tracts, *The Drapier Letters* (1724–25), the *Proposal for the Universal Use of Irish Manufacture* (1720), and, of course, *A Modest Proposal* (1729), considered the best short satire in the English language.

In the early 1720s, while he was working on *Gulliver's Travels,* Swift found that he could not ignore what was happening around him in Ireland. As he remarked in a letter around this time, ". . . as the world is now turned, no Cloyster is retired enough to keep Politicks out. . . ."[1] What concerned Swift most was the degree to which he saw the Whig government in London encroaching upon the liberties of the Irish people. Rather than trying to influence the Irish clergy or public officials, however, Swift decided to see what he could do to arouse the common people, especially shopkeepers, and convince them that passivity in the face of English economic exploitation would only lead to economic slavery. In his *Proposal for the Universal Use of Irish Manufacture,* Swift proposed that the Irish boycott all clothing imported from England. Despite a sluggish response from the Irish, Swift used the same approach four years later in response

---

1. Herbert Davis, *Jonathan Swift, Essays on His Satire and Other Studies* (New York: Oxford University Press, 1964), p. 136.

to the Whig government's attempts to impose on Ireland what was, in effect, a debased coinage. In 1722, the government granted a patent to an English iron merchant, William Wood, to coin and distribute in Ireland a certain number of copper coins (Ireland possessed no mint of its own). Irish opposition to the patent centered around the fear that the real intent was to flood Ireland with so many of these coins that the Irish monetary system would be thrown into chaos. When the Irish Parliament condemned the patent, the Whig Prime Minister ordered an inquiry in 1724. It was at this precise moment that Swift attempted to prod the Irish into action by publishing the first of seven letters signed "M. B. Drapier." In subsequent weeks, three more letters by the pseudonymous "M. B. Drapier" appeared. They were all written with one aim in mind: to persuade the Irish to boycott Woods' coins and to insist that Walpole revoke the patent. The letters were written in the plain, unornamented idiom of a Dublin shopkeeper. They spell out the facts of the matter, propose a plan of action for the boycott, and even come dangerously close to suggesting rebellion if the English insist on forcing the coinage on the Irish. Dubliners responded by demonstrating in the streets and there were petitions to Parliament and declarations against Wood. There was little doubt that Swift had succeeded in arousing popular sentiment.

Two weeks after the fourth letter appeared, Lord Carteret, the new Lord Lieutenant of Ireland, announced a reward of £300 for any "such person or persons as shall . . . discover the author of that wicked and malicious pamphlet." This was, in reality, a sham, since everyone in Ireland, including Carteret, knew that M. B. Drapier was Swift. No one came forward to claim the reward and several months later, the Prime Minister, Sir Robert Walpole, withdrew Woods' patent. The most powerful man in England and one of the great Prime Ministers in English history had been humbled by the power of Swift's pen. To this day, the Irish have never forgotten that.

This crisis over, Swift returned to the manuscript of *Gulli-*

ver's *Travels* which appeared in 1726. Originally conceived as part of "The Memoirs of Martinus Scriblerus," the *Travels* was to be a parody of travel books and scientific pedantry. But as Swift worked on the manuscript in the years after 1714, it became much more than that. His mock-hero became Lemuel Gulliver, a sailor who over the years is stranded on a series of islands in different parts of the Pacific. In contrast to Swift's other works, *Gulliver's Travels* is a sustained narrative, related by a fictional character who becomes progressively more and more disillusioned by his experiences and ends up a complete misanthrope. It is a sweeping satire that focuses as much on the general weaknesses of human nature as it does on the absurdities of eighteenth-century society. Parts of the satire are quite topical, reflecting the experiences of the Tories at the end of Queen Anne's reign as well as Swift's contempt for George I and the Whig ministry that followed. Some of the scientific satire in the third book was very clearly aimed at what Swift regarded as some of the excesses and absurdities of the Royal Society and scientific speculation generally. But the most powerful satire—and one for which *Gulliver's Travels* still resonates today—is contained in the fourth book, the Voyage to Houyhnhnm-land. Swift rejects as nonsense the popular notion that Man is naturally good and capable of perfectibility. Although he sees Man as a fallen being, Swift refuses, however, to go so far as extreme Puritans who condemned Man as irrational, depraved, decadent. Instead, he sees Man as having the capacity to live a productive moral existence because he is capable of rationality and somehow has the capacity to balance the animal and the rational. As Swift noted in a letter to Pope just before *Gulliver's Travels* was published, "I have got materials toward a treatise proving the falsity of that definition *animal rationale* [rational animal], and to show that it would be only *rationis capax* [capable of reason]. Upon this great foundation of misanthropy, . . . the whole building of my *Travels* is erected. . . ." The result was a book that has been described in our century as "the most powerful indictment of man's inhumanity ever written. . . ."[1]

Like so much satire, *Gulliver's Travels* walks that thin line between laughter and pain. Swift's ultimate intent was to force his reader to see clearly the nature of the world he inhabits, to feel its brutality, and to recognize the ways in which Man constantly deceives himself in order to avoid accepting what he sees in the mirror. If at the conclusion of *Gulliver's Travels*, we are left with the absurd picture of a madman who stuffs his nose with herbs to avoid the smell of his family and spends the most pleasant part of the day in the stable conversing with his horses, we are also left with a profoundly disturbing series of images of Man at his worst.

The anger and moral anguish that lay behind *Gulliver's Travels* diminished perhaps as those years in exile wore on, but they did not die out. In fact, they continued to smolder as Swift produced numerous poems and a variety of essays, a number of them for a new periodical, *The Intelligencer* (1728). Although he had won the battle over the coinage, the war with the Whig ministry in London was far from over. Swift continued to be enraged over the suffering he saw around him in Dublin, the poverty, the hunger, the increasing numbers of beggars—especially among children. He became convinced that the English were seriously intent on the utter impoverishment of the Irish. In a letter to Pope in 1729, he described Ireland as having suffered through "three terrible years' dearth of corn, and every place strewed with beggars. . . ." Swift was frustrated by what he saw as the hopelessness of the situation and weary with reading one silly proposal after another from well-meaning but ineffective schemers. He finally vented that frustration in 1729 in what was probably the greatest of his Irish tracts, *A Modest Proposal*.

This time, Swift chose a different tactic. Rather than denounce the government in London or berate the Irish Parlia-

---

1. Maynard Mack, ed., Introduction to *The Augustans* (Englewood Cliffs, N.J.: Prentice-Hall, 1961), p. 16.

ment for its passivity, or attack absentee English landowners for siphoning off revenues from their Irish estates and returning nothing, Swift selects a tone of voice that is quiet, dispassionate, and a point of view that is, if anything, eminently rational. He carries the idea of exploitation and deliberate impoverishment to a horrifying, rational conclusion by proposing—with chilling irony—that the Irish resolve their economic problems by resorting to cannibalism of their children. Citing numerous authorities to establish his credibility, he uses the impersonal vocabulary of a political pollster and presents the horrendous as eminently desirable. The final irony is, of course, that this is an accommodating Irishman—not an Englishman—who proposes the ultimate ironic alternative to death by starvation.

Swift's increasing isolation and loneliness in the final decade of his life were documented in the correspondence he maintained with Pope, Gay, Arbuthnot, and others. Gay died in 1732, Arbuthnot in 1735, his close friend, Thomas Sheridan, in 1738, and he felt their loss keenly. But the death earlier, in 1728, of Esther Johnson (Stella), with whom he had maintained a close, affectionate relationship for many years, was especially difficult to bear. He was also made uncomfortable by increasing deafness and frequent attacks of dizziness which he described as "that old vertigo in my head." We know now that Swift was suffering from what modern medicine has identified as Ménière's Syndrome. And his eyes began to weaken noticeably. Despite the discomforts and isolation, however, Swift continued to be engaged in politics. In 1736, furious over the Irish Parliament's response to a controvery between farmers and graziers over a tax matter, he wrote *The Legion Club*, a poem attacking Parliament's integrity and intelligence. He portrays the new Parliament building as a madhouse and its inhabitants as demonic. The poem is in effect a tour of Bedlam which quickly degenerates into Hades.

These later years also had their lighter moments. During periods of relief from the vertigo, Swift managed to finish one of his more comic pieces, *A Complete Collection of Genteel and Ingenious*

Conversation (1738), a parody of the inanities of everyday conversation among the gentry. Even as his body began to fail, his mind was as sharp as ever.

But by 1742, there were signs of mental deterioration, probably as a result of brain lesions[1] or perhaps senility. In order to protect Swift and his affairs, a group of friends asked the court to appoint a committee of guardians.[2] A series of strokes deprived him of his speech for much of the time. He finally died in 1745 at the age of seventy-eight, and was buried in St. Patrick's Cathedral, not too far from Stella. In his will, Swift had stipulated that the following be inscribed on his memorial: "Ubi Saeva Indignatio/Ulterius/Collacerare Nequit" (He has gone where fierce indignation can lacerate him no more). According to William Butler Yeats, "Swift sleeps under the greatest epitaph in history."

George R. Levine
University of Buffalo
State University of New York

---

1. Irvin Ehrenpreis, *Swift: The Man, His Works, The Age* (Cambridge, Mass.: Harvard University Press, 1983), III, 908.
2. Ehrenpeis, III, 915.

A Tale of a Tub

TO THE RIGHT HONOURABLE

JOHN LORD SOMERS.

My Lord,

THOUGH the Author has written a large Dedication, yet that being addressed to a Prince whom I am never likely to have the honour of being known to; a person, besides, as far as I can observe, not at all regarded or thought on by any of our present writers; and I being wholly free from that slavery which booksellers usually lie under to the caprices of authors, I think it a wise piece of presumption to inscribe these papers to your Lordship, and to implore your Lordship's protection of them. God and your Lordship know their faults and their merits; for as to my own particular, I am altogether a stranger to the matter; and though everybody else should be equally ignorant, I do not fear the sale of the book at all the worse upon that score. Your Lordship's name on the front in capital letters will at any time get off one edition: neither would I desire any other help to grow an alderman than a patent for the sole privilege of dedicating to your Lordship.

I should now, in right of a dedicator, give your Lordship a list of your own virtues, and at the same time be very unwilling to offend your modesty; but chiefly I should celebrate your liberality towards men of great parts and small fortunes, and give you broad hints that I mean myself. And I was just going on in the usual method to peruse a hundred or two of dedications, and transcribe an abstract to be applied to your Lordship, but I was diverted by a certain accident. For upon the covers of these papers I casually observed written in large letters the two following words, DETUR DIGNISSIMO, which, for aught I knew, might contain some important meaning. But it unluckily fell out that none of the Authors I employ understood Latin (though I have them often in pay to translate out of that language). I was therefore compelled to have recourse to the Curate of our Parish, who Englished it thus, *Let it be given to the worthiest;* and his comment was that the Author meant his work should be dedicated to the sublimest genius of the age for wit, learning, judgment, eloquence, and wisdom. I called at a poet's chamber (who works for my shop) in an alley hard by, showed him the translation, and desired his opinion who it was that the Author could mean. He told me, after some consideration, that vanity was a thing he abhorred, but by the description he thought himself to be the person aimed at; and at the same time he very kindly offered his own assistance gratis towards penning a dedication to himself. I desired him, however, to give a second guess. Why then, said he, it must be I, or my Lord Somers. From thence I went to several other wits of my acquaintance, with no small hazard and weariness to my person, from a prodigious number of dark winding stairs; but found them all in the same story, both of your Lordship and themselves. Now your Lordship is to understand that this proceeding was not of my own invention; for I have somewhere heard it is a maxim that those to whom everybody allows the second place have an undoubted title to the first.

This infallibly convinced me that your Lordship was the person intended by the Author. But being very unacquainted in the style and form of dedications, I employed those wits aforesaid to furnish me with hints and materials towards a panegyric upon your Lordship's virtues.

In two days they brought me ten sheets of paper filled up on every side. They swore to me that they had ransacked whatever could be found in the characters of Socrates, Aristides, Epaminondas, Cato, Tully, Atticus, and other hard names which I cannot now recollect. However, I have reason to believe they imposed upon my ignorance, because when I came to read over their collections, there was not a syllable there but what I and everybody else knew as well as themselves : therefore I grievously suspect a cheat; and that these Authors of mine stole and transcribed every word from the universal report of mankind. So that I look upon myself as fifty shillings out of pocket to no manner of purpose.

If by altering the title I could make the same materials serve for another dedication (as my betters have done), it would help to make up my loss; but I have made several persons dip here and there in those papers, and before they read three lines they have all assured me plainly that they cannot possibly be applied to any person besides your Lordship.

I expected, indeed, to have heard of your Lordship's bravery at the head of an army; of your undaunted courage in mounting a breach or scaling a wall; or to have had your pedigree traced in a lineal descent from the House of Austria; or of your wonderful talent at dress and dancing; or your profound knowledge in algebra, metaphysics, and the Oriental tongues: but to ply the world with an old beaten story of your wit, and eloquence, and learning, and wisdom, and justice, and politeness, and candour, and evenness of temper in all scenes of life; of that great discernment in discovering and readiness in favouring deserving men; with forty other common topics : I confess I have neither conscience nor countenance to do it. Because there is no virtue either of a public or private life which some circumstances of your own have not often produced upon the stage of the world; and those few which for want of occasions to exert them might otherwise have passed unseen or unobserved by your friends, your enemies have at length brought to light.

It is true I should be very loth the bright example of your Lordship's virtues should be lost to after-ages, both for their sake and your own ; but chiefly because they will be so very necessary to adorn the history of a late reign ; and that is another reason why I would forbear to make a recital of them here; because I have been told by wise men that as dedications have run for some years past, a good historian will not be apt to have recourse thither in search of characters.

There is one point wherein I think we dedicators would do well to change our measures; I mean, instead of running on so far upon the praise of our patron's liberality, to spend a word or two in admiring their patience. I can put no greater compliment on your Lordship's than by giving you so ample an occasion to exercise it at present. Though perhaps I shall not be apt to reckon much merit to your Lordship upon that score, who having been formerly used to tedious harangues, and sometimes to as little purpose, will be the readier to pardon this, especially when it is offered by one who is, with all respect and veneration,

MY LORD,

Your Lordship's most obedient

and most faithful Servant,

THE BOOKSELLER.

THE

BOOKSELLER TO THE READER.

IT is now six years since these papers came first to my hands, which seems to have been about a twelvemonth after they were written, for the Author tells us in his preface to the first treatise that he had calculated it for the year 1697; and in several passages of that discourse, as well as the second, it appears they were written about that time.

As to the Author, I can give no manner of satisfaction. However, I am credibly informed that this publication is without his knowledge, for he concludes the copy is lost, having lent it to a person since dead, and being never in possession of it after; so that, whether the work received his last hand, or whether he intended to fill up the defective places, is like to remain a secret.

If I should go about to tell the reader by what accident I became master of these papers, it would, in this unbelieving age, pass for little more than the cant or jargon of the trade. I therefore gladly spare both him and myself so unnecessary a trouble. There yet remains a difficult question—why I published them no sooner? I forbore upon two accounts. First, because I thought I had better work upon my hands; and secondly, because I was not without some hope of hearing from the Author and receiving his directions. But I have been lately alarmed with intelligence of a surreptitious copy which a certain great wit had new polished and refined, or, as our present writers express themselves, "fitted to the humour of the age," as they have already done with great felicity to Don Quixote, Boccalini, La Bruyère, and other authors. However, I thought it fairer dealing to offer the whole work in its naturals. If any gentleman will please to furnish me with a key, in order to explain the more difficult parts, I shall very gratefully acknowledge the favour, and print it by itself.

THE EPISTLE DEDICATORY

HIS ROYAL HIGHNESS PRINCE POSTERITY.

SIR,

I HERE present your Highness with the fruits of a very few leisure hours, stolen from the short intervals of a world of business, and of an employment quite alien from such amusements as this; the poor production of that refuse of time which has lain heavy upon my hands during a long prorogation of Parliament, a great dearth of foreign news, and a tedious fit of rainy weather. For which, and other reasons, it cannot choose extremely to deserve such a patronage as that of your Highness, whose numberless virtues in so few years, make the world look upon you as the future example to all princes. For although your Highness is hardly got clear of infancy, yet has the universal learned world already resolved upon appealing to your future dictates with the lowest and most resigned submission, fate having decreed you sole arbiter of the productions of human wit in this polite and most accomplished age. Methinks the number of appellants were enough to shock and startle any judge of a genius less unlimited than yours; but in order to prevent such glorious trials, the person, it seems, to whose care the education of your Highness is committed, has resolved, as I am told, to keep you in almost an universal ignorance of our studies, which it is your inherent birthright to inspect.

It is amazing to me that this person should have assurance, in the face of the sun, to go about persuading your Highness that our age is almost wholly illiterate and has hardly produced one writer upon any subject. I know very well that when your Highness shall come to riper years, and have gone through the learning of antiquity, you will be too curious to neglect inquiring into the authors of the very age before you; and to think that this insolent, in the account he is preparing for your view, designs to reduce them to a number so insignificant as I am ashamed to mention; it moves my zeal and my spleen for the honour and interest of our vast flourishing body, as well as of myself, for whom I know by long experience he has professed, and still continues, a peculiar malice.

It is not unlikely that, when your Highness will one day peruse what I am now writing, you may be ready to expostulate with your governor upon the credit of what I here affirm, and command him to show you some of our productions. To which he will answer—for I am well informed of his designs—by asking your Highness where they are, and what is become of them? and pretend it a demonstration that there never were any, because they are not then to be found. Not to be found! Who has mislaid them? Are they sunk in the abyss of things? It is certain that in their own nature they were light enough to swim upon the surface for all eternity; therefore, the fault is in him who tied weights so heavy to their heels as to depress them to the centre. Is their very essence destroyed? Who has annihilated them? Were they drowned by purges or martyred by pipes? Who administered them to the posteriors of ———. But that it may no longer be a doubt with your Highness who is to be the author of this universal ruin, I beseech you to observe that large and terrible scythe which your governor affects to bear continually about him. Be pleased to remark the length and strength, the sharpness and hardness, of his nails and teeth; consider his baneful, abominable breath, enemy to life and matter, infectious and corrupting, and then reflect whether it be possible for any mortal ink and paper of this generation to make a suitable resistance. Oh, that your Highness would one day resolve to disarm this usurping *maître de palais* of his furious engines, and bring your empire *hors du page.*

It were endless to recount the several methods of tyranny and destruction which your governor is pleased to practise upon this occasion. His inveterate malice is such to the writings of our age, that, of several thousands produced yearly from this renowned city, before the next revolution of the sun there is not one to be heard of. Unhappy infants! many of them barbarously destroyed before they have so much as learnt their mother-tongue to beg for pity. Some he stifles in their cradles, others he frights into convulsions, whereof they suddenly die, some he flays alive, others he tears limb from limb, great numbers are offered to Moloch, and the rest, tainted by his breath, die of a languishing consumption.

But the concern I have most at heart is for our Corporation of Poets, from whom I am preparing a petition to your Highness, to be subscribed with the names of one hundred and thirty-six of the first race, but whose immortal productions are never likely to reach your eyes, though each of them is now an humble and an earnest appellant for the laurel, and has large comely volumes ready to show for a support to his pretensions. The never-dying works of these illustrious persons your governor, sir, has devoted to unavoidable death, and your Highness is to be made believe that our age has never arrived at the honour to produce one single poet.

We confess immortality to be a great and powerful goddess, but in vain we offer up to her our devotions and our sacrifices if your Highness's governor, who has usurped the priesthood, must, by an unparalleled ambition and avarice, wholly intercept and devour them.

To affirm that our age is altogether unlearned and devoid of writers in any kind, seems to be an assertion so bold and so false, that I have been sometimes thinking the contrary may almost be proved by uncontrollable demonstration. It is true, indeed, that although their numbers be vast and their productions numerous in proportion, yet are they hurried so hastily off the scene that they escape our memory and delude our sight. When I first thought of this address, I had prepared a copious list of titles to present your Highness as an undisputed argument for what I affirm. The originals were posted fresh upon all gates and corners of streets; but returning in a very few hours to take a review, they were all torn down and fresh ones in their places. I inquired after them among readers and booksellers, but I inquired in vain; the memorial of them was lost among men, their place was no more to be found; and I was laughed to scorn for a clown and a pedant, devoid of all taste and refinement, little versed in the course of present affairs, and that knew nothing of what had passed in the best companies of court and town. So that I can only avow in general to your Highness that we do abound in learning and wit, but to fix upon particulars is a task too slippery for my slender abilities. If I should venture, in a windy day, to affirm to your Highness that there is a large cloud near the horizon in the form of a bear, another in the zenith with the head of an ass, a third to the westward with claws like a dragon; and your Highness should in a few minutes think fit to examine the truth, it is certain they would be all changed in figure and position, new ones would arise, and all we could agree upon would be, that clouds there were, but that I was grossly mistaken in the zoography and topography of them.

But your governor, perhaps, may still insist, and put the question, What is then become of those immense bales of paper which must needs have been employed in such numbers of books? Can these also be wholly annihilated, and so of a sudden, as I pretend? What shall I say in return of so invidious an objection? It ill befits the distance between your Highness and me to send you for ocular conviction to a jakes or an oven, to the windows of a bawdyhouse, or to a sordid lanthorn. Books, like men their authors, have no more than one way of coming into the world, but there are ten thousand to go out of it and return no more.

I profess to your Highness, in the integrity of my heart, that what I am going to say is literally true this minute I am writing;

what revolutions may happen before it shall be ready for your perusal I can by no means warrant ; however, I beg you to accept it as a specimen of our learning, our politeness, and our wit. I do therefore affirm, upon the word of a sincere man, that there is now actually in being a certain poet called John Dryden, whose translation of Virgil was lately printed in large folio, well bound, and if diligent search were made, for aught I know, is yet to be seen. There is another called Nahum Tate, who is ready to make oath that he has caused many reams of verse to be published, whereof both himself and his bookseller, if lawfully required, can still produce authentic copies, and therefore wonders why the world is pleased to make such a secret of it. There is a third, known by the name of Tom Durfey, a poet of a vast comprehension, an universal genius, and most profound learning. There are also one Mr. Rymer and one Mr. Dennis, most profound critics. There is a person styled Dr. Bentley, who has wrote near a thousand pages of immense erudition, giving a full and true account of a certain squabble of wonderful importance between himself and a bookseller ; he is a writer of infinite wit and humour, no man rallies with a better grace and in more sprightly turns. Further, I avow to your Highness that with these eyes I have beheld the person of William Wotton, B.D., who has written a good-sized volume against a friend of your governor, from whom, alas! he must therefore look for little favour, in a most gentlemanly style, adorned with utmost politeness and civility, replete with discoveries equally valuable for their novelty and use, and embellished with traits of wit so poignant and so apposite, that he is a worthy yoke-mate to his fore-mentioned friend.

Why should I go upon farther particulars, which might fill a volume with the just eulogies of my contemporary brethren? I shall bequeath this piece of justice to a larger work, wherein I intend to write a character of the present set of wits in our nation; their persons I shall describe particularly and at length, their genius and understandings in miniature.

In the meantime, I do here make bold to present your Highness with a faithful abstract drawn from the universal body of all arts and sciences, intended wholly for your service and instruction. Nor do I doubt in the least but your Highness will peruse it as carefully and make as considerable improvements as other young princes have already done by the many volumes of late years written for a help to their studies.

That your Highness may advance in wisdom and virtue, as well as years, and at last outshine all your royal ancestors, shall be the daily prayer of,

Sir,

Your Highness's most devoted, &c.

Decemb. 1697.

THE PREFACE.

THE wits of the present age being so very numerous and penetrating, it seems the grandees of Church and State begin to fall under horrible apprehensions lest these gentlemen, during the intervals of a long peace, should find leisure to pick holes in the weak sides of religion and government. To prevent which, there has been much thought employed of late upon certain projects for taking off the force and edge of those formidable inquirers from canvassing and reasoning upon such delicate points. They have at length fixed upon one, which will require some time as well as cost to perfect. Meanwhile, the danger hourly increasing, by new levies of wits, all appointed (as there is reason to fear) with pen, ink, and paper, which may at an hour's warning be drawn out into pamphlets and other offensive weapons ready for immediate execution, it was judged of absolute necessity that some present expedient be thought on till the main design can be brought to maturity. To this end, at a grand committee, some days ago, this important discovery was made by a certain curious and refined observer, that seamen have a custom when they meet a Whale to fling him out an empty Tub, by way of amusement, to divert him from laying violent hands upon the Ship. This parable was immediately mythologised; the Whale was interpreted to be Hobbes's "Leviathan," which tosses and plays with all other schemes of religion and government, whereof a great many are hollow, and dry, and empty, and noisy, and wooden, and given to rotation. This is the Leviathan from whence the terrible wits of our age are said to borrow their weapons. The Ship in danger is easily understood to be its old antitype the commonwealth. But how to analyse the Tub was a matter of difficulty, when, after long inquiry and debate, the literal meaning was preserved, and it was decreed that, in order to prevent these Leviathans from tossing and sporting with the commonwealth, which of itself is too apt to fluctuate, they should be diverted from that game by "A Tale of a Tub." And my genius being conceived to lie not unhappily that way, I had the honour done me to be engaged in the performance.

This is the sole design in publishing the following treatise, which I hope will serve for an interim of some months to employ those unquiet spirits till the perfecting of that great work, into the secret of which it is reasonable the courteous reader should have some little light.

It is intended that a large Academy be erected, capable of containing nine thousand seven hundred forty and three persons, which, by modest computation, is reckoned to be pretty near the current number of wits in this island.[1] These are to be disposed into the several schools of this Academy, and there pursue those studies to which their genius most inclines them. The under-taker himself will publish his proposals with all convenient speed, to which I shall refer the curious reader for a more particular account, mentioning at present only a few of the principal schools. There is, first, a large pederastic school, with French and Italian masters; there is also the spelling school, a very spacious build-ing; the school of looking-glasses; the school of swearing; the school of critics; the school of salivation; the school of hobby-horses; the school of poetry; the school of tops; the school of spleen; the school of gaming; with many others too tedious to recount. No person to be admitted member into any of these schools without an attestation under two sufficient persons' hands certifying him to be a wit.

But to return. I am sufficiently instructed in the principal duty of a preface if my genius were capable of arriving at it. Thrice have I forced my imagination to take the tour of my

1. The number of livings in England—Will Pate, a friend of Swift who contributed several notes to the 1720 edition of *A Tale.* Swift referred to Pate as "a learned woolen-draper."

invention, and thrice it has returned empty, the latter having been wholly drained by the following treatise. Not so my more successful brethren the moderns, who will by no means let slip a preface or dedication without some notable distinguishing stroke to surprise the reader at the entry, and kindle a wonderful expectation of what is to ensue. Such was that of a most ingenious poet, who, soliciting his brain for something new, compared himself to the hangman and his patron to the patient. This was *insigne, recens, indictum ore alio.*[1] When I went through that necessary and noble course of study,[2] I had the happiness to observe many such egregious touches, which I shall not injure the authors by transplanting, because I have remarked that nothing is so very tender as a modern piece of wit, and which is apt to suffer so much in the carriage. Some things are extremely witty to-day, or fasting, or in this place, or at eight o'clock, or over a bottle, or spoke by Mr. Whatdyecall'm, or in a summer's morning, any of which, by the smallest transposal or misapplication, is utterly annihilate. Thus wit has its walks and purlieus, out of which it may not stray the breadth of a hair, upon peril of being lost. The moderns have artfully fixed this Mercury, and reduced it to the circumstances of time, place, and person. Such a jest there is that will not pass out of Covent Garden, and such a one that is nowhere intelligible but at Hyde Park Corner. Now, though it sometimes tenderly affects me to consider that all the towardly passages I shall deliver in the following treatise will grow quite out of date and relish with the first shifting of the present scene, yet I must need subscribe to the justice of this proceeding, because I cannot imagine why we should be at expense to furnish wit for succeeding ages, when the former have made no sort of provision for ours; wherein I speak the sentiment of the very newest, and consequently the most orthodox refiners, as well as my own. However, being extremely solicitous that every accomplished person who has got into the taste of wit calculated for this present month of August 1697 should descend

---

1 " Distinguished, new, told by no other tongue."—*Horace.*
2 " Reading prefaces, &c."—*Swift's note in the margin.*

to the very bottom of all the sublime throughout this treatise, I hold it fit to lay down this general maxim. Whatever reader desires to have a thorough comprehension of an author's thoughts, cannot take a better method than by putting himself into the circumstances and posture of life that the writer was in upon every important passage as it flowed from his pen, for this will introduce a parity and strict correspondence of ideas between the reader and the author. Now, to assist the diligent reader in so delicate an affair—as far as brevity will permit—I have recollected that the shrewdest pieces of this treatise were conceived in bed in a garret. At other times (for a reason best known to myself) I thought fit to sharpen my invention with hunger, and in general the whole work was begun, continued, and ended under a long course of physic and a great want of money. Now, I do affirm it will be absolutely impossible for the candid peruser to go along with me in a great many bright passages, unless upon the several difficulties emergent he will please to capacitate and prepare himself by these directions. And this I lay down as my principal *postulatum.*

Because I have professed to be a most devoted servant of all modern forms, I apprehend some curious wit may object against me for proceeding thus far in a preface without declaiming, according to custom, against the multitude of writers whereof the whole multitude of writers most reasonably complain. I am just come from perusing some hundreds of prefaces, wherein the authors do at the very beginning address the gentle reader concerning this enormous grievance. Of these I have preserved a few examples, and shall set them down as near as my memory has been able to retain them.

One begins thus : " For a man to set up for a writer when the press swarms with," &c.

Another : " The tax upon paper does not lessen the number of scribblers who daily pester," &c.

Another : " When every little would-be wit takes pen in hand, 'tis in vain to enter the lists," &c.

Another : " To observe what trash the press swarms with," &c.

Another : "Sir, it is merely in obedience to your commands that I venture into the public, for who upon a less consideration would be of a party with such a rabble of scribblers," &c.

Now, I have two words in my own defence against this objection. First, I am far from granting the number of writers a nuisance to our nation, having strenuously maintained the contrary in several parts of the following discourse; secondly, I do not well understand the justice of this proceeding, because I observe many of these polite prefaces to be not only from the same hand, but from those who are most voluminous in their several productions; upon which I shall tell the reader a short tale.

A mountebank in Leicester Fields had drawn a huge assembly about him. Among the rest, a fat unwieldy fellow, half stifled in the press, would be every fit crying out, "Lord! what a filthy crowd is here. Pray, good people, give way a little. Bless me! what a devil has raked this rabble together. Z——ds, what squeezing is this? Honest friend, remove your elbow." At last a weaver that stood next him could hold no longer. "A plague confound you," said he, "for an overgrown sloven; and who in the devil's name, I wonder, helps to make up the crowd half so much as yourself? Don't you consider that you take up more room with that carcass than any five here? Is not the place as free for us as for you? Bring your own guts to a reasonable compass, and then I'll engage we shall have room enough for us all."

There are certain common privileges of a writer, the benefit whereof I hope there will be no reason to doubt; particularly, that where I am not understood, it shall be concluded that something very useful and profound is couched underneath; and again, that whatever word or sentence is printed in a different character shall be judged to contain something extraordinary either of wit or sublime.

As for the liberty I have thought fit to take of praising myself, upon some occasions or none, I am sure it will need no excuse if a multitude of great examples be allowed sufficient authority; for it is here to be noted that praise was originally a pension paid by the world, but the moderns, finding the trouble and charge too great in collecting it, have lately bought out the fee-simple, since which time the right of presentation is wholly in ourselves. For this reason it is that when an author makes his own eulogy, he uses a certain form to declare and insist upon his title, which is commonly in these or the like words, " I speak without vanity," which I think plainly shows it to be a matter of right and justice. Now, I do here once for all declare, that in every encounter of this nature through the following treatise the form aforesaid is implied, which I mention to save the trouble of repeating it on so many occasions.

It is a great ease to my conscience that I have written so elaborate and useful a discourse without one grain of satire intermixed, which is the sole point wherein I have taken leave to dissent from the famous originals of our age and country. I have observed some satirists to use the public much at the rate that pedants do a naughty boy ready horsed for discipline. First expostulate the case, then plead the necessity of the rod from great provocations, and conclude every period with a lash. Now, if I know anything of mankind, these gentlemen might very well spare their reproof and correction, for there is not through all Nature another so callous and insensible a member as the world's posteriors, whether you apply to it the toe or the birch. Besides, most of our late satirists seem to lie under a sort of mistake, that because nettles have the prerogative to sting, therefore all other weeds must do so too. I make not this comparison out of the least design to detract from these worthy writers, for it is well known among mythologists that weeds have the pre-eminence over all other vegetables ; and therefore the first monarch of this island whose taste and judgment were so acute and refined, did very wisely root out the roses from the collar of the order and plant the thistles in their stead, as the nobler flower of the two. For which reason it is conjectured by profounder antiquaries that the satirical itch, so prevalent in this part of our island, was first brought among us from beyond the Tweed. Here may it long flourish and abound ; may it survive and neglect the scorn of the world with as much ease and contempt as the world is insensible to the lashes of it. May their own dulness, or that of their party, be no discouragement for the authors to proceed ; but let them remember it is with wits as with razors, which are never so apt to cut those they are employed on as when they have lost their edge. Besides, those whose teeth are too rotten to bite are best of all others qualified to revenge that defect with their breath.

I am not, like other men, to envy or undervalue the talents I cannot reach, for which reason I must needs bear a true honour to this large eminent sect of our British writers. And I hope this little panegyric will not be offensive to their ears, since it has the advantage of being only designed for themselves. Indeed, Nature herself has taken order that fame and honour should be purchased at a better pennyworth by satire than by any other productions of the brain, the world being soonest provoked to praise by lashes, as men are to love. There is a problem in an ancient author why dedications and other bundles of flattery run all upon stale musty topics, without the smallest tincture of anything new, not only to the torment and nauseating of the Christian reader, but, if not suddenly prevented, to the universal spreading of that pestilent disease the lethargy in this island, whereas there is very little satire which has not something in it untouched before. The defects of the former are usually imputed to the want of invention among those who are dealers in that kind ; but I think with a great deal of injustice, the solution being easy and natural, for the materials of panegyric, being very few in number, have been long since exhausted ; for as health is but one thing, and has been always the same, whereas diseases are by thousands, besides new and daily additions, so all the virtues that have been ever in mankind are to be counted upon a few fingers, but his follies and vices are innumerable, and time adds hourly to the heap. Now the utmost a poor poet can do is to get by heart a list of the cardinal virtues and deal them with his utmost liberality to his hero or his patron. He may ring the changes as far as it will go, and vary his phrase till he has talked round, but the reader quickly finds it is all pork,[1] with a little variety of sauce, for there is no inventing terms of art beyond our ideas, and when ideas are exhausted, terms of art must be so too.

But though the matter for panegyric were as fruitful as the topics of satire, yet would it not be hard to find out a sufficient reason why the latter will be always better received than the first; for this being bestowed only upon one or a few persons at a time, is sure to raise envy, and consequently ill words, from the rest who have no share in the blessing. But satire, being levelled at all, is never resented for an offence by any, since every individual person makes bold to understand it of others, and very wisely removes his particular part of the burden upon the shoulders of the World, which are broad enough and able to bear it. To this purpose I have sometimes reflected upon the difference between Athens and England with respect to the point before us. In the Attic[2] commonwealth it was the privilege and birthright of every citizen and poet to rail aloud and in public, or to expose upon the stage by name any person they pleased, though of the greatest figure, whether a Creon, an Hyperbolus, an Alcibiades, or a Demosthenes. But, on the other side, the least reflecting word let fall against the people in general was immediately caught up and revenged upon the authors, however considerable for their quality or their merits; whereas in England it is just the reverse of all this. Here you may securely display your utmost rhetoric against mankind in the face of the world; tell them that all are gone astray; that there is none that doeth good, no, not one; that we live in the very dregs of time; that knavery and atheism are epidemic as the pox; that honesty is fled with Astræa ; with any other common-places equally new and eloquent, which are furnished by the *splendida bilis ;*[3] and when you have done, the whole audience, far from

---

[1] Plutarch.—*Swift's note in the margin.*
[2] Xenophon.—*Swift's note in the margin, marked, in future,* S.
[3] Spleen.—*Horace.*

being offended, shall return you thanks as a deliverer of precious and useful truths. Nay, further, it is but to venture your lungs, and you may preach in Covent Garden against foppery and fornication, and something else; against pride, and dissimulation, and bribery at Whitehall. You may expose rapine and injustice in the Inns-of-Court chapel, and in a City pulpit be as fierce as you please against avarice, hypocrisy, and extortion. It is but a ball bandied to and fro, and every man carries a racket about him to strike it from himself among the rest of the company. But, on the other side, whoever should mistake the nature of things so far as to drop but a single hint in public how such a one starved half the fleet, and half poisoned the rest; how such a one, from a true principle of love and honour, pays no debts but for wenches and play; how such a one runs out of his estate; how Paris, bribed by Juno and Venus, loath to offend either party, slept out the whole cause on the bench; or how such an orator makes long speeches in the Senate, with much thought, little sense, and to no purpose ;—whoever, I say, should venture to be thus particular, must expect to be imprisoned for *scandalum magnatum*, to have challenges sent him, to be sued for defamation, and to be brought before the bar of the House.

But I forget that I am expatiating on a subject wherein I have no concern, having neither a talent nor an inclination for satire. On the other side, I am so entirely satisfied with the whole present procedure of human things, that I have been for some years preparing material towards "A Panegyric upon the World;" to which I intended to add a second part, entitled "A Modest Defence of the Proceedings of the Rabble in all Ages." Both these I had thoughts to publish by way of appendix to the following treatise ; but finding my common-place book fill much slower than I had reason to expect, I have chosen to defer them to another occasion. Besides, I have been unhappily prevented in that design by a certain domestic misfortune, in the particulars whereof, though it would be very seasonable, and much in the modern way, to inform the gentle reader, and would also be of great assistance towards extending this preface into the size

now in vogue—which by rule ought to be large in proportion
as the subsequent volume is small—yet I shall now dismiss
our impatient reader from any further attendance at the
porch; and having duly prepared his mind by a preliminary
discourse, shall gladly introduce him to the sublime mysteries
that ensue.

A TALE OF A TUB, &c.

SECTION I.

THE INTRODUCTION.

WHOEVER has an ambition to be heard in a crowd must press, and squeeze, and thrust, and climb with indefatigable pains, till he has exalted himself to a certain degree of altitude above them. Now, in all assemblies, though you wedge them ever so close, we may observe this peculiar property, that over their heads there is room enough; but how to reach it is the difficult point, it being as hard to get quit of number as of hell.

> " ——Evadere ad auras,
> Hoc opus, hic labor est." [1]

To this end the philosopher's way in all ages has been by erecting certain edifices in the air; but whatever practice and reputation these kind of structures have formerly possessed, or may still continue in, not excepting even that of Socrates when he was suspended in a basket to help contemplation, I think, with due submission, they seem to labour under two inconveniences. First, that the foundations being laid too high, they have been often out of sight and ever out of hearing. Secondly, that the

---

[1] " But to return, and view the cheerful skies,
In this the task and mighty labour lies."
—Dryden's " Virgil."

materials being very transitory, have suffered much from inclemencies of air, especially in these north-west regions.

Therefore, towards the just performance of this great work
there remain but three methods that I can think on; whereof
the wisdom of our ancestors being highly sensible, has, to encou-
.rage all aspiring adventures, thought fit to erect three wooden
machines for the use of those orators who desire to talk much
without interruption. These are the Pulpit, the Ladder, and the
Stage-itinerant. For as to the Bar, though it be compounded of
the same matter and designed for the same use, it cannot, however, be well allowed the honour of a fourth, by reason of its level
or inferior situation exposing it to perpetual interruption from
collaterals. Neither can the Bench itself, though raised to a
proper eminency, put in a better claim, whatever its advocates
insist on. For if they please to look into the original design
of its erection, and the circumstances or adjuncts subservient to
that design, they will soon acknowledge the present practice
exactly correspondent to the primitive institution, and both to
answer the etymology of the name, which in the Phœnician
tongue is a word of great signification, importing, if literally
interpreted, " The place of sleep," but in common acceptation,
" A seat well bolstered and cushioned, for the repose of old and
gouty limbs;" *senes ut in otia tuta recedant.*[1] Fortune being
indebted to them this part of retaliation, that as formerly they
have long talked whilst others slept, so now they may sleep as
long whilst others talk.

But if no other argument could occur to exclude the Bench
and the Bar from the list of oratorical machines, it were sufficient
that the admission of them would overthrow a number which I
was resolved to establish, whatever argument it might cost me;
in imitation of that prudent method observed by many other
philosophers and great clerks, whose chief art in division has
been to grow fond of some proper mystical number, which their
imaginations have rendered sacred to a degree that they force
common reason to find room for it in every part of Nature,

---

[1] " That the old may withdraw into safe ease."

reducing, including, and adjusting every genus and species within that compass by coupling some against their wills and banishing others at any rate. Now, among all the rest, the profound number THREE [1] is that which has most employed my sublimest speculations, nor ever without wonderful delight. There is now in the press, and will be published next term, a panegyrical essay of mine upon this number, wherein I have, by most convincing proofs, not only reduced the senses and the elements under its banner, but brought over several deserters from its two great rivals, SEVEN and NINE.

Now, the first of these oratorical machines, in place as well as dignity, is the Pulpit. Of pulpits there are in this island several sorts, but I esteem only that made of timber from the *Sylva Caledonia*, which agrees very well with our climate. If it be upon its decay, it is the better, both for conveyance of sound and for other reasons to be mentioned by and by. The degree of perfection in shape and size I take to consist in being extremely narrow, with little ornament, and, best of all, without a cover; for, by ancient rule, it ought to be the only uncovered vessel in every assembly where it is rightfully used, by which means, from its near resemblance to a pillory, it will ever have a mighty influence on human ears.

Of Ladders I need say nothing. It is observed by foreigners themselves, to the honour of our country, that we excel all nations in our practice and understanding of this machine. The ascending orators do not only oblige their audience in the agreeable delivery, but the whole world in their early publication of their speeches, which I look upon as the choicest treasury of our British eloquence, and whereof I am informed that worthy

---

[1] In his subsequent apology for "The Tale of a Tub," Swift wrote of these machines that, "In the original manuscript there was a description of a fourth, which those who had the papers in their power blotted out, as having something in it of satire that I suppose they thought was too particular; and therefore they were forced to change it to the number three, whence some have endeavoured to squeeze out a dangerous meaning that was never thought on. And indeed the conceit was half spoiled by changing the numbers; that of four being much more cabalistic, and therefore better exposing the pretended virtue of numbers, a superstition then intended to be ridiculed."

citizen and bookseller, Mr. John Dunton, has made a faithful and a painful collection, which he shortly designs to publish in twelve volumes in folio, illustrated with copper-plates,—a work highly useful and curious, and altogether worthy of such a hand.

The last engine of orators is the· Stage-itinerant, erected with much sagacity, *sub Jove pluvio, in triviis et quadriviis.*[1] It is the great seminary of the two former, and its orators are sometimes preferred to the one and sometimes to the other, in proportion to their deservings, there being a strict and perpetual intercourse between all three.

From this accurate deduction it is manifest that for obtaining attention in public there is of necessity required a superior position of place. But although this point be generally granted, yet the cause is little agreed in; and it seems to me that very few philosophers have fallen into a true natural solution of this phenomenon. The deepest account, and the most fairly digested of any I have yet met with is this, that air being a heavy body, and therefore, according to the system of Epicurus,[2] continually descending, must needs be more so when laden and pressed down by words, which are also bodies of much weight and gravity, as is manifest from those deep impressions they make and leave upon us, and therefore must be delivered from a due altitude, or else they will neither carry a good aim nor fall down with a sufficient force.

> " Corpoream quoque enim vocem constare fatendum est,
> Et sonitum, quoniam possunt impellere sensus."
> *—Lucr.* lib. 4.[3]

And I am the readier to favour this conjecture from a common observation, that in the several assemblies of these orators Nature itself has instructed the hearers to stand with their mouths open and erected parallel to the horizon, so as they may be intersected by a perpendicular line from the zenith to the centre of the earth.

---

[1] " Under the rainy sky, in the meetings of three and of four ways."
[2] Lucretius, lib. 2.—S.
[3] " 'Tis certain, then, the voice that thus can wound
    Is all material; body, every sound."

In which position, if the audience be well compact, every one carries home a share, and little or nothing is lost.

I confess there is something yet more refined in the contrivance and structure of our modern theatres. For, first, the pit is sunk below the stage with due regard to the institution above deduced, that whatever weighty matter shall be delivered thence, whether it be lead or gold, may fall plump into the jaws of certain critics, as I think they are called, which stand ready open to devour them. Then the boxes are built round and raised to a level with the scene, in deference to the ladies, because that large portion of wit laid out in raising pruriences and protuberances is observed to run much upon a line, and ever in a circle. The whining passions and little starved conceits are gently wafted up by their own extreme levity to the middle region, and there fix and are frozen by the frigid understandings of the inhabitants. Bombast and buffoonery, by nature lofty and light, soar highest of all, and would be lost in the roof if the prudent architect had not, with much foresight, contrived for them a fourth place, called the twelve-penny gallery, and there planted a suitable colony, who greedily intercept them in their passage.

Now this physico-logical scheme of oratorical receptacles or machines contains a great mystery, being a type, a sign, an emblem, a shadow, a symbol, bearing analogy to the spacious commonwealth of writers and to those methods by which they must exalt themselves to a certain eminency above the inferior world. By the Pulpit are adumbrated the writings of our modern saints in Great Britain, as they have spiritualised and refined them from the dross and grossness of sense and human reason. The matter, as we have said, is of rotten wood, and that upon two considerations : because it is the quality of rotten wood to light in the dark ; and secondly, because its cavities are full of worms— which is a type with a pair of handles, having a respect to the two principal qualifications of the orator and the two different fates attending upon his works.[1]

The Ladder is an adequate symbol of faction and of poetry,

[1] To be burnt or worm-eaten.

to both of which so noble a number of authors are indebted for their fame. Of faction, because . . *Hiatus* . .
. . . . *in MS.* .
Of poetry, because its orators do *perorare* with a song; and because, climbing up by slow degrees, fate is sure to turn them off before they can reach within many steps of the top; and because it is a preferment attained by transferring of propriety and a confounding of *meum* and *tuum.*

Under the Stage-itinerant are couched those productions designed for the pleasure and delight of mortal man, such as "Six Pennyworth of Wit," "Westminster Drolleries," "Delightful Tales," "Complete Jesters," and the like, by which the writers of and for Grub Street have in these later ages so nobly triumphed over time, have clipped his wings, pared his nails, filed his teeth, turned back his hour-glass, blunted his scythe, and drawn the hobnails out of his shoes. It is under this class I have presumed to list my present treatise, being just come from having the honour conferred upon me to be adopted a member of that illustrious fraternity.

Now, I am not unaware how the productions of the Grub Street brotherhood have of late years fallen under many prejudices, nor how it has been the perpetual employment of two junior start-up societies to ridicule them and their authors as unworthy their established post in the commonwealth of wit and learning. Their own consciences will easily inform them whom I mean ; nor has the world been so negligent a looker-on as not to observe the continual efforts made by the societies of Gresham and of Will's,[1] to edify a name and reputation upon the ruin of ours. And this is yet a more feeling grief to us, upon the regards of tenderness as well as of justice, when we reflect on their proceedings not only as unjust, but as ungrateful, undutiful, and unnatural. For how can it be forgot by the world or themselves, to say nothing of our own records, which are full and clear in the point, that they both are seminaries, not only of our planting, but our

[1] The Royal Society first met at Gresham College, the resort of men of science. Will's Coffee-House was the resort of wits and men of letters.

watering too. I am informed our two rivals have lately made an offer to enter into the lists with united forces and challenge us to a comparison of books, both as to weight and number. In return to which, with license from our president, I humbly offer two answers. First, we say the proposal is like that which Archimedes made upon a smaller affair,[1] including an impossibility in the practice; for where can they find scales of capacity enough for the first, or an arithmetician of capacity enough for the second. Secondly, we are ready to accept the challenge, but with this condition, that a third indifferent person be assigned, to whose impartial judgment it shall be left to decide which society each book, treatise, or pamphlet do most properly belong to. This point, God knows, is very far from being fixed at present, for we are ready to produce a catalogue of some thousands which in all common justice ought to be entitled to our fraternity, but by the revolted and new-fangled writers most perfidiously ascribed to the others. Upon all which we think it very unbecoming our prudence that the determination should be remitted to the authors themselves, when our adversaries by briguing and caballing have caused so universal a defection from us, that the greatest part of our society has already deserted to them, and our nearest friends begin to stand aloof, as if they were half ashamed to own us.

This is the utmost I am authorised to say upon so ungrateful and melancholy a subject, because we are extremely unwilling to inflame a controversy whose continuance may be so fatal to the interests of us all, desiring much rather that things be amicably composed; and we shall so far advance on our side as to be ready to receive the two prodigals with open arms whenever they shall think fit to return from their husks and their harlots, which I think, from the present course of their studies,[2] they most properly may be said to be engaged in, and, like an indulgent parent, continue to them our affection and our blessing.

But the greatest maim given to that general reception which the writings of our society have formerly received, next to the

---

[1] Viz., about moving the earth.—S.

[2] "Virtuoso experiments and modern comedies."—S.

transitory state of all sublunary things, has been a superficial
vein among many readers of the present age, who will by no
means be persuaded to inspect beyond the surface and the rind
of things; whereas wisdom is a fox, who, after long hunting, will
at last cost you the pains to dig out.   It is a cheese which, by
how much the richer, has the thicker, the homelier, and the
coarser coat, and whereof to a judicious palate the maggots are
the best.   It is a sack-posset, wherein the deeper you go you will
find it the sweeter.   Wisdom is a hen whose cackling we must
value and consider, because it is attended with an egg.   But
then, lastly, it is a nut, which, unless you choose with judgment,
may cost you a tooth, and pay you with nothing but a worm.   In
consequence of these momentous truths, the Grubæan sages have
always chosen to convey their precepts and their arts shut up
within the vehicles of types and fables, which having been perhaps more careful and curious in adorning than was altogether
necessary, it has fared with these vehicles after the usual fate of
coaches over-finely painted and gilt, that the transitory gazers
have so dazzled their eyes and filled their imaginations with the
outward lustre, as neither to regard nor consider the person or
the parts of the owner within.   A misfortune we undergo with
somewhat less reluctancy, because it has been common to us
with Pythagoras, Æsop, Socrates, and other of our predecessors.

However, that neither the world nor ourselves may any longer
suffer by such misunderstandings, I have been prevailed on, after
much importunity from my friends, to travail in a complete and
laborious dissertation upon the prime productions of our society,
which, besides their beautiful externals for the gratification of
superficial readers, have darkly and deeply couched under them
the most finished and refined systems of all sciences and arts, as
I do not doubt to lay open by untwisting or unwinding, and either
to draw up by exantlation or display by incision.

This great work was entered upon some years ago by one of
our most eminent members.   He began with the " History of
Reynard the Fox," but neither lived to publish his essay nor to
proceed farther in so useful an attempt, which is very much to be

lamented, because the discovery he made and communicated to his friends is now universally received; nor do I think any of the learned will dispute that famous treatise to be a complete body of civil knowledge, and the revelation, or rather the apocalypse, of all state arcana. But the progress I have made is much greater, having already finished my annotations upon several dozens, from some of which I shall impart a few hints to the candid reader, as far as will be necessary to the conclusion at which I aim.

The first piece I have handled is that of "Tom Thumb," whose author was a Pythagorean philosopher. This dark treatise contains the whole scheme of the metempsychosis, deducing the progress of the soul through all her stages.

The next is " Dr. Faustus," penned by Artephius, an author *bonæ notæ* and an adeptus; he published it in the nine hundred and eighty-fourth year [1] of his age; this writer proceeds wholly by reincrudation, or in the *via humida ;* and the marriage between Faustus and Helen does most conspicuously dilucidate the fermenting of the male and female dragon.

"Whittington and his Cat " is the work of that mysterious Rabbi, Jehuda Hannasi, containing a defence of the Gemara of the Jerusalem Misna, and its just preference to that of Babylon, contrary to the vulgar opinion.

"The Hind and Panther." This is the masterpiece of a famous writer now living,[2] intended for a complete abstract of sixteen thousand schoolmen from Scotus to Bellarmine.

"Tommy Potts." Another piece, supposed by the same hand, by way of supplement to the former.

The "Wise Men of Gotham," *cum* Appendice. This is a treatise of immense erudition, being the great original and fountain of those arguments, bandied about both in France and England, for a just defence of modern learning and wit, against the presumption, the pride, and the ignorance of the ancients. This unknown

---

[1] He lived a thousand.—S.

[2] Viz., in the year 1697.—S. Dryden died in 1700, and the publication of the " Tale of a Tub," written in 1697, was not until 1704.

author hath so exhausted the subject, that a penetrating reader will easily discover whatever has been written since upon that dispute to be little more than repetition. An abstract of this treatise has been lately published by a worthy member of our society.

These notices may serve to give the learned reader an idea as well as a taste of what the whole work is likely to produce, wherein I have now altogether circumscribed my thoughts and my studies; and if I can bring it to a perfection before I die, shall reckon I have well employed the poor remains of an unfortunate life. This indeed is more than I can justly expect from a quill worn to the pith in the service of the State, in pros and cons upon Popish Plots, and Meal Tubs, and Exclusion Bills, and Passive Obedience, and Addresses of Lives and Fortunes; and Prerogative, and Property, and Liberty of Conscience, and Letters to a Friend: from an understanding and a conscience, threadbare and ragged with perpetual turning; from a head broken in a hundred places by the malignants of the opposite factions, and from a body spent with poxes ill cured, by trusting to bawds and surgeons, who (as it afterwards appeared) were professed enemies to me and the Government, and revenged their party's quarrel upon my nose and shins. Fourscore and eleven pamphlets have I written under three reigns, and for the service of six-and-thirty factions. But finding the State has no farther occasion for me and my ink, I retire willingly to draw it out into speculations more becoming a philosopher, having, to my unspeakable comfort, passed a long life with a conscience void of offence towards God and towards men.

But to return. I am assured from the reader's candour that the brief specimen I have given will easily clear all the rest of our society's productions from an aspersion grown, as it is manifest, out of envy and ignorance, that they are of little farther use or value to mankind beyond the common entertainments of their wit and their style; for these I am sure have never yet been disputed by our keenest adversaries; in both which, as well as the more profound and most mystical part, I have throughout this treatise closely followed the most applauded originals. And to render all complete, I have with much thought and application of mind so ordered that the chief title prefixed to it (I mean that under which I design it shall pass in the common conversation of court and town) is modelled exactly after the manner peculiar to our society.

I confess to have been somewhat liberal in the business of titles,[1] having observed the humour of multiplying them, to bear great vogue among certain writers, whom I exceedingly reverence. And indeed it seems not unreasonable that books, the children of the brain, should have the honour to be christened with variety of names, as well as other infants of quality. Our famous Dryden has ventured to proceed a point farther, endeavouring to introduce also a multiplicity of godfathers,[2] which is an improvement of much more advantage, upon a very obvious account. It is a pity this admirable invention has not been better cultivated, so as to grow by this time into general imitation, when such an authority serves it for a precedent. Nor have my endeavours been wanting to second so useful an example, but it seems there is an unhappy expense usually annexed to the calling of a godfather, which was clearly out of my head, as it is very reasonable to believe. Where the pinch lay, I cannot certainly affirm ; but having employed a world of thoughts and pains to split my treatise into forty sections, and having entreated forty Lords of my acquaintance that they would do me the honour to stand, they all made it matter of conscience, and sent me their excuses.

[1] The title-page in the original was so torn that it was not possible to recover several titles which the author here speaks of.—S.

[2] See Virgil translated, &c.—S.

SECTION II.

ONCE upon a time there was a man who had three sons by one wife [1] and all at a birth, neither could the midwife tell certainly which was the eldest. Their father died while they were young, and upon his death-bed, calling the lads to him, spoke thus :—

"Sons, because I have purchased no estate, nor was born to any, I have long considered of some good legacies to bequeath you, and at last, with much care as well as expense, have provided each of you (here they are) a new coat. Now, you are to understand that these coats have two virtues contained in them ; one is, that with good wearing they will last you fresh and sound as long as you live ; the other is, that they will grow in the same proportion with your bodies, lengthening and widening of themselves, so as to be always fit. Here, let me see them on you before I die. So, very well ! Pray, children, wear them clean and brush them often. You will find in my will (here it is) full instructions in every particular concerning the wearing and management of your coats, wherein you must be very exact to avoid the penalties I have appointed for every transgression or neglect, upon which your future fortunes will entirely depend. I have also commanded in my will that you should live together in one house like brethren and friends, for then you will be sure to thrive and not otherwise."

Here the story says this good father died, and the three sons went all together to seek their fortunes.

1 Peter, the Church of Rome ; Martin, the Reformed Church as established by authority in England ; Jack, the dissenters from the English Church Establishment. Martin, named probably from Martin Luther ; Jack, from John Calvin. The coats are the coats of righteousness, in which all servants of God should be clothed ; alike in love and duty, however they may differ in opinion.

I shall not trouble you with recounting what adventures they met for the first seven years, any farther than by taking notice that they carefully observed their father's will and kept their coats in very good order; that they travelled through several countries, encountered a reasonable quantity of giants, and slew certain dragons.

Being now arrived at the proper age for producing themselves, they came up to town and fell in love with the ladies, but especially three, who about that time were in chief reputation, the Duchess d'Argent, Madame de Grands-Titres, and the Countess d'Orgueil.[1] On their first appearance, our three adventurers met with a very bad reception, and soon with great sagacity guessing out the reason, they quickly began to improve in the good qualities of the town. They wrote, and rallied, and rhymed, and sung, and said, and said nothing; they drank, and fought, and slept, and swore, and took snuff; they went to new plays on the first night, haunted the chocolate-houses, beat the watch; they bilked hackney-coachmen, ran in debt with shopkeepers, and lay with their wives; they killed bailiffs, kicked fiddlers down-stairs, ate at Locket's, loitered at Will's; they talked of the drawing-room and never came there; dined with lords they never saw; whispered a duchess and spoke never a word; exposed the scrawls of their laundress for billet-doux of quality; came ever just from court and were never seen in it; attended the levee *sub dio;* got a list of peers by heart in one company, and with great familiarity retailed them in another. Above all, they constantly attended those committees of Senators who are silent in the House and loud in the coffee-house, where they nightly adjourn to chew the cud of politics, and are encompassed with a ring of disciples who lie in wait to catch up their droppings. The three brothers had acquired forty other qualifications of the like stamp too tedious to recount, and by consequence were justly reckoned the most accomplished persons in town. But all would not suffice, and the ladies afore-

[1] Covetousness, ambition, and pride, which were the three great vices that the ancient fathers inveighed against as the first corruptions of Christianity.— *W. Wotton.*

said continued still inflexible. To clear up which difficulty, I must, with the reader's good leave and patience, have recourse to some points of weight which the authors of that age have not sufficiently illustrated.

For about this time it happened a sect arose whose tenets obtained and spread very far, especially in the *grand monde*, and among everybody of good fashion. They worshipped a sort of idol,[1] who, as their doctrine delivered, did daily create men by a kind of manufactory operation. This idol they placed in the highest parts of the house on an altar erected about three feet. He was shown in the posture of a Persian emperor sitting on a superficies with his legs interwoven under him. This god had a goose for his ensign, whence it is that some learned men pretend to deduce his original from Jupiter Capitolinus. At his left hand, beneath the altar, Hell seemed to open and catch at the animals the idol was creating, to prevent which, certain of his priests hourly flung in pieces of the uninformed mass or substance, and sometimes whole limbs already enlivened, which that horrid gulph insatiably swallowed, terrible to behold. The goose was also held a subaltern divinity or *Deus minorum gentium*, before whose shrine was sacrificed that creature whose hourly food is human gore, and who is in so great renown abroad for being the delight and favourite of the Egyptian Cercopithecus.[2] Millions of these animals were cruelly slaughtered every day to appease the hunger of that consuming deity. The chief idol was also worshipped as the inventor of the yard and the needle, whether as the god of seamen, or on account of certain other mystical attributes, hath not been sufficiently cleared.

The worshippers of this deity had also a system of their belief which seemed to turn upon the following fundamental. They held the universe to be a large suit of clothes which invests everything; that the earth is invested by the air; the air is invested by the stars; and the stars are invested by the *Primum Mobile*. Look on this globe of earth, you will find it to be a very complete and fashionable dress. What is that which some call land but

---

[1] The tailor.   [2] A sacred monkey.

a fine coat faced with green, or the sea but a waistcoat of water-tabby? Proceed to the particular works of the creation, you will find how curious journeyman Nature hath been to trim up the vegetable beaux; observe how sparkish a periwig adorns the head of a beech, and what a fine doublet of white satin is worn by the birch. To conclude from all, what is man himself but a micro-coat, or rather a complete suit of clothes with all its trimmings? As to his body there can be no dispute, but examine even the acquirements of his mind, you will find them all contribute in their order towards furnishing out an exact dress. To instance no more, is not religion a cloak, honesty a pair of shoes worn out in the dirt, self-love a surtout, vanity a shirt, and conscience a pair of breeches, which, though a cover for lewdness as well as nastiness, is easily slipped down for the service of both.

These *postulata* being admitted, it will follow in due course of reasoning that those beings which the world calls improperly suits of clothes are in reality the most refined species of animals, or to proceed higher, that they are rational creatures or men. For is it not manifest that they live, and move, and talk, and perform all other offices of human life? Are not beauty, and wit, and mien, and breeding their inseparable proprieties? In short, we see nothing but them, hear nothing but them. Is it not they who walk the streets, fill up Parliament-, coffee-, play-, bawdy-houses. It is true, indeed, that these animals, which are vulgarly called suits of clothes or dresses, do according to certain compositions receive different appellations. If one of them be trimmed up with a gold chain, and a red gown, and a white rod, and a great horse, it is called a Lord Mayor; if certain ermines and furs be placed in a certain position, we style them a Judge, and so an apt conjunction of lawn and black satin we entitle a Bishop.

Others of these professors, though agreeing in the main system, were yet more refined upon certain branches of it; and held that man was an animal compounded of two dresses, the natural and the celestial suit, which were the body and the soul; that the soul was the outward, and the body the inward clothing; that the latter was *ex traduce,* but the former of daily creation and circumfusion. This last they proved by Scripture, because in them we live, and move, and have our being: as likewise by philosophy, because they are all in all, and all in every part. Besides, said they, separate these two, and you will find the body to be only a senseless unsavoury carcass. By all which it is manifest that the outward dress must needs be the soul.

To this system of religion were tagged several subaltern doctrines, which were entertained with great vogue; as particularly the faculties of the mind were deduced by the learned among them in this manner: embroidery was sheer wit, gold fringe was agreeable conversation, gold lace was repartee, a huge long periwig was humour, and a coat full of powder was very good raillery. All which required abundance of finesse and delicatesse to manage with advantage, as well as a strict observance after times and fashions.

I have with much pains and reading collected out of ancient authors this short summary of a body of philosophy and divinity which seems to have been composed by a vein and race of thinking very different from any other systems, either ancient or modern. And it was not merely to entertain or satisfy the reader's curiosity, but rather to give him light into several circumstances of the following story, that, knowing the state of dispositions and opinions in an age so remote, he may better comprehend those great events which were the issue of them. I advise, therefore, the courteous reader to peruse with a world of application, again and again, whatever I have written upon this matter. And so leaving these broken ends, I carefully gather up the chief thread of my story, and proceed.

These opinions, therefore, were so universal, as well as the practices of them, among the refined part of court and town, that our three brother adventurers, as their circumstances then stood, were strangely at a loss. For, on the one side, the three ladies they addressed themselves to (whom we have named already) were ever at the very top of the fashion, and abhorred all that were below it but the breadth of a hair. On the other

side, their father's will was very precise, and it was the main precept in it, with the greatest penalties annexed, not to add to or
diminish from their coats one thread without a positive command
in the will.   Now the coats their father had left them were, it is
true, of very good cloth, and besides, so neatly sewn you would
swear they were all of a piece, but, at the same time, very plain,
with little or no ornament; and it happened that before they were
a month in town great shoulder-knots came up.   Straight all the
world was shoulder-knots; no approaching the ladies' *ruelles* without the quota of shoulder-knots.   "That fellow," cries one, "has no
soul: where is his shoulder-knot?"[1]   Our three brethren soon discovered their want by sad experience, meeting in their walks with
forty mortifications and indignities.   If they went to the playhouse, the doorkeeper showed them into the twelve-penny gallery.
If they called a boat, says a waterman, "I am first sculler."   If
they stepped into the "Rose" to take a bottle, the drawer would
cry, "Friend, we sell no ale."   If they went to visit a lady, a footman met them at the door with " Pray, send up your message."
In this unhappy case they went immediately to consult their
father's will, read it over and over, but not a word of the
shoulder-knot.   What should they do?   What temper should
they find?   Obedience was absolutely necessary, and yet shoulder-
knots appeared extremely requisite.   After much thought, one of
the brothers, who happened to be more book-learned than the
other two, said he had found an expedient.   "It is true," said he,
"there is nothing here in this will, *totidem verbis*, making mention of shoulder-knots, but I dare conjecture we may find them

---

[1] The Roman Catholics were considered by the Reformers to have added to the
simple doctrines of Christianity inventions of their own, and to have laid especial
stress on the adoption of them.   Upon Swift's saying of the three brothers, "Now
the coats their father had left them were, it is true, of very good cloth, and besides
so neatly sewn that you would swear they were all of a piece, but, at the same
time, very plain, with little or no ornament," W. Wotton observes: "This is the
distinguishing character of the Christian religion.   *Christiana religio absoluta et
simplex*, was Ammianus Marcellinus's description of it, who was himself a heathen."
But the learned Peter argues that if a doctrine cannot be found, *totidem verbis*, in
so many words, it may be found in so many syllables, or, if that way fail, we shall
make them out in a third way, of so many letters.

inclusive, or *totidem syllabis.*" This distinction was immediately approved by all; and so they fell again to examine the will. But their evil star had so directed the matter that the first syllable was not to be found in the whole writing; upon which disappointment, he who found the former evasion took heart, and said, "Brothers, there is yet hopes; for though we cannot find them *totidem verbis* nor *totidem syllabis,* I dare engage we shall make them out *tertio modo* or *totidem literis.*" This discovery was also highly commended, upon which they fell once more to the scrutiny, and soon picked out S, H, O, U, L, D, E, R, when the same planet, enemy to their repose, had wonderfully contrived that a K was not to be found. Here was a weighty difficulty! But the distinguishing brother (for whom we shall hereafter find a name), now his hand was in, proved by a very good argument that K was a modern illegitimate letter, unknown to the learned ages, nor anywhere to be found in ancient manuscripts. "It is true," said he, "the word *Calendæ* had in Q. V. C.[1] been sometimes writ with a K, but erroneously, for in the best copies it is ever spelt with a C; and by consequence it was a gross mistake in our language to spell 'knot' with a K," but that from henceforward he would take care it should be writ with a C. Upon this all further difficulty vanished; shoulder-knots were made clearly out to be *jure paterno,* and our three gentlemen swaggered with as large and as flaunting ones as the best.

But as human happiness is of a very short duration, so in those days were human fashions, upon which it entirely depends. Shoulder-knots had their time, and we must now imagine them in their decline, for a certain lord came just from Paris with fifty yards of gold lace upon his coat, exactly trimmed after the court fashion of that month. In two days all mankind appeared closed up in bars of gold lace. Whoever durst peep abroad without his complement of gold lace was as scandalous as a ——, and as ill received among the women. What should our three knights do in this momentous affair? They had sufficiently strained a point

---

1 *Quibusdam veteribus codicibus* [some ancient MSS.].—S.

already in the affair of shoulder-knots. Upon recourse to the will, nothing appeared there but *altum silentium.* That of the shoulder-knots was a loose, flying, circumstantial point, but this of gold lace seemed too considerable an alteration without better warrant. It did *aliquo modo essentiæ adhærere,* and therefore required a positive precept. But about this time it fell out that the learned brother aforesaid had read "Aristotelis Dialectica," and especially that wonderful piece *de Interpretatione,* which has the faculty of teaching its readers to find out a meaning in everything but itself, like commentators on the Revelations, who proceed prophets without understanding a syllable of the text. "Brothers," said he, "you are to be informed that of wills, *duo sunt genera,* nuncupatory and scriptory,[1] that in the scriptory will here before us there is no precept or mention about gold lace, *conceditur,* but *si idem affirmetur de nuncupatorio negatur.* For, brothers, if you remember, we heard a fellow say when we were boys that he heard my father's man say that he heard my father say that he would advise his sons to get gold lace on their coats as soon as ever they could procure money to buy it." "That is very true," cries the other. "I remember it perfectly well," said the third. And so, without more ado, they got the largest gold lace in the parish, and walked about as fine as lords.

A while after, there came up all in fashion a pretty sort of flame-coloured satin [2] for linings, and the mercer brought a pattern of it immediately to our three gentlemen. "An please your worships," said he, "my Lord C—— and Sir J. W. had linings out of this very piece last night; it takes wonderfully, and I shall not have a remnant left enough to make my wife a pin-cushion by to-morrow morning at ten o'clock." Upon this they fell again to rummage the will, because the present case also required a positive precept, the lining being held by orthodox writers to be of the essence of the coat. After long search they could fix upon nothing to the

---

[1] There are two kinds—oral tradition and the written record,—reference to the value attached to tradition in the Roman Church.

[2] The flame-coloured lining figures the doctrine of Purgatory; and the codicil annexed, the Apocryphal books annexed to the Bible. The dog-keeper is said to be an allusion to the Apocryphal book of Tobit.

matter in hand, except a short advice in their father's will to take care of fire and put out their candles before they went to sleep.[1] This, though a good deal for the purpose, and helping very far towards self-conviction, yet not seeming wholly of force to establish a command, and being resolved to avoid further scruple, as well as future occasion for scandal, says he that was the scholar, "I remember to have read in wills of a codicil annexed, which is indeed a part of the will, and what it contains hath equal authority with the rest. Now I have been considering of this same will here before us, and I cannot reckon it to be complete for want of such a codicil. I will therefore fasten one in its proper place very dexterously. I have had it by me some time; it was written by a dog-keeper of my grandfather's, and talks a great deal, as good luck would have it, of this very flame-coloured satin." The project was immediately approved by the other two; an old parchment scroll was tagged on according to art, in the form of a codicil annexed, and the satin bought and worn.

Next winter a player, hired for the purpose by the Corporation of Fringemakers, acted his part in a new comedy, all covered with silver fringe,[2] and according to the laudable custom gave rise to that fashion. Upon which the brothers, consulting their father's will, to their great astonishment found these words : " Item, I charge and command my said three sons to wear no sort of silver fringe upon or about their said coats," &c., with a penalty in case of disobedience too long here to insert. However, after some pause, the brother so often mentioned for his erudition, who was well skilled in criticisms, had found in a certain author, which he said should be nameless, that the same word which in the will is called fringe does also signify a broom-stick, and doubtless ought to have the same interpretation in this paragraph. This another of the brothers disliked, because of that epithet silver, which could not, he humbly conceived, in propriety of speech be reasonably applied to a broom-stick; but it was replied upon him that this epithet was understood in a mythological and allegorical sense.

---

[1] Dread hell and subdue their lusts.
[2] Strained glosses and interpretations of the simple text.

However, he objected again why their father should forbid them to wear a broom-stick on their coats, a caution that seemed unnatural and impertinent; upon which he was taken up short, as one that spoke irreverently of a mystery which doubtless was very useful and significant, but ought not to be over-curiously pried into or nicely reasoned upon. And in short, their father's authority being now considerably sunk, this expedient was allowed to serve as a lawful dispensation for wearing their full proportion of silver fringe.

A while after was revived an old fashion, long antiquated, of embroidery with Indian figures of men, women, and children.[1] Here they had no occasion to examine the will. They remembered but too well how their father had always abhorred this fashion; that he made several paragraphs on purpose, importing his utter detestation of it, and bestowing his everlasting curse to his sons whenever they should wear it. For all this, in a few days they appeared higher in the fashion than anybody else in the town. But they solved the matter by saying that these figures were not at all the same with those that were formerly worn and were meant in the will; besides, they did not wear them in that sense, as forbidden by their father, but as they were a commendable custom, and of great use to the public. That these rigorous clauses in the will did therefore require some allowance and a favourable interpretation, and ought to be understood *cum grano salis.*

But fashions perpetually altering in that age, the scholastic brother grew weary of searching further evasions and solving everlasting contradictions. Resolved, therefore, at all hazards to comply with the modes of the world, they concerted matters together, and agreed unanimously to lock up their father's will in a strong-box, brought out of Greece or Italy[2] (I have forgot which), and trouble themselves no farther to examine it, but only refer to its authority whenever they thought fit. In consequence

[1] Images in churches.
[2] The locking up of the Gospel in the original Greek or in the Latin of the Vulgate, and forbidding its diffusion in the language of the people.

whereof, a while after it grew a general mode to wear an infinite number of points, most of them tagged with silver; upon which the scholar pronounced *ex cathedrâ*[1] that points were absolutely *jure paterno*, as they might very well remember. It is true, indeed, the fashion prescribed somewhat more than were directly named in the will; however, that they, as heirs-general of their father, had power to make and add certain clauses for public emolument, though not deducible *todidem verbis* from the letter of the will, or else *multa absurda sequerentur.* This was understood for canonical, and therefore on the following Sunday they came to church all covered with points.

The learned brother so often mentioned was reckoned the best scholar in all that or the next street to it; insomuch, as having run something behindhand with the world, he obtained the favour from a certain lord[2] to receive him into his house and to teach his children. A while after the lord died, and he, by long practice upon his father's will, found the way of contriving a deed of conveyance of that house to himself and his heirs; upon which he took possession, turned the young squires out, and received his brothers in their stead.

[1] The Pope's bulls and decretals, issued by his paternal authority, that must determine questions of interpretation and tradition, or else many absurd things would follow.

[2] Constantine the Great, from whom the Church of Rome was said to have received the donation of St. Peter's patrimony, and first derived the wealth described by our old Reformers as "the fatal gift of Constantine."

SECTION III.

A DIGRESSION CONCERNING CRITICS.

THOUGH I have been hitherto as cautious as I could, upon all occasions, most nicely to follow the rules and methods of writing laid down by the example of our illustrious moderns, yet has the unhappy shortness of my memory led me into an error, from which I must immediately extricate myself, before I can decently pursue my principal subject. I confess with shame it was an unpardonable omission to proceed so far as I have already done before I had performed the due discourses, expostulatory, supplicatory, or deprecatory, with my good lords the critics. Towards some atonement for this grievous neglect, I do here make humbly bold to present them with a short account of themselves and their art, by looking into the original and pedigree of the word, as it is generally understood among us, and very briefly considering the ancient and present state thereof.

By the word critic, at this day so frequent in all conversations, there have sometimes been distinguished three very different species of mortal men, according as I have read in ancient books and pamphlets. For first, by this term were understood such persons as invented or drew up rules for themselves and the world, by observing which a careful reader might be able to pronounce upon the productions of the learned, form his taste to a true relish of the sublime and the admirable, and divide every beauty of matter or of style from the corruption that apes it. In their common perusal of books, singling out the errors and defects, the nauseous, the fulsome, the dull, and the impertinent, with the caution of a man that walks through Edinburgh streets in a

morning, who is indeed as careful as he can to watch diligently
and spy out the filth in his way; not that he is curious to observe
the colour and complexion of the ordure or take its dimensions,
much less to be paddling in or tasting it, but only with a design
to come out as cleanly as he may.   These men seem, though
very erroneously, to have understood the appellation of critic in a
literal sense; that one principal part of his office was to praise
and acquit, and that a critic who sets up to read only for an
occasion of censure and reproof is a creature as barbarous as a
judge who should take up a resolution to hang all men that came
before him upon a trial.

Again, by the word critic have been meant the restorers of
ancient learning from the worms, and graves, and dust of manuscripts.

Now the races of these two have been for some ages utterly
extinct, and besides to discourse any further of them would not
be at all to my purpose.

The third and noblest sort is that of the true critic, whose
original is the most ancient of all.   Every true critic is a hero
born, descending in a direct line from a celestial stem, by Momus
and Hybris, who begat Zoilus, who begat Tigellius, who begat
Etcætera the elder, who begat Bentley, and Rymer, and Wotton,
and Perrault, and Dennis, who begat Etcætera the younger.

And these are the critics from whom the commonwealth of
learning has in all ages received such immense benefits, that the
gratitude of their admirers placed their origin in heaven, among
those of Hercules, Theseus, Perseus, and other great deservers
of mankind.   But heroic virtue itself hath not been exempt from
the obloquy of evil tongues.   For it hath been objected that
those ancient heroes, famous for their combating so many giants,
and dragons, and robbers, were in their own persons a greater
nuisance to mankind than any of those monsters they subdued;
and therefore, to render their obligations more complete, when
all other vermin were destroyed, should in conscience have concluded with the same justice upon themselves, as Hercules most
generously did, and hath upon that score procured for himself

more temples and votaries than the best of his fellows. For these reasons I suppose it is why some have conceived it would be very expedient for the public good of learning that every true critic, as soon as he had finished his task assigned, should immediately deliver himself up to ratsbane or hemp, or from some convenient altitude, and that no man's pretensions to so illustrious a character should by any means be received before that operation was performed.

Now, from this heavenly descent of criticism, and the close analogy it bears to heroic virtue, it is easy to assign the proper employment of a true, ancient, genuine critic: which is, to travel through this vast world of writings; to peruse and hunt those monstrous faults bred within them ; to drag out the lurking errors, like Cacus from his den ; to multiply them like Hydra's heads ; and rake them together like Augeas's dung; or else to drive away a sort of dangerous fowl who have a perverse inclination to plunder the best branches of the tree of knowledge, like those Stymphalian birds that ate up the fruit.

These reasonings will furnish us with an adequate definition of a true critic: that he is a discoverer and collector of writers' faults; which may be further put beyond dispute by the following demonstration :—That whoever will examine the writings in all kinds wherewith this ancient sect hath honoured the world, shall immediately find from the whole thread and tenor of them that the ideas of the authors have been altogether conversant and taken up with the faults, and blemishes, and oversights, and mistakes of other writers, and let the subject treated on be whatever it will, their imaginations are so entirely possessed and replete with the defects of other pens, that the very quintessence of what is bad does of necessity distil into their own, by which means the whole appears to be nothing else but an abstract of the criticisms themselves have made.

Having thus briefly considered the original and office of a critic, as the word is understood in its most noble and universal acceptation, I proceed to refute the objections of those who argue from the silence and pretermission of authors, by which they pretend to prove that the very art of criticism, as now exercised, and by me explained, is wholly modern, and consequently that the critics of Great Britain and France have no title to an original so ancient and illustrious as I have deduced. Now, if I can clearly make out, on the contrary, that the most ancient writers have particularly described both the person and the office of a true critic agreeable to the definition laid down by me, their grand objection—from the silence of authors—will fall to the ground.

I confess to have for a long time borne a part in this general error, from which I should never have acquitted myself but through the assistance of our noble moderns, whose most edifying volumes I turn indefatigably over night and day, for the improvement of my mind and the good of my country. These have with unwearied pains made many useful searches into the weak sides of the ancients, and given us a comprehensive list of them.[1] Besides, they have proved beyond contradiction that the very finest things delivered of old have been long since invented and brought to light by much later pens, and that the noblest discoveries those ancients ever made in art or nature have all been produced by the transcending genius of the present age, which clearly shows how little merit those ancients can justly pretend to, and takes off that blind admiration paid them by men in a corner, who have the unhappiness of conversing too little with present things. Reflecting maturely upon all this, and taking in the whole compass of human nature, I easily concluded that these ancients, highly sensible of their many imperfections, must needs have endeavoured, from some passages in their works, to obviate, soften, or divert the censorious reader, by satire or panegyric upon the true critics, in imitation of their masters, the moderns. Now, in the commonplaces[2] of both these I was plentifully instructed by a long course of useful study in prefaces and prologues, and therefore immediately resolved to try what I could discover of either, by a diligent perusal of the most ancient writers, and especially those who treated of the earliest times.

---

[1] See Wotton "Of Ancient and Modern Learning."—S.
[2] Satire and panegyric upon critics.—S.

Here I found, to my great surprise, that although they all entered upon occasion into particular descriptions of the true critic, according as they were governed by their fears or their hopes, yet whatever they touched of that kind was with abundance of caution, adventuring no further than mythology and hieroglyphic. This, I suppose, gave ground to superficial readers for urging the silence of authors against the antiquity of the true critic, though the types are so apposite, and the applications so necessary and natural, that it is not easy to conceive how any reader of modern eye and taste could overlook them. I shall venture from a great number to produce a few which I am very confident will put this question beyond doubt.

It well deserves considering that these ancient writers, in treating enigmatically upon this subject, have generally fixed upon the very same hieroglyph, varying only the story according to their affections or their wit. For first, Pausanias is of opinion that the perfection of writing correct was entirely owing to the institution of critics, and that he can possibly mean no other than the true critic is, I think, manifest enough from the following description. He says they were a race of men who delighted to nibble at the superfluities and excrescences of books, which the learned at length observing, took warning of their own accord to lop the luxuriant, the rotten, the dead, the sapless, and the overgrown branches from their works. But now all this he cunningly shades under the following allegory : That the Nauplians in Argia learned the art of pruning their vines by observing that when an ass had browsed upon one of them, it thrived the better and bore fairer fruit. But Herodotus holding the very same hieroglyph, speaks much plainer and almost *in terminis.* He hath been so bold as to tax the true critics of ignorance and malice, telling us openly, for I think nothing can be plainer, that in the western part of Libya there were asses with horns, upon which relation Ctesias [1] yet refines, mehtioning the very same animal about India ; adding, that whereas all other asses wanted a gall, these horned

---

[1] *Vide* excerpta ex eo apud Photium—S.

ones were so redundant in that part that their flesh was not to be eaten because of its extreme bitterness.

Now, the reason why those ancient writers treated this subject only by types and figures was because they durst not make open attacks against a party so potent and so terrible as the critics of those ages were, whose very voice was so dreadful that a legion of authors would tremble and drop their pens at the sound.   For so Herodotus tells us expressly in another place how a vast army of Scythians was put to flight in a panic terror by the braying of an ass.   From hence it is conjectured by certain profound philologers, that the great awe and reverence paid to a true critic by the writers of Britain have been derived to us from those our Scythian ancestors.   In short, this dread was so universal, that in process of time those authors who had a mind to publish their sentiments more freely in describing the true critics of their several ages, were forced to leave off the use of the former hieroglyph as too nearly approaching the prototype, and invented other terms instead thereof that were more cautious and mystical. So Diodorus, speaking to the same purpose, ventures no farther than to say that in the mountains of Helicon there grows a certain weed which bears a flower of so damned a scent as to poison those who offer to smell it.   Lucretius gives exactly the same relation.

> "Est etiam in magnis Heliconis montibus arbos,
> Floris odore hominem retro consueta necare."—*Lib.* 6.[1]

But Ctesias, whom we lately quoted, has been a great deal bolder; he had been used with much severity by the true critics of his own age, and therefore could not forbear to leave behind him at least one deep mark of his vengeance against the whole tribe.   His meaning is so near the surface that I wonder how it possibly came to be overlooked by those who deny the antiquity of the true critics.   For pretending to make a description of many strange animals about India, he has set down these remarkable

[1] " Near Helicon and round the learned hill
Grow trees whose blossoms with their odour kill."—*Hawkesworth.*

words. "Among the rest," says he, "there is a serpent that wants
teeth, and consequently cannot bite, but if its vomit (to which it is
much addicted) happens to fall upon anything, a certain rottenness or corruption ensues. These serpents are generally found
among the mountains where jewels grow, and they frequently
emit a poisonous juice, whereof whoever drinks, that person's
brain flies out of his nostrils."

There was also among the ancients a sort of critic, not distinguished in specie from the former but in growth or degree, who
seem to have been only the tyros or junior scholars, yet because
of their differing employments they are frequently mentioned as
a sect by themselves. The usual exercise of these young students
was to attend constantly at theatres, and learn to spy out the worst
parts of the play, whereof they were obliged carefully to take note,
and render a rational account to their tutors. Fleshed at these
smaller sports, like young wolves, they grew up in time to be
nimble and strong enough for hunting down large game. For it
has been observed, both among ancients and moderns, that a true
critic has one quality in common with a whore and an alderman,
never to change his title or his nature ; that a grey critic has been
certainly a green one, the perfections and acquirements of his age
being only the improved talents of his youth, like hemp, which
some naturalists inform us is bad for suffocations, though taken
but in the seed. I esteem the invention, or at least the refinement
of prologues, to have been owing to these younger proficients, of
whom Terence makes frequent and honourable.mention, under
the name of Malevoli.

Now it is certain the institution of the true critics was of absolute necessity to the commonwealth of learning. For all human
actions seem to be divided like Themistocles and his company.
One man can fiddle, and another can make a small town a great
city ; and he that cannot do either one or the other deserves to
be kicked out of the creation. The avoiding of which penalty
has doubtless given the first birth to the nation of critics, and
withal an occasion for their secret detractors to report that a
true critic is a sort of mechanic set up with a stock and tools for

his trade, at as little expense as a tailor; and that there is much analogy between the utensils and abilities of both. That the "Tailor's Hell" is the type of a critic's commonplace-book, and his wit and learning held forth by the goose. That it requires at least as many of these to the making up of one scholar as of the others to the composition of a man. That the valour of both is equal, and their weapons near of a size. Much may be said in answer to these invidious reflections; and I can positively affirm the first to be a falsehood: for, on the contrary, nothing is more certain than that it requires greater layings out to be free of the critic's company than of any other you can name. For as to be a true beggar, it will cost the richest candidate every groat he is worth, so before one can commence a true critic, it will cost a man all the good qualities of his mind, which perhaps for a less purchase would be thought but an indifferent bargain.

Having thus amply proved the antiquity of criticism and de-scribed the primitive state of it, I shall now examine the present condition of this Empire, and show how well it agrees with its ancient self.[1] A certain author, whose works have many ages since been entirely lost, does in his fifth book and eighth chapter say of critics that "their writings are the mirrors of learning." This I understand in a literal sense, and suppose our author must mean that whoever designs to be a perfect writer must inspect into the books of critics, and correct his inventions there as in a mirror. Now, whoever considers that the mirrors of the ancients were made of brass and fine mercurio, may presently apply the two principal qualifications of a true modern critic, and conse-quently must needs conclude that these have always been and must be for ever the same. For brass is an emblem of duration, and when it is skilfully burnished will cast reflections from its own superficies without any assistance of mercury from behind. All the other talents of a critic will not require a particular mention, being included or easily deducible to these. However, I shall conclude with three maxims, which may serve both as charac-

---

[1] A quotation after the manner of a great author. *Vide* Bentley's "Dissertation," &c.—S.

teristics to distinguish a true modern critic from a pretender, and will be also of admirable use to those worthy spirits who engage in so useful and honourable an art.

The first is, that criticism, contrary to all other faculties of the intellect, is ever held the truest and best when it is the very first result of the critic's mind; as fowlers reckon the first aim for the surest, and seldom fail of missing the mark if they stay not for a second.

Secondly, the true critics are known by their talent of swarming about the noblest writers, to which they are carried merely by instinct, as a rat to the best cheese, or a wasp to the fairest fruit. So when the king is a horseback he is sure to be the dirtiest person of the company, and they that make their court best are such as bespatter him most.

Lastly, a true critic in the perusal of a book is like a dog at a feast, whose thoughts and stomach are wholly set upon what the guests fling away, and consequently is apt to snarl most when there are the fewest bones.[1]

Thus much I think is sufficient to serve by way of address to my patrons, the true modern critics, and may very well atone for my past silence, as well as that which I am like to observe for the future. I hope I have deserved so well of their whole body as to meet with generous and tender usage at their hands. Supported by which expectation I go on boldly to pursue those adventures already so happily begun.

[1] "And how they're disappointed when they're pleased."—*Congreve, quoted by Pate.*

SECTION IV.

A TALE OF A TUB.

I HAVE now with much pains and study conducted the reader
to a period where he must expect to hear of great revolutions.
For no sooner had our learned brother, so often mentioned, got
a warm house of his own over his head, than he began to look big
and to take mightily upon him, insomuch that unless the gentle
reader out of his great candour will please a little to exalt his idea,
I am afraid he will henceforth hardly know the hero of the play
when he happens to meet him, his part, his dress, and his mien
being so much altered.

He told his brothers he would have them to know that he
was their elder, and consequently his father's sole heir; nay, a
while after, he would not allow them to call him brother, but Mr.
Peter; and then he must be styled Father Peter, and sometimes
My Lord Peter.   To support this grandeur, which he soon began
to consider could not be maintained without a better *fonde* than
what he was born to, after much thought he cast about at last to
turn projector and virtuoso, wherein he so well succeeded, that
many famous discoveries, projects, and machines which bear great
vogue and practice at present in the world, are owing entirely to
Lord Peter's invention.   I will deduce the best account I have
been able to collect of the chief amongst them, without considering much the order they came out in, because I think authors
are not well agreed as to that point.

I hope when this treatise of mine shall be translated into foreign
languages (as I may without vanity affirm that the labour of
collecting, the faithfulness in recounting, and the great usefulness

of the matter to the public, will amply deserve that justice), that the worthy members of the several Academies abroad, especially those of France and Italy, will favourably accept these humble offers for the advancement of universal knowledge. I do also advertise the most reverend fathers the Eastern missionaries that I have purely for their sakes made use of such words and phrases as will best admit an easy turn into any of the Oriental languages, especially the Chinese. And so I proceed with great content of mind upon reflecting how much emolument this whole globe of earth is like to reap by my labours.

The first undertaking of Lord Peter was to purchase a large continent, lately said to have been discovered in *Terra Australis incognita.* This tract of land he bought at a very great penny-worth from the discoverers themselves (though some pretended to doubt whether they had ever been there), and then retailed it into several cantons to certain dealers, who carried over colonies, but were all shipwrecked in the voyage; upon which Lord Peter sold the said continent to other customers again and again, and again and again, with the same success.

The second project I shall mention was his sovereign remedy for the worms, especially those in the spleen. The patient was to eat nothing after supper for three nights; as soon as he went to bed, he was carefully to lie on one side, and when he grew weary, to turn upon the other. He must also duly confine his two eyes to the same object, and by no means break wind at both ends together without manifest occasion. These prescriptions diligently observed, the worms would void insensibly by perspiration ascending through the brain.

A third invention was the erecting of a whispering-office for the public good and ease of all such as are hypochondriacal or troubled with the cholic, as likewise of all eavesdroppers, physicians, midwives, small politicians, friends fallen out, repeating poets, lovers happy or in despair, bawds, privy-counsellors, pages, parasites and buffoons, in short, of all such as are in danger of bursting with too much wind. An ass's head was placed so conveniently, that the party affected might easily with his mouth accost either of the animal's ears, which he was to apply close for a certain space, and by a fugitive faculty peculiar to the ears of that animal, receive immediate benefit, either by eructation, or expiration, or evomition.

Another very beneficial project of Lord Peter's was an office of insurance for tobacco-pipes, martyrs of the modern zeal, volumes of poetry, shadows .... and rivers, that these, nor any of these, shall receive damage by fire. From whence our friendly societies may plainly find themselves to be only transcribers from this original, though the one and the other have been of great benefit to the undertakers as well as of equal to the public.

Lord Peter was also held the original author of puppets and raree-shows, the great usefulness whereof being so generally known, I shall not enlarge farther upon this particular.

But another discovery for which he was much renowned was his famous universal pickle. For having remarked how your common pickle in use among housewives was of no farther benefit than to preserve dead flesh and certain kinds of vegetables, Peter with great cost as well as art had contrived a pickle proper for houses, gardens, towns, men, women, children, and cattle, wherein he could preserve them as sound as insects in amber. Now this pickle to the taste, the smell, and the sight, appeared exactly the same with what is in common service for beef, and butter, and herrings (and has been often that way applied with great success), but for its may sovereign virtues was quite a different thing. For Peter would put in a certain quantity of his powder pimperlim-pimp, after which it never failed of success. The operation was performed by spargefaction in a proper time of the moon. The patient who was to be pickled, if it were a house, would infallibly be preserved from all spiders, rats, and weasels; if the party affected were a dog, he should be exempt from mange, and madness, and hunger. It also infallibly took away all scabs and lice, and scalled heads from children, never hindering the patient from any duty, either at bed or board.

But of all Peter's rarities, he most valued a certain set of bulls, whose race was by great fortune preserved in a lineal descent from those that guarded the golden-fleece. Though some who pretended to observe them curiously doubted the breed had not been kept entirely chaste, because they had degenerated from their ancestors in some qualities, and had acquired others very extraordinary, but a foreign mixture. The bulls of Colchis are recorded to have brazen feet; but whether it happened by ill pasture and running, by an alloy from intervention of other parents from stolen intrigues; whether a weakness in their progenitors had impaired the seminal virtue, or by a decline necessary through a long course of time, the originals of nature being depraved in these latter sinful ages of the world—whatever was the cause, it is certain that Lord Peter's bulls were extremely vitiated by the rust of time in the metal of their feet, which was now sunk into common lead. However, the terrible roaring peculiar to their lineage was preserved, as likewise that faculty of breathing out fire from their nostrils; which notwithstanding many of their detractors took to be a feat of art, and to be nothing so terrible as it appeared, proceeding only from their usual course of diet, which was of squibs and crackers. However, they had two peculiar marks which extremely distinguished them from the bulls of Jason, and which I have not met together in the description of any other monster beside that in Horace, "Varias inducere plumas," and "Atrum definit in piscem." For these had fishes tails, yet upon occasion could outfly any bird in the air. Peter put these bulls upon several employs. Sometimes he would set them a roaring to fright naughty boys and make them quiet. Sometimes he would send them out upon errands of great importance, where it is wonderful to recount, and perhaps the cautious reader may think much to believe it; an *appetitus sensibilis* deriving itself through the whole family from their noble ancestors, guardians of the *Golden Fleece*, they continued so extremely fond of gold, that if Peter sent them abroad, though it were only upon a compliment, they would roar, and spit, and belch, and snivel out fire, and keep a perpetual coil till you flung them a bit of gold; but then *pulveris exigui jactu,* they would grow calm and quiet as lambs. In short, whether by secret connivance or encouragement from their master, or out of their own liquorish affection to gold, or both, it is certain they were no better than a sort of sturdy, swaggering beggars; and where they could not prevail to get an alms, would make women miscarry and children fall into fits; who to this very day usually call sprites and hobgoblins by the name of bull-beggars. They grew at last so very troublesome to the neighbourhood, that some gentlemen of the North-West got a parcel of right English bull-dogs, and baited them so terribly, that they felt it ever after.

I must needs mention one more of Lord Peter's projects, which was very extraordinary, and discovered him to be master of a high reach and profound invention. Whenever it happened that any rogue of Newgate was condemned to be hanged, Peter would offer him a pardon for a certain sum of money, which when the poor caitiff had made all shifts to scrape up and send, his lordship would return a piece of paper in this form :—

"To all mayors, sheriffs, jailors, constables, bailiffs, hangmen, &c. Whereas we are informed that A. B. remains in the hands of you, or any of you, under the sentence of death. We will and command you, upon sight hereof, to let the said prisoner depart to his own habitation, whether he stands condemned for murder, sodomy, rape, sacrilege, incest, treason, blasphemy, &c., for which this shall be your sufficient warrant. And if you fail hereof, G— d—mn you and yours to all eternity. And so we bid you heartily farewell. Your most humble man's man,

"EMPEROR PETER."

The wretches trusting to this lost their lives and money too.

I desire of those whom the learned among posterity will appoint for commentators upon this elaborate treatise, that they will proceed with great caution upon certain dark points, wherein all who are not *verè adepti* may be in danger to form rash and hasty conclusions, especially in some mysterious paragraphs, where certain arcana are joined for brevity sake, which in the operation must be divided. And I am certain that future sons of art will return large thanks to my memory for so grateful, so useful an inmuendo.

It will be no difficult part to persuade the reader that so many worthy discoveries met with great success in the world; though I may justly assure him that I have related much the smallest number; my design having been only to single out such as will be of most benefit for public imitation, or which best served to give some idea of the reach and wit of the inventor. And therefore it need not be wondered if by this time Lord Peter was become exceeding rich. But alas! he had kept his brain so long and so violently upon the rack, that at last it shook itself, and began to turn round for a little ease. In short, what with pride, projects, and knavery, poor Peter was grown distracted, and conceived the strangest imaginations in the world. In the height of his fits (as it is usual with those who run mad out of pride) he would call himself God Almighty, and sometimes monarch of the universe. I have seen him (says my author) take three old high-crowned hats, and clap them all on his head, three storey high, with a huge bunch of keys at his girdle, and an angling rod in his hand. In which guise, whoever went to take him by the hand in the way of salutation, Peter with much grace, like a well-educated spaniel, would present them with his foot, and if they refused his civility, then he would raise it as high as their chops, and give them a damned kick on the mouth, which hath ever since been called a salute. Whoever walked by without paying him their compliments, having a wonderful strong breath, he would blow their hats off into the dirt. Meantime his affairs at home went upside down, and his two brothers had a wretched time, where his first *boutade* was to kick both their wives one morning out of doors, and his own too, and in their stead gave orders to pick up the first three strollers could be met with in the streets. A while after he nailed up the cellar door, and would not allow his brothers a drop of drink to their victuals.[1] Dining

---

[1] Refusing the cup of sacrament to the laity. Thomas Warton observes on the following passage its close resemblance to the speech of Panurge in Rabelais, and says that Swift formed himself upon Rabelais.

one day at an alderman's in the city, Peter observed him expatiating after the manner of his brethren in the praises of his sirloin of beef. "Beef," said the sage magistrate, "is the king of meat; beef comprehends in it the quintessence of partridge, and quail, and venison, and pheasant, and plum-pudding, and custard." When Peter came home, he would needs take the fancy of cooking up this doctrine into use, and apply the precept in default of a sirloin to his brown loaf. "Bread," says he, "dear brothers, is the staff of life, in which bread is contained inclusive the quintessence of beef, mutton, veal, venison, partridge, plum-pudding, and custard, and to render all complete, there is intermingled a due quantity of water, whose crudities are also corrected by yeast or barm, through which means it becomes a wholesome fermented liquor, diffused through the mass of the bread." Upon the strength of these conclusions, next day at dinner was the brown loaf served up in all the formality of a City feast. "Come, brothers," said Peter, "fall to, and spare not; here is excellent good mutton;[1] or hold, now my hand is in, I'll help you." At which word, in much ceremony, with fork and knife, he carves out two good slices of a loaf, and presents each on a plate to his brothers. The elder of the two, not suddenly entering into Lord Peter's conceit, began with very civil language to examine the mystery. "My lord," said he, "I doubt, with great submission, there may be some mistake." "What!" says Peter, "you are pleasant; come then, let us hear this jest your head is so big with." "None in the world, my Lord; but unless I am very much deceived, your Lordship was pleased a while ago to let fall a word about mutton, and I would be glad to see it with all my heart." "How," said Peter, appearing in great surprise, "I do not comprehend this at all;" upon which the younger, interposing to set the business right, "My Lord," said he, "my brother, I suppose, is hungry, and longs for the mutton your Lordship hath promised us to dinner." "Pray," said Peter, "take me along with you, either you are both mad, or disposed to be merrier than I approve of; if you there do not like your piece, I will carve you another,

---

[1] Transubstantiation.

though I should take that to be the choice bit of the whole shoulder." "What, then, my Lord?" replied the first; "it seems this is a shoulder of mutton all this while." "Pray, sir," says Peter, "eat your victuals and leave off your impertinence, if you please, for I am not disposed to relish it at present;" but the other could not forbear, being over-provoked at the affected seriousness of Peter's countenance. "My Lord," said he, "I can only say, that to my eyes and fingers, and teeth and nose, it seems to be nothing but a crust of bread." Upon which the second put in his word: "I never saw a piece of mutton in my life so nearly resembling a slice from a twelve-penny loaf." "Look ye, gentlemen," cries Peter in a rage, "to convince you what a couple of blind, positive, ignorant, wilful puppies you are, I will use but this plain argument; by G——, it is true, good, natural mutton as any in Leadenhall Market; and G—— confound you both eternally if you offer to believe otherwise." Such a thundering proof as this left no further room for objection; the two unbelievers began to gather and pocket up their mistake as hastily as they could. "Why, truly," said the first, "upon more mature consideration"—"Ay," says the other, interrupting him, "now I have thought better on the thing, your Lordship seems to have a great deal of reason." "Very well," said Peter. "Here, boy, fill me a beer-glass of claret. Here's to you both with all my heart." The two brethren, much delighted to see him so readily appeased, returned their most humble thanks, and said they would be glad to pledge his Lordship. "That you shall," said Peter, "I am not a person to refuse you anything that is reasonable; wine moderately taken is a cordial. Here is a glass apiece for you; it is true natural juice from the grape; none of your damned vintner's brewings." Having spoke thus, he presented to each of them another large dry crust, bidding them drink it off, and not be bashful, for it would do them no hurt. The two brothers, after having performed the usual office in such delicate conjunctures, of staring a sufficient period at Lord Peter and each other, and finding how matters were like to go, resolved not to enter on a new dispute, but let him carry the point as he pleased; for he was now got into one of his mad fits, and to argue or expostulate further would only serve to render him a hundred times more untractable.

I have chosen to relate this worthy matter in all its circumstances, because it gave a principal occasion to that great and famous rupture[1] which happened about the same time among these brethren, and was never afterwards made up. But of that I shall treat at large in another section.

However, it is certain that Lord Peter, even in his lucid intervals, was very lewdly given in his common conversation, extreme wilful and positive, and would at any time rather argue to the death than allow himself to be once in an error. Besides, he had an abominable faculty of telling huge palpable lies upon all occasions, and swearing not only to the truth, but cursing the whole company to hell if they pretended to make the least scruple of believing him. One time he swore he had a cow at home which gave as much milk at a meal as would fill three thousand churches, and what was yet more extraordinary, would never turn sour. Another time he was telling of an old sign-post[2] that belonged to his father, with nails and timber enough on it to build sixteen large men-of-war. Talking one day of Chinese waggons, which were made so light as to sail over mountains, "Z——nds," said Peter, "where's the wonder of that? By G——, I saw a large house of lime and stone travel over sea and land (granting that it stopped sometimes to bait) above two thousand German leagues."[3] And that which was the good of it, he would swear desperately all the while that he never told a lie in his life, and at every word: "By G——, gentlemen, I tell you nothing but the truth, and the d——l broil them eternally that will not believe me."

In short, Peter grew so scandalous that all the neighbourhood began in plain words to say he was no better than a knave; and his two brothers, long weary of his ill-usage, resolved at last to

---

[1] The Reformation.

[2] The cross (*in hoc signo vinces*). Pieces of the wood said to be part of it were many in the churches.

[3] One miracle to be believed was that the Chapel of Loretto travelled from the Holy Land to Italy.

leave him; but first they humbly desired a copy of their father's will, which had now lain by neglected time out of mind. Instead of granting this request, he called them rogues, traitors, and the rest of the vile names he could muster up. However, while he was abroad one day upon his projects, the two youngsters watched their opportunity, made a shift to come at the will, and took a *copia vera*,[1] by which they presently saw how grossly they had been abused, their father having left them equal heirs, and strictly commanded that whatever they got should lie in common among them all. Pursuant to which, their next enterprise was to break open the cellar-door and get a little good drink to spirit and comfort their hearts.[2] In copying the will, they had met another precept against whoring, divorce, and separate maintenance; upon which, their next work was to discard their concubines and send for their wives.[3] Whilst all this was in agitation, there enters a solicitor from Newgate, desiring Lord Peter would please to procure a pardon for a thief that was to be hanged to-morrow. But the two brothers told him he was a coxcomb to seek pardons from a fellow who deserved to be hanged much better than his client, and discovered all the method of that imposture in the same form I delivered it a while ago, advising the solicitor to put his friend upon obtaining a pardon from the king. In the midst of all this clatter and revolution in comes Peter with a file of dragoons at his heels, and gathering from all hands what was in the wind, he and his gang, after several millions of scurrilities and curses not very important here to repeat, by main force very fairly kicks them both out of doors, and would never let them come under his roof from that day to this.

1 Made a true copy of the Bible in the language of the people.
2 Gave the cup to the laity.
3 Allowed marriages of priests.

SECTION V.

A DIGRESSION IN THE MODERN KIND.

WE whom the world is pleased to honour with the title of modern authors, should never have been able to compass our great design of an everlasting remembrance and never-dying fame if our endeavours had not been so highly serviceable to the general good of mankind. This, O universe! is the adventurous attempt of me, thy secretary—

> " Quemvis perferre laborem
> Suadet, et inducit noctes vigilare serenas."

To this end I have some time since, with a world of pains and art, dissected the carcass of human nature, and read many useful lectures upon the several parts, both containing and contained, till at last it smelt so strong I could preserve it no longer. Upon which I have been at a great expense to fit up all the bones with exact contexture and in due symmetry, so that I am ready to show a very complete anatomy thereof to all curious gentlemen and others. But not to digress further in the midst of a digression, as I have known some authors enclose digressions in one another like a nest of boxes, I do affirm that, having carefully cut up human nature, I have found a very strange, new, and important discovery: that the public good of mankind is performed by two ways—instruction and diversion. And I have further proved my said several readings (which, perhaps, the world may one day see, if I can prevail on any friend to steal a copy, or on certain gentlemen of my admirers to be very importunate) that, as mankind is now disposed, he receives much greater advantage by being diverted than instructed, his epidemical diseases being fastidiosity, amorphy, and oscitation; whereas, in the present universal empire of wit and learning, there seems but little matter left for instruction. However, in compliance with a lesson of great age and authority, I have attempted carrying the point in all its heights, and accordingly throughout this divine treatise have skilfully kneaded up both together with a layer of *utile* and a layer of *dulce*.

When I consider how exceedingly our illustrious moderns have eclipsed the weak glimmering lights of the ancients, and turned them out of the road of all fashionable commerce to a degree that our choice town wits of most refined accomplishments are in grave dispute whether there have been ever any ancients or no; in which point we are like to receive wonderful satisfaction from the most useful labours and lucubrations of that worthy modern, Dr. Bentley. I say, when I consider all this, I cannot but bewail that no famous modern hath ever yet attempted an univcrsal system in a small portable volume of all things that are to be known, or believed, or imagined, or practised in life. I am, however, forced to acknowledge that such an enterprise was thought on some time ago by a great philosopher of O-Brazile. The method he proposed was by a certain curious receipt, a nostrum, which after his untimely death I found among his papers, and do here, out of my great affection to the modern learned, present them with it, not doubting it may one day encourage some worthy undertaker.

You take fair correct copies, well bound in calf's skin and lettered at the back, of all modern bodies of arts and sciences whatsoever, and in what language you please. These you distil in *balneo Mariæ*, infusing quintessence of poppy Q.S., together with three pints of lethe, to be had from the apothecaries. You cleanse away carefully the *sordes* and *caput mortuum*, letting all that is volatile evaporate. You preserve only the first running, which is again to be distilled seventeen times, till what remains will amount to about two drams. This you keep in a glass vial hermetically sealed for one-and-twenty days. Then you begin your catholic treatise, taking every morning fasting (first shaking the vial) three drops of this elixir, snuffing it strongly up your nose. It will dilate itself about the brain (where there is any) in fourteen minutes, and you immediately perceive in your head an infinite number of abstracts, summaries, compendiums, extracts, collections, medullas, excerpta quædams, florilegias and the like, all disposed into great order and reducible upon paper.

I must needs own it was by the assistance of this arcanum that I, though otherwise *impar*, have adventured upon so daring an attempt, never achieved or undertaken before but by a certain author called Homer, in whom, though otherwise a person not without some abilities, and for an ancient of a tolerable genius, I have discovered many gross errors which are not to be forgiven his very ashes, if by chance any of them are left. For whereas we are assured he designed his work for a complete body of all knowledge, human, divine, political, and mechanic,[1] it is manifest he hath wholly neglected some, and been very imperfect in the rest. For, first of all, as eminent a cabalist as his disciples would represent him, his account of the *opus magnum* is extremely poor and deficient; he seems to have read but very superficially either Sendivogus, Behmen, or Anthroposophia Theomagica.[2] He is also quite mistaken about the *sphæra pyroplastica*, a neglect not to be atoned for, and (if the reader will admit so severe a censure) *vix crederem autorem hunc unquam audivisse ignis vocem.* His failings are not less prominent in several parts of the mechanics. For having read his writings with the utmost application usual among modern wits, I could never yet discover the least direction about the structure of that useful instrument a save-all; for want of which, if the moderns had not lent their assistance, we might yet have wandered in the dark. But I have still behind a fault far more notorious to tax this author with; I mean his gross ignorance in the common

---

[1] Homerus omnes res humanas poematis complexus est.—*Xenophon in Conviv.*—S.

[2] A treatise written about fifty years ago by a Welsh gentleman of Cambridge. His name, as I remember, Vaughan, as appears by the answer to it by the learned Dr. Henry More. It is a piece of the most unintelligible fustian that perhaps was ever published in any language.—S. This piece was by the brother of Henry Vaughan, the poet.

laws of this realm, and in the doctrine as well as discipline of the Church of England. A defect, indeed, for which both he and all the ancients stand most justly censured by my worthy and ingenious friend Mr. Wotton, Bachelor of Divinity, in his incomparable treatise of ancient and modern learning ; a book never to be sufficiently valued, whether we consider the happy turns and flowings of the author's wit, the great usefulness of his sublime discoveries upon the subject of flies and spittle, or the laborious eloquence of his style. And I cannot forbear doing that author the justice of my public acknowledgments for the great helps and liftings I had out of his incomparable piece while I was penning this treatise.

But besides these omissions in Homer already mentioned, the curious reader will also observe several defects in that author's writings for which he is not altogether so accountable. For whereas every branch of knowledge has received such wonderful acquirements since his age, especially within these last three years or thereabouts, it is almost impossible he could be so very perfect in modern discoveries as his advocates pretend. We freely acknowledge him to be the inventor of the compass, of gunpowder, and the circulation of the blood ; but I challenge any of his admirers to show me in all his writings a complete account of the spleen. Does he not also leave us wholly to seek in the art of political wagering? What can be more defective and unsatisfactory than his long dissertation upon tea? and as to his method of salivation without mercury, so much celebrated of late, it is to my own knowledge and experience a thing very little to be relied on.

It was to supply such momentous defects that I have been prevailed on, after long solicitation, to take pen in hand, and I dare venture to promise the judicious reader shall find nothing neglected here that can be of use upon any emergency of life. I am confident to have included and exhausted all that human imagination can rise or fall to. Particularly I recommend to the perusal of the learned certain discoveries that are wholly untouched by others, whereof I shall only mention, among a great many more, my " New Help of Smatterers, or the Art of being Deep Learned and Shallow Read," "A Curious Invention about Mouse-traps," "A Universal Rule of Reason, or Every Man his own Carver," together with a most useful engine for catching of owls. All which the judicious reader will find largely treated on in the several parts of this discourse.

I hold myself obliged to give as much light as possible into the beauties and excellences of what I am writing, because it is become the fashion and humour most applauded among the first authors of this polite and learned age, when they would correct the ill nature of critical or inform the ignorance of courteous readers. Besides, there have been several famous pieces lately published, both in verse and prose, wherein if the writers had not been pleased, out of their great humanity and affection to the public, to give us a nice detail of the sublime and the admirable they contain, it is a thousand to one whether we should ever have discovered one grain of either. For my own particular, I cannot deny that whatever I have said upon this occasion had been more proper in a preface, and more agreeable to the mode which usually directs it there. But I here think fit to lay hold on that great and honourable privilege of being the last writer. I claim an absolute authority in right as the freshest modern, which gives me a despotic power over all authors before me. In the strength of which title I do utterly disapprove and declare against that pernicious custom of making the preface a bill of fare to the book For I have always looked upon it as a high point of indiscretion in monstermongers and other retailers of strange sights to hang out a fair large picture over the door, drawn after the life, with a most eloquent description underneath. This has saved me many a threepence, for my curiosity was fully satisfied, and I never offered to go in, though often invited by the urging and attending orator with his last moving and standing piece of rhetoric, "Sir, upon my word, we are just going to begin." Such is exactly the fate at this time of Prefaces, Epistles, Advertisements, Introductions, Prolegomenas, Apparatuses, To the Readers's. This expedient was admirable at first; our great Dryden has long carried it as far as it would go, and with incredible success. He has often said

to me in confidence that the world would never have suspected
him to be so great a poet if he had not assured them so frequently
in his prefaces, that it was impossible they could either doubt or
forget it. Perhaps it may be so. However, I much fear his instructions have edified out of their place, and taught men to grow
wiser in certain points where he never intended they should; for
it is lamentable to behold with what a lazy scorn many of the
yawning readers in our age do now-a-days twirl over forty or fifty
pages of preface and dedication (which is the usual modern stint),
as if it were so much Latin. Though it must be also allowed, on
the other hand, that a very considerable number is known to proceed critics and wits by reading nothing else. Into which two
factions I think all present readers may justly be divided. Now,
for myself, I profess to be of the former sort, and therefore having
the modern inclination to expatiate upon the beauty of my own
productions, and display the bright parts of my discourse, I
thought best to do it in the body of the work, where as it now lies
it makes a very considerable addition to the bulk of the volume,
a circumstance by no means to be neglected by a skilful writer.

Having thus paid my due deference and acknowledgment to
an established custom of our newest authors, by a long digression
unsought for and a universal censure unprovoked, by forcing into
the light, with much pains and dexterity, my own excellences and
other men's defaults, with great justice to myself and candour to
them, I now happily resume my subject, to the infinite satisfaction
both of the reader and the author.

SECTION VI.

A TALE OF A TUB.

WE left Lord Peter in open rupture with his two brethren, both for ever discarded from his house, and resigned to the wide world with little or nothing to trust to. Which are circumstances that render them proper subjects for the charity of a writer's pen to work on, scenes of misery ever affording the fairest harvest for great adventures. And in this the world may perceive the difference between the integrity of a generous author and that of a common friend. The latter is observed to adhere close in prosperity, but on the decline of fortune to drop suddenly off; whereas the generous author, just on the contrary, finds his hero on the dunghill, from thence, by gradual steps, raises him to a throne, and then immediately withdraws, expecting not so much as thanks for his pains; in imitation of which example I have placed Lord Peter in a noble house, given him a title to wear and money to spend. There I shall leave him for some time, returning, where common charity directs me, to the assistance of his two brothers at their lowest ebb. However, I shall by no means forget my character of a historian, to follow the truth step by step whatever happens, or wherever it may lead me.

The two exiles so nearly united in fortune and interest took a lodging together, where at their first leisure they began to reflect on the numberless misfortunes and vexations of their life past, and could not tell of the sudden to what failure in their conduct they ought to impute them, when, after some recollection, they called to mind the copy of their father's will which they had so happily recovered. This was immediately produced, and a firm resolution taken between them to alter whatever was already amiss, and reduce all their future measures to the strictest obedience prescribed therein. The main body of the will (as the reader cannot easily have forgot) consisted in certain admirable rules about the wearing of their coats, in the perusal whereof the two brothers at every period duly comparing the doctrine with the practice, there was never seen a wider difference between two things, horrible downright transgressions of every point. Upon which they both resolved without further delay to fall immediately upon reducing the whole exactly after their father's model.

But here it is good to stop the hasty reader, ever impatient to see the end of an adventure before we writers can duly prepare him for it. I am to record that these two brothers began to be distinguished at this time by certain names. One of them desired to be called Martin, and the other took the appellation of Jack. These two had lived in much friendship and agreement under the tyranny of their brother Peter, as it is the talent of fellow-sufferers to do, men in misfortune being like men in the dark, to whom all colours are the same. But when they came forward into the world, and began to display themselves to each other and to the light, their complexions appeared extremely different, which the present posture of their affairs gave them sudden opportunity to discover.

But here the severe reader may justly tax me as a writer of short memory, a deficiency to which a true modern cannot but of necessity be a little subject. Because, memory being an employment of the mind upon things past, is a faculty for which the learned in our illustrious age have no manner of occasion, who deal entirely with invention and strike all things out of themselves, or at least by collision from each other; upon which account, we think it highly reasonable to produce our great forgetfulness as an argument unanswerable for our great wit. I ought in method to have informed the reader about fifty pages ago of a fancy Lord Peter took, and infused into his brothers, to wear on their coats whatever trimmings came up in fashion, never pulling off any as they went out of the mode, but keeping on all together, which amounted in time to a medley the most antic you can possibly conceive, and this to a degree that, upon the time of their falling out, there was hardly a thread of the original coat to be seen, but an infinite quantity of lace, and ribbands, and fringe, and embroidery, and points (I mean only those tagged with silver, for the rest fell off). Now this material circumstance having been forgot in due place, as good fortune hath ordered, comes in very properly here, when the two brothers are just going to reform their vestures into the primitive state prescribed by their father's will.

They both unanimously entered upon this great work, looking sometimes on their coats and sometimes on the will. Martin laid the first hand; at one twitch brought off a large handful of points, and with a second pull stripped away ten dozen yards of fringe. But when he had gone thus far he demurred a while. He knew very well there yet remained a great deal more to be done; however, the first heat being over, his violence began to cool, and he resolved to proceed more moderately in the rest of the work, having already very narrowly escaped a swinging rent in pulling off the points, which being tagged with silver (as we have observed before), the judicious workman had with much sagacity double sewn to preserve them from falling. Resolving therefore to rid his coat of a huge quantity of gold lace, he picked up the stitches with much caution and diligently gleaned out all the loose threads as he went, which proved to be a work of time. Then he fell about the embroidered Indian figures of men, women, and children, against which, as you have heard in its due place, their father's testament was extremely exact and severe. These, with much dexterity and application, were after a while quite eradicated or utterly defaced. For the rest, where he observed the embroidery to be worked so close as not to be got away without damaging the cloth, or where it served to hide or strengthened any flaw in the body of the coat, contracted by the perpetual tampering of workmen upon it, he concluded the wisest course was to let it remain, resolving in no case whatsoever that the substance of the stuff should suffer injury, which he thought the best method for serving the true intent and meaning of his father's will. And this is the nearest account I have been able to collect of Martin's proceedings upon this great revolution.

But his brother Jack, whose adventures will be so extraordinary as to furnish a great part in the remainder of this discourse, entered upon the matter with other thoughts and a quite different spirit. For the memory of Lord Peter's injuries produced a degree of hatred and spite which had a much greater share of inciting him than any regards after his father's commands, since these appeared at best only secondary and subservient to the other. However, for this medley of humour he made a shift to find a very plausible name, honouring it with the title of zeal, which is, perhaps, the most significant word that has been ever yet produced in any language, as, I think, I have fully proved in my excellent analytical discourse upon that subject, wherein I have deduced a histori-theo-physiological account of zeal, showing how it first proceeded from a notion into a word, and from thence in a hot summer ripened into a tangible substance. This work, containing three large volumes in folio, I design very shortly to publish by the modern way of subscription, not doubting but the nobility and gentry of the land will give me all possible encouragement, having already had such a taste of what I am able to perform.

I record, therefore, that brother Jack, brimful of this miraculous compound, reflecting with indignation upon Peter's tyranny, and further provoked by the despondency of Martin, prefaced his resolutions to this purpose. "What!" said he, "a rogue that locked up his drink, turned away our wives, cheated us of our fortunes, palmed his crusts upon us for mutton, and at last kicked us out of doors; must we be in his fashions? A rascal, besides, that all the street cries out against." Having thus kindled and inflamed himself as high as possible, and by consequence in a delicate temper for beginning a reformation, he set about the work immediately, and in three minutes made more dispatch than Martin had done in as many hours. For, courteous reader, you are given to understand that zeal is never so highly obliged as when you set it a-tearing; and Jack, who doted on that quality in himself, allowed it at this time its full swing. Thus it happened that, stripping down a parcel of gold lace a little too hastily, he rent the main body of his coat from top to bottom;[1] and whereas his talent was not of the happiest in taking up a stitch, he knew no better way than to darn it again with packthread and a skewer. But the matter was yet infinitely worse (I record it with tears) when he proceeded to the embroidery; for being clumsy of nature, and of temper impatient withal, beholding millions of stitches that required the nicest hand and sedatest constitution to extricate, in a great rage he tore off the whole piece, cloth and all, and flung it into the kennel, and furiously thus continuing his career, "Ah! good brother Martin," said he, "do as I do, for the love of God; strip, tear, pull, rend, flay off all, that we may appear as unlike that rogue Peter as it is possible. I would not for a hundred pounds carry the least mark about me that might give occasion to the neighbours of suspecting I was related to such a rascal." But Martin, who at this time happened to be extremely phlegmatic and sedate, begged his brother, of all love, not to damage his coat by any means, for he never would get such another; desired him to consider that it was not their business to form their actions by any reflection upon Peter's, but by observing the rules prescribed in their father's will. That he should remember Peter was still their brother, whatever faults or injuries he had committed, and therefore they should by all means avoid such a thought as that of taking measures for good and evil from no other rule than of opposition to him. That it was true the testament of their good father was very exact in what related to the wearing of their coats; yet was it no less penal and strict in prescribing agreement, and friendship, and affection between them. And therefore, if straining a point were at all defensible, it would certainly be so rather to the advance of unity than increase of contradiction.

---

[1] After the changes made by Martin that transformed the Church of Rome into the Church of England, Jack's proceedings made a rent from top to bottom by the separation of the Presbyterians from the Church Establishment.

Martin had still proceeded as gravely as he began, and doubt-less would have delivered an admirable lecture of morality, which might have exceedingly contributed to my reader's repose both of body and mind (the true ultimate end of ethics), but Jack was already gone a flight-shot beyond his patience. And as in scho-lastic disputes nothing serves to rouse the spleen of him that opposes so much as a kind of pedantic affected calmness in the respondent, disputants being for the most part like unequal scales, where the gravity of one side advances the lightness of the other, and causes it to fly up and kick the beam; so it happened here that the weight of Martin's arguments exalted Jack's levity, and made him fly out and spurn against his brother's moderation. In short, Martin's patience put Jack in a rage; but that which most afflicted him was to observe his brother's coat so well reduced into the state of innocence, while his own was either wholly rent to his shirt, or those places which had escaped his cruel clutches were still in Peter's livery. So that he looked like a drunken beau half rifled by bullies, or like a fresh tenant of Newgate when he has refused the payment of garnish, or like a discovered shop-lifter left to the mercy of Exchange-women,[1] or like a bawd in her old velvet petticoat resigned into the secular hands of the mobile.[2] Like any or like all of these, a medley of rags, and lace, and fringes, unfortunate Jack did now appear; he would have been extremely glad to see his coat in the condition of Martin's, but infinitely gladder to find that of Martin in the same predicament with his. However, since neither of these was likely to come to pass, he thought fit to lend the whole business another turn, and to dress up necessity into a virtue. Therefore, after as many of the fox's arguments as he could muster up for bringing Martin to reason, as he called it, or as he meant it, into his own ragged, bobtailed condition, and observing he said all to little purpose, what alas! was left for the forlorn Jack to do, but, after a million

---

[1] The galleries over the piazzas in the old Royal Exchange were formerly filled with shops, kept chiefly by women. Illustrations of this feature in London life are to be found in Dekker's "Shoemaker's Holiday," and other plays.

[2] The contraction of the word *mobile* to *mob* first appeared in the time of Charles the Second.

of scurrilities against his brother, to run mad with spleen, and spite, and contradiction. To be short, here began a mortal breach between these two. Jack went immediately to new lodgings, and in a few days it was for certain reported that he had run out of his wits. In a short time after he appeared abroad, and confirmed the report by falling into the oddest whimsies that ever a sick brain conceived.

And now the little boys in the streets began to salute him with several names. Sometimes they would call him Jack the Bald, sometimes Jack with a Lanthorn, sometimes Dutch Jack, sometimes French Hugh, sometimes Tom the Beggar, and sometimes Knocking Jack of the North.[1] And it was under one or some or all of these appellations (which I leave the learned reader to determine) that he hath given rise to the most illustrious and epidemic sect of Æolists, who, with honourable commemoration, do still acknowledge the renowned Jack for their author and founder. Of whose originals as well as principles I am now advancing to gratify the world with a very particular account.

"Mellæo contingens cuncta lepore." [2]

1. Jack the Bald, Calvin, from calvus, bald; Jack with a Lanthorn professing inward lights, Quakers; Dutch Jack, Jack of Leyden, Anabaptists; French Hugh, the Huguenots; Tom the Beggar, the Gueuses of Flanders; Knocking Jack of the North, John Knox of Scotland, Aeolists, pretenders to inspiration.

2. "Touching everything with honeyed wit."

SECTION VII.

A DIGRESSION IN PRAISE OF DIGRESSIONS.

I HAVE sometimes heard of an Iliad in a nut-shell, but it has been my fortune to have much oftener seen a nut-shell in an Iliad. There is no doubt that human life has received most wonderful advantages from both; but to which of the two the world is chiefly indebted, I shall leave among the curious as a problem worthy of their utmost inquiry. For the invention of the latter, I think the commonwealth of learning is chiefly obliged to the great modern improvement of digressions. The late refinements in knowledge, running parallel to those of diet in our nation, which among men of a judicious taste are dressed up in various compounds, consisting in soups and olios, fricassees and ragouts.

It is true there is a sort of morose, detracting, ill-bred people who pretend utterly to disrelish these polite innovations. And as to the similitude from diet, they allow the parallel, but are so bold as to pronounce the example itself a corruption and degeneracy of taste. They tell us that the fashion of jumbling fifty things together in a dish was at first introduced in compliance to a depraved and debauched appetite, as well as to a crazy constitution, and to see a man hunting through an olio after the head and brains of a goose, a widgeon, or a woodcock, is a sign he wants a stomach and digestion for more substantial victuals. Further, they affirm that digressions in a book are like foreign troops in a state, which argue the nation to want a heart and hands of its own, and often either subdue the natives, or drive them into the most unfruitful corners.

But after all that can be objected by these supercilious censors, it is manifest the society of writers would quickly be reduced to a very inconsiderable number if men were put upon making books with the fatal confinement of delivering nothing beyond what is to the purpose. It is acknowledged that were the case the same among us as with the Greeks and Romans, when learning was in its cradle, to be reared and fed and clothed by invention, it would be an easy task to fill up volumes upon particular occasions without further expatiating from the subject than by moderate excursions, helping to advance or clear the main design. But with knowledge it has fared as with a numerous army encamped in a fruitful country, which for a few days maintains itself by the product of the soil it is on, till provisions being spent, they send to forage many a mile among friends or enemies, it matters not. Meanwhile the neighbouring fields, trampled and beaten down, become barren and dry, affording no sustenance but clouds of dust.

The whole course of things being thus entirely changed between us and the ancients, and the moderns wisely sensible of it, we of this age have discovered a shorter and more prudent method to become scholars and wits, without the fatigue of reading or of thinking. The most accomplished way of using books at present is twofold: either first to serve them as some men do lords, learn their titles exactly, and then brag of their acquaintance; or, secondly, which is indeed the choicer, the profounder, and politer method, to get a thorough insight into the index by which the whole book is governed and turned, like fishes by the tail. For to enter the palace of learning at the great gate requires an expense of time and forms, therefore men of much haste and little ceremony are content to get in by the back-door. For the arts are all in a flying march, and therefore more easily subdued by attacking them in the rear. Thus physicians discover the state of the whole body by consulting only what comes from behind. Thus men catch knowledge by throwing their wit on the posteriors of a book, as boys do sparrows with flinging salt upon their tails. Thus human life is best understood by the wise man's rule of regarding the end. Thus are the sciences found, like Hercules' oxen, by tracing them backwards. Thus are old sciences unravelled like old stockings, by beginning at the foot.

Besides all this, the army of the sciences hath been of late with a world of martial discipline drawn into its close order, so that a view or a muster may be taken of it with abundance of expedition. For this great blessing we are wholly indebted to systems and abstracts, in which the modern fathers of learning, like prudent usurers, spent their sweat for the ease of us their children. For labour is the seed of idleness, and it is the peculiar happiness of our noble age to gather the fruit.

Now the method of growing wise, learned, and sublime having become so regular an affair, and so established in all its forms, the number of writers must needs have increased accordingly, and to a pitch that has made it of absolute necessity for them to interfere continually with each other. Besides, it is reckoned that there is not at this present a sufficient quantity of new matter left in Nature to furnish and adorn any one particular subject to the extent of a volume. This I am told by a very skilful computer, who hath given a full demonstration of it from rules of arithmetic.

This perhaps may be objected against by those who maintain the infinity of matter, and therefore will not allow that any species of it can be exhausted. For answer to which, let us examine the noblest branch of modern wit or invention planted and cultivated by the present age, and which of all others hath borne the most and the fairest fruit. For though some remains of it were left us by the ancients, yet have not any of those, as I remember, been translated or compiled into systems for modern use. Therefore we may affirm, to our own honour, that it has in some sort been both invented and brought to a perfection by the same hands. What I mean is, that highly celebrated talent among the modern wits of deducing similitudes, allusions, and applications, very surprising, agreeable, and apposite, from the signs of either sex, together with their proper uses. And truly, having observed how little invention bears any vogue besides what is derived into these channels, I have sometimes had a thought that the happy genius of our age and country was prophetically held forth by that ancient typical description of the Indian pigmies whose stature did not exceed above two feet, *sed quorum pudenda crassa, et ad talos usque pertingentia.* Now I have been very curious to inspect the late productions, wherein the beauties of this kind have most prominently appeared. And although this vein hath bled so freely, and all endeavours have been used in the power of human breath to dilate, extend, and keep it open, like the Scythians,[1] who had a custom and an instrument to blow up those parts of their mares, that they might yield the more milk; yet I am under an apprehension it is near growing dry and past all recovery, and that either some new *fonde* of wit should, if possible, be provided, or else that we must e'en be content with repetition here as well as upon all other occasions.

This will stand as an uncontestable argument that our modern wits are not to reckon upon the infinity of matter for a constant supply. What remains, therefore, but that our last recourse must be had to large indexes and little compendiums? Quotations must be plentifully gathered and booked in alphabet. To this end, though authors need be little consulted, yet critics, and commentators, and lexicons carefully must. But above all, those judicious collectors of bright parts, and flowers, and observandas are to be nicely dwelt on by some called the sieves and boulters of learning, though it is left undetermined whether they dealt in pearls or meal, and consequently whether we are more to value that which passed through or what stayed behind.

By these methods, in a few weeks there starts up many a writer capable of managing the profoundest and most universal subjects. For what though his head be empty, provided his common-place book be full? And if you will bate him but the circumstances of method, and style, and grammar, and invention; allow him but the common privileges of transcribing from others, and digressing from himself as often as he shall see occasion, he will desire no more ingredients towards fitting up a treatise that shall make a very comely figure on a bookseller's shelf, there to

---

[1] Herodotus, l. 4.—*S.*

be preserved neat and clean for a long eternity, adorned with the heraldry of its title fairly inscribed on a label, never to be thumbed or greased by students, nor bound to everlasting chains of dark-ness in a library, but when the fulness of time is come shall happily undergo the trial of purgatory in order to ascend the sky.

Without these allowances how is it possible we modern wits should ever have an opportunity to introduce our collections listed under so many thousand heads of a different nature, for want of which the learned world would be deprived of infinite delight as well as instruction, and we ourselves buried beyond redress in an inglorious and undistinguished oblivion?

From such elements as these I am alive to behold the day wherein the corporation of authors can outvie all its brethren in the field—a happiness derived to us, with a great many others, from our Scythian ancestors, among whom the number of pens was so infinite that the Grecian eloquence had no other way of expressing it than by saying that in the regions far to the north it was hardly possible for a man to travel, the very air was so replete with feathers.

The necessity of this digression will easily excuse the length, and I have chosen for it as proper a place as I could readily find. If the judicious reader can assign a fitter, I do here empower him to remove it into any other corner he please. And so I return with great alacrity to pursue a more important concern.

SECTION VIII.

A TALE OF A TUB.

THE learned Æolists maintain the original cause of all things
   to be wind, from which principle this whole universe was
at first produced, and into which it must at last be resolved, that
the same breath which had kindled and blew up the flame of
Nature should one day blow it out.

"Quod procul à nobis flectat Fortuna gubernans."

This is what the Adepti understand by their *anima mundi*,
that is to say, the spirit, or breath, or wind of the world; or
examine the whole system by the particulars of Nature, and you
will find it not to be disputed. For whether you please to call
the *forma informans* of man by the name of *spiritus, animus,
afflatus,* or *anima,* what are all these but several appellations for
wind, which is the ruling element in every compound, and into
which they all resolve upon their corruption. Further, what is
life itself but, as it is commonly called, the breath of our nostrils,
whence it is very justly observed by naturalists that wind still
continues of great emolument in certain mysteries not to be
named, giving occasion for those happy epithets of *turgidus* and
inflatus, applied either to the emittent or recipient organs.

By what I have gathered out of ancient records, I find the
compass of their doctrine took in two-and-thirty points, wherein
it would be tedious to be very particular. However, a few
of their most important precepts deducible from it are by no
means to be omitted; among which, the following maxim was of
much weight: That since wind had the master share as well as

operation in every compound, by consequence those beings must be of chief excellence wherein that primordium appears most prominently to abound, and therefore man is in highest perfection of all created things, as having, by the great bounty of philosophers, been endued with three distinct *animas* or winds, to which the sage Æolists, with much liberality, have added a fourth, of equal necessity as well as ornament with the other three, by this *quartum principium* taking in the four corners of the world. Which gave occasion to that renowned cabalist Bombastus [1] of placing the body of man in due position to the four cardinal points.

In consequence of this, their next principle was that man brings with him into the world a peculiar portion or grain of wind, which may be called a *quinta essentia* extracted from the other four. This quintessence is of catholic use upon all emergencies of life, is improveable into all arts and sciences, and may be wonderfully refined as well as enlarged by certain methods in education. This, when blown up to its perfection, ought not to be covetously hoarded up, stifled, or hid under a bushel, but freely communicated to mankind. Upon these reasons, and others of equal weight, the wise Æolists affirm the gift of belching to be the noblest act of a rational creature. To cultivate which art, and render it more serviceable to mankind, they made use of several methods. At certain seasons of the year you might behold the priests amongst them in vast numbers with their mouths gaping wide against a storm. At other times were to be seen several hundreds linked together in a circular chain, with every man a pair of bellows applied to his neighbour, by which they blew up each other to the shape and size of a tun; and for that reason with great propriety of speech did usually call their bodies their vessels.[2] When, by these and the like performances, they were grown sufficiently replete, they would immediately depart, and disembogue for the public good a plentiful share of their acquirements into their disciples' chaps. For we must here observe that

---

1 Bombast von Hohenheim—Paracelsus.
2 Fanatical preachers of rebellion.

all learning was esteemed among them to be compounded from the same principle.   Because, first, it is generally affirmed or confessed that learning puffeth men up; and, secondly, they proved it by the following syllogism : "Words are but wind, and learning is nothing but words; ergo, learning is nothing but wind."   For this reason the philosophers among them did in their schools deliver to their pupils all their doctrines and opinions by eructation, wherein they had acquired a wonderful eloquence, and of incredible variety.   But the great characteristic by which their chief sages were best distinguished was a certain position of countenance, which gave undoubted intelligence to what degree or proportion the spirit agitated the inward mass.   For after certain gripings, the wind and vapours issuing forth, having first by their turbulence and convulsions within caused an earthquake in man's little world, distorted the mouth, bloated the cheeks, and gave the eyes a terrible kind of relievo.   At which junctures all their belches were received for sacred, the sourer the better, and swallowed with infinite consolation by their meagre devotees. And to render these yet more complete, because the breath of man's life is in his nostrils, therefore the choicest, most edifying, and most enlivening belches were very wisely conveyed through that vehicle to give them a tincture as they passed.

Their gods were the four winds, whom they worshipped as the spirits that pervade and enliven the universe, and as those from whom alone all inspiration can properly be said to proceed. However, the chief of these, to whom they performed the adoration of Latria, was the Almighty North, an ancient deity, whom the inhabitants of Megalopolis in Greece had likewise in highest reverence.   "Omnium deorum Boream maxime celebrant."[1] This god, though endued with ubiquity, was yet supposed by the profounder Æolists to possess one peculiar habitation, or (to speak in form) a *cælum empyræum*, wherein he was more intimately present.   This was situated in a certain region well known to the ancient Greeks, by them called Σκοτία, or the Land of Darkness. And although many controversies have arisen upon that matter,

[1] Pausanias, l. 8.—S.

yet so much is undisputed, that from a region of the like denomination the most refined Æolists have borrowed their original,
from whence in every age the zealous among their priesthood have
brought over their choicest inspiration, fetching it with their own
hands from the fountain-head in certain bladders, and disploding
it among the sectaries in all nations, who did, and do, and ever
will, daily gasp and pant after it.

Now their mysteries and rites were performed in this manner.
It is well known among the learned that the virtuosos of former
ages had a contrivance for carrying and preserving winds in casks
or barrels, which was of great assistance upon long sea-voyages, and
the loss of so useful an art at present is very much to be lamented,
though, I know not how, with great negligence omitted by Panci-
rollus. It was an invention ascribed to Æolus himself, from
whom this sect is denominated, and who, in honour of their
founder's memory, have to this day preserved great numbers of
those barrels, whereof they fix one in each of their temples, first
beating out the top. Into this barrel upon solemn days the priest
enters, where, having before duly prepared himself by the methods
already described, a secret funnel is also conveyed to the bottom of
the barrel, which admits new supplies of inspiration from a northern
chink or cranny. Whereupon you behold him swell immediately
to the shape and size of his vessel. In this posture he disembogues
whole tempests upon his auditory, as the spirit from beneath gives
him utterance, which issuing *ex adytis* and *penetralibus,* is not
performed without much pain and gripings. And the wind in
breaking forth deals with his face as it does with that of the sea,
first blackening, then wrinkling, and at last bursting it into a foam.
It is in this guise the sacred Æolist delivers his oracular belches
to his panting disciples, of whom some are greedily gaping after
the sanctified breath, others are all the while hymning out the
praises of the winds, and gently wafted to and fro by their own
humming, do thus represent the soft breezes of their deities
appeased.

It is from this custom of the priests that some authors maintain
these Æolists to have been very ancient in the world, because

the delivery of their mysteries, which I have just now mentioned, appears exactly the same with that of other ancient oracles, whose inspirations were owing to certain subterraneous effluviums of wind delivered with the same pain to the priest, and much about the same influence on the people. It is true indeed that these were frequently managed and directed by female officers, whose organs were understood to be better disposed for the admission of those oracular gusts, as entering and passing up through a receptacle of greater capacity, and causing also a pruriency by the way, such as with due management has been refined from carnal into a spiritual ecstasy. And to strengthen this profound conjecture, it is further insisted that this custom of female priests is kept up still in certain refined colleges of our modern Æolists,[1] who are agreed to receive their inspiration, derived through the receptacle aforesaid, like their ancestors the Sybils.

And whereas the mind of man, when he gives the spur and bridle to his thoughts, does never stop, but naturally sallies out into both extremes of high and low, of good and evil, his first flight of fancy commonly transports him to ideas of what is most perfect, finished, and exalted, till, having soared out of his own reach and sight, not well perceiving how near the frontiers of height and depth border upon each other, with the same course and wing he falls down plump into the lowest bottom of things, like one who travels the east into the west, or like a straight line drawn by its own length into a circle. Whether a tincture of malice in our natures makes us fond of furnishing every bright idea with its reverse, or whether reason, reflecting upon the sum of things, can, like the sun, serve only to enlighten one half of the globe, leaving the other half by necessity under shade and darkness, or whether fancy, flying up to the imagination of what is highest and best, becomes over-short, and spent, and weary, and suddenly falls, like a dead bird of paradise, to the ground; or whether, after all these metaphysical conjectures, I have not entirely missed the true reason ; the proposition, however, which has stood me in so much circumstance is altogether true, that as the most

[1] The Quakers allowed women to preach.

uncivilised parts of mankind have some way or other climbed up into the conception of a God or Supreme Power, so they have seldom forgot to provide their fears with certain ghastly notions, which, instead of better, have served them pretty tolerably for a devil. And this proceeding seems to be natural enough, for it is with men whose imaginations are lifted up very high after the same rate as with those whose bodies are so, that as they are delighted with the advantage of a nearer contemplation upwards, so they are equally terrified with the dismal prospect of the precipice below. Thus in the choice of a devil it has been the usual method of mankind to single out some being, either in act or in vision, which was in most antipathy to the god they had framed. Thus also the sect of the Æolists possessed themselves with a dread and horror and hatred of two malignant natures, betwixt whom and the deities they adored perpetual enmity was established. The first of these was the chameleon, sworn foe to inspiration, who in scorn devoured large influences of their god, without refunding the smallest blast by eructation. The other was a huge terrible monster called Moulinavent, who with four strong arms waged eternal battle with all their divinities, dexterously turning to avoid their blows and repay them with interest.[1]

Thus furnished, and set out with gods as well as devils, was the renowned sect of Æolists, which makes at this day so illustrious a figure in the world, and whereof that polite nation of Laplanders are beyond all doubt a most authentic branch, of whom I therefore cannot without injustice here omit to make honourable mention, since they appear to be so closely allied in point of interest as well as inclinations with their brother Æolists among us, as not only to buy their winds by wholesale from the same merchants, but also to retail them after the same rate and method, and to customers much alike.

Now whether the system here delivered was wholly compiled by Jack, or, as some writers believe, rather copied from the

---

[1] The worshippers of wind or air found their evil spirits in the chameleon, by which it was eaten, and the windmill, Moulin-à-vent, by whose four hands it was beaten.

original at Delphos, with certain additions and emendations suited to times and circumstances, I shall not absolutely determine. This I may affirm, that Jack gave it at least a new turn, and formed it into the same dress and model as it lies deduced by me.

I have long sought after this opportunity of doing justice to a society of men for whom I have a peculiar honour, and whose opinions as well as practices have been extremely misrepresented and traduced by the malice or ignorance of their adversaries. For I think it one of the greatest and best of human actions to remove prejudices and place things in their truest and fairest light, which I therefore boldly undertake, without any regards of my own beside the conscience, the honour, and the thanks.

SECTION IX.

A DIGRESSION CONCERNING THE ORIGINAL, THE USE, AND IMPROVEMENT OF MADNESS IN A COMMON-WEALTH.

NOR shall it any ways detract from the just reputation of this famous sect that its rise and institution are owing to such an author as I have described Jack to be, a person whose intellectuals were overturned and his brain shaken out of its natural position, which we commonly suppose to be a distemper, and call by the name of madness or frenzy. For if we take a survey of the greatest actions that have been performed in the world under the influence of single men, which are the establishment of new empires by conquest, the advance and progress of new schemes in philosophy, and the contriving as well as the propagating of new religions, we shall find the authors of them all to have been persons whose natural reason hath admitted great revolutions from their diet, their education, the prevalency of some certain temper, together with the particular influence of air and climate. Besides, there is something individual in human minds that easily kindles at the accidental approach and collision of certain circumstances, which, though of paltry and mean appearance, do often flame out into the greatest emergencies of life. For great turns are not always given by strong hands, but by lucky adaptation and at proper seasons, and it is of no import where the fire was kindled if the vapour has once got up into the brain. For the upper region of man is furnished like the middle region of the air; the materials are formed from causes of the widest difference, yet produce at last the same substance and effect. Mists arise from the earth, steams from dunghills, exhalations from the sea, and smoke from fire; yet all clouds are the same in composition as well as consequences, and the fumes issuing from a jakes will furnish as comely and useful a vapour as incense from an altar. Thus far, I suppose, will easily be granted me; and then it will follow that as the face of Nature never produces rain but when it is overcast and disturbed, so human understanding seated in the brain must be troubled and overspread by vapours ascending from the lower faculties to water the invention and render it fruitful. Now although these vapours (as it hath been already said) are of as various original as those of the skies, yet the crop they produce differs both in kind and degree, merely according to the soil. I will produce two instances to prove and explain what I am now advancing.

A certain great prince [1] raised a mighty army, filled his coffers with infinite treasures, provided an invincible fleet, and all this without giving the least part of his design to his greatest ministers or his nearest favourites. Immediately the whole world was alarmed, the neighbouring crowns in trembling expectation towards what point the storm would burst, the small politicians everywhere forming profound conjectures. Some believed he had laid a scheme for universal monarchy; others, after much insight, determined the matter to be a project for pulling down the Pope and setting up the Reformed religion, which had once been his own. Some again, of a deeper sagacity, sent him into Asia to subdue the Turk and recover Palestine. In the midst of all these projects and preparations, a certain state-surgeon,[2] gathering the nature of the disease by these symptoms, attempted the cure, at one blow performed the operation, broke the bag and out flew the vapour; nor did anything want to render it a complete remedy, only that the prince unfortunately happened to die in the performance. Now is the reader exceeding curious to learn from whence this vapour took its rise, which had so long set the nations at a gaze? What secret wheel, what hidden spring, could

---

[1] Henry IV. of France.
[2] Ravaillac, who stabbed Henry IV.

put into motion so wonderful an engine? It was afterwards discovered that the movement of this whole machine had been directed by an absent female, who was removed into an enemy's country. What should an unhappy prince do in such ticklish circumstances as these? He tried in vain the poet's never-failing receipt of *corpora quæque*, for

> " Idque petit corpus mens unde est saucia amore ;
> Unde feritur, eo tendit, gestitque coire."—*Lucr.*

Having to no purpose used all peaceable endeavours, the collected part of the semen, raised and inflamed, became adust, converted to choler, turned head upon the spinal duct, and ascended to the brain. The very same principle that influences a bully to break the windows of a woman who has jilted him naturally stirs up a great prince to raise mighty armies and dream of nothing but sieges, battles, and victories.

The other instance is what I have read somewhere in a very ancient author of a mighty king,[1] who, for the space of above thirty years, amused himself to take and lose towns, beat armies and be beaten, drive princes out of their dominions, fright children from their bread and butter, burn, lay waste, plunder, dragoon, massacre subject and stranger, friend and foe, male and female. It is recorded that the philosophers of each country were in grave dispute upon causes natural, moral, and political, to find out where they should assign an original solution of this phenomenon. At last the vapour or spirit which animated the hero's brain, being in perpetual circulation, seized upon that region of the human body so renowned for furnishing the *zibeta occidentalis*,[2] and gathering there into a tumour, left the rest of the world for that time in peace. Of such mighty consequence is it where those exhalations fix, and of so little from whence they proceed.

---

[1] Swift's contemporary, Louis XIV. of France.

[2] Western civet. Paracelsus was said to have endeavoured to extract a perfume from human excrement that might become as fashionable as civet from the cat. It was called *zibeta occidentalis*, the back being, according to Paracelsus, the western part of the body.

The same spirits which in their superior progress would conquer a kingdom descending upon the anus, conclude in a fistula.

Let us next examine the great introducers of new schemes in philosophy, and search till we can find from what faculty of the soul the disposition arises in mortal man of taking it into his head to advance new systems with such an eager zeal in things agreed on all hands impossible to be known ; from what seeds this disposition springs, and to what quality of human nature these grand innovators have been indebted for their number of disciples, because it is plain that several of the chief among them, both ancient and modern, were usually mistaken by their adversaries, and, indeed, by all, except their own followers, to have been persons crazed or out of their wits, having generally proceeded in the common course of their words and actions by a method very different from the vulgar dictates of unrefined reason, agreeing for the most part in their several models with their present undoubted successors in the academy of modern Bedlam, whose merits and principles I shall further examine in due place. Of this kind were Epicurus, Diogenes, Apollonius, Lucretius, Paracelsus, Des Cartes, and others, who, if they were now in the world, tied fast and separate from their followers; would in this our undistinguishing age incur manifest danger of phlebotomy, and whips, and chains, and dark chambers, and straw. For what man in the natural state or course of thinking did ever conceive it in his power to reduce the notions of all mankind exactly to the same length, and breadth, and height of his own? Yet this is the first humble and civil design of all innovators in the empire of reason. Epicurus modestly hoped that one time or other a certain fortuitous concourse of all men's opinions, after perpetual jostlings, the sharp with the smooth, the light and the heavy, the round and the square, would, by certain clinamina, unite in the notions of atoms and void, as these did in the originals of all things. Cartesius reckoned to see before he died the sentiments of all philosophers, like so many lesser stars in his romantic system, rapt and drawn within his own vortex. Now I would gladly be informed how it is possible to account for such imaginations as these in particular men, without recourse to my phenomenon of vapours ascending from the lower faculties to overshadow the brain, and there distilling into conceptions, for which the narrowness of our mother-tongue has not yet assigned any other name beside that of madness or frenzy. Let us therefore now conjecture how it comes to pass that none of these great prescribers do ever fail providing themselves and their notions with a number of implicit disciples, and I think the reason is easy to be assigned, for there is a peculiar string in the harmony of human understanding, which in several individuals is exactly of the same tuning. This, if you can dexterously screw up to its right key, and then strike gently upon it whenever you have the good fortune to light among those of the same pitch, they will by a secret necessary sympathy strike exactly at the same time. And in this one circumstance lies all the skill or luck of the matter; for, if you chance to jar the string among those who are either above or below your own height, instead of subscribing to your doctrine, they will tie you fast, call you mad, and feed you with bread and water. It is therefore a point of the nicest conduct to distinguish and adapt this noble talent with respect to the differences of persons and of times. Cicero understood this very well, when, writing to a friend in England, with a caution, among other matters, to beware of being cheated by our hackney-coachmen (who, it seems, in those days were as arrant rascals as they are now), has these remarkable words, *Est quod gaudeas te in ista loca venisse, ubi aliquid sapere viderere.*[1] For, to speak a bold truth, it is a fatal miscarriage so ill to order affairs as to pass for a fool in one company, when in another you might be treated as a philosopher; which I desire some certain gentlemen of my acquaintance to lay up in their hearts as a very seasonable innuendo.

This, indeed, was the fatal mistake of that worthy gentleman, my most ingenious friend Mr. Wotton, a person in appearance ordained for great designs as well as performances, whether you will

[1] Ep. Fam. vii. 10, to Trebatius, who, as the next sentence in the letter shows, had not gone into England.

consider his notions or his looks. Surely no man ever advanced into the public with fitter qualifications of body and mind for the propagation of a new religion. Oh, had those happy talents, misapplied to vain philosophy, been turned into their proper channels of dreams and visions, where distortion of mind and countenance are of such sovereign use, the base, detracting world would not then have dared to report that something is amiss, that his brain hath undergone an unlucky shake, which even his brother modernists themselves, like ungrates, do whisper so loud that it reaches up to the very garret I am now writing in.

Lastly, whoever pleases to look into the fountains of enthusiasm, from whence in all ages have eternally proceeded such fattening streams, will find the spring-head to have been as troubled and muddy as the current. Of such great emolument is a tincture of this vapour, which the world calls madness, that without its help the world would not only be deprived of those two great blessings, conquests and systems, but even all mankind would unhappily be reduced to the same belief in things invisible. Now the former *postulatum* being held, that it is of no import from what originals this vapour proceeds, but either in what angles it strikes and spreads over the understanding, or upon what species of brain it ascends, it will be a very delicate point to cut the feather and divide the several reasons to a nice and curious reader, how this numerical difference in the brain can produce effects of so vast a difference from the same vapour as to be the sole point of individuation between Alexander the Great, Jack of Leyden, and Monsieur Des Cartes. The present argument is the most abstracted that ever I engaged in; it strains my faculties to their highest stretch, and I desire the reader to attend with utmost perpensity, for I now proceed to unravel this knotty point.

There is in mankind a certain   .   .   .   *Hic multa*   .
.   .   .   .   *desiderantur.*   .
and this I take to be a clear solution of the matter.

Having, therefore, so narrowly passed through this intricate difficulty, the reader will, I am sure, agree with me in the conclusion that, if the moderns mean by madness only a disturbance or transposition of the brain, by force of certain vapours issuing up from the lower faculties, then has this madness been the parent of all those mighty revolutions that have happened in empire, in philosophy, and in religion. For the brain in its natural position and state of serenity disposeth its owner to pass his life in the common forms, without any thought of subduing multitudes to his own power, his reasons, or his visions, and the more he shapes his understanding by the pattern of human learning, the less he is inclined to form parties after his particular notions, because that instructs him in his private infirmities, as well as in the stubborn ignorance of the people. But when a man's fancy gets astride on his reason, when imagination is at cuffs with the senses, and common understanding as well as common sense is kicked out of doors, the first proselyte he makes is himself; and when that is once compassed, the difficulty is not so great in bringing over others, a strong delusion always operating from without as vigorously as from within. For cant and vision are to the ear and the eye the same that tickling is to the touch. Those entertainments and pleasures we most value in life are such as dupe and play the wag with the senses. For if we take an examination of what is generally understood by happiness, as it has respect either to the understanding or the senses, we shall find all its properties and adjuncts will herd under this short definition, that it is a perpetual possession of being well deceived. And first, with relation to the mind or understanding, it is manifest what mighty advantages fiction has over truth, and the reason is just at our elbow: because imagination can build nobler scenes and produce more wonderful revolutions than fortune or Nature will be at the expense to furnish. Nor is mankind so much to blame in his choice thus determining him, if we consider that the debate merely lies between things past and things conceived, and so the question is only this: whether things that have place in the imagination may not as properly be said to exist as those that are seated in the memory? which may be justly held in the affirmative, and very much to the advantage of the former, since this is acknowledged to be the womb of things, and the other allowed to be no more than the grave. Again, if we take this definition of happiness and examine it with reference to the senses, it will be acknowledged wonderfully adapt. How sad and insipid do all objects accost us that are not conveyed in the vehicle of delusion! How shrunk is everything as it appears in the glass of Nature, so that if it were not for the assistance of artificial mediums, false lights, refracted angles, varnish, and tinsel, there would be a mighty level in the felicity and enjoyments of mortal men. If this were seriously considered by the world, as I have a certain reason to suspect it hardly will, men would no longer reckon among their high points of wisdom the art of exposing weak sides and publishing infirmities—an employment, in my opinion, neither better nor worse than that of unmasking, which, I think, has never been allowed fair usage, either in the world or the playhouse.

In the proportion that credulity is a more peaceful possession of the mind than curiosity, so far preferable is that wisdom which converses about the surface to that pretended philosophy which enters into the depths of things and then comes gravely back with informations and discoveries, that in the inside they are good for nothing. The two senses to which all objects first address themselves are the sight and the touch; these never examine farther than the colour, the shape, the size, and whatever other qualities dwell or are drawn by art upon the outward of bodies; and then comes reason officiously, with tools for cutting, and opening, and mangling, and piercing, offering to demonstrate that they are not of the same consistence quite through. Now I take all this to be the last degree of perverting Nature, one of whose eternal laws it is to put her best furniture forward. And therefore, in order to save the charges of all such expensive anatomy for the time to come, I do here think fit to inform the reader that in such conclusions as these reason is certainly in the right; and that in most corporeal beings which have fallen under my cognisance, the outside hath been infinitely preferable to the in, whereof I have been further convinced from some late experiments. Last week I saw a woman flayed, and you will hardly believe how much it altered her person for the worse. Yesterday I ordered the carcass of a beau to be stripped in my presence, when we were all amazed to find so many unsuspected faults under one suit of clothes. Then I laid open his brain, his heart, and his spleen, but I plainly perceived at every operation that the farther we proceeded, we found the defects increase upon us in number and bulk; from all which I justly formed this conclusion to myself, that whatever philosopher or projector can find out an art to sodder and patch up the flaws and imperfections of Nature, will deserve much better of mankind and teach us a more useful science than that so much in present esteem, of widening and exposing them (like him who held anatomy to be the ultimate end of physic). And he whose fortunes and dispositions have placed him in a convenient station to enjoy the fruits of this noble art, he that can with Epicurus content his ideas with the films and images that fly off upon his senses from the superfices of things, such a man, truly wise, creams off Nature, leaving the sour and the dregs for philosophy and reason to lap up. This is the sublime and refined point of felicity called the possession of being well-deceived, the serene peaceful state of being a fool among knaves.

But to return to madness. It is certain that, according to the system I have above deduced, every species thereof proceeds from a redundancy of vapour; therefore, as some kinds of frenzy give double strength to the sinews, so there are of other species which add vigour, and life, and spirit to the brain. Now it usually happens that these active spirits, getting possession of the brain, resemble those that haunt other waste and empty dwellings, which for want of business either vanish and carry away a piece of the house, or else stay at home and fling it all out of the windows. By which are mystically displayed the two principal branches of madness, and which some philosophers, not considering so well as I, have mistook to be different in their causes, over-hastily assigning the first to deficiency and the other to redundance.

I think it therefore manifest, from what I have here advanced, that the main point of skill and address is to furnish employment for this redundancy of vapour, and prudently to adjust the seasons of it, by which means it may certainly become of cardinal and catholic emolument in a commonwealth. Thus one man, choosing a proper juncture, leaps into a gulf, from thence proceeds a hero, and is called the saviour of his country. Another achieves the same enterprise, but unluckily timing it, has left the brand of madness fixed as a reproach upon his memory. Upon so nice a distinction are we taught to repeat the name of Curtius with reverence and love, that of Empedocles with hatred and contempt. Thus also it is usually conceived that the elder Brutus only personated the fool and madman for the good of the public; but this was nothing else than a redundancy of the same vapour long misapplied, called by the Latins *ingenium par negotiis,* or (to translate it as nearly as I can), a sort of frenzy never in its right element till you take it up in business of the state.

Upon all which, and many other reasons of equal weight, though not equally curious, I do here gladly embrace an opportunity I have long sought for, of recommending it as a very noble undertaking to Sir Edward Seymour, Sir Christopher Musgrave, Sir John Bowles, John Howe, Esq., and other patriots concerned, that they would move for leave to bring in a Bill for appointing commissioners to inspect into Bedlam and the parts adjacent, who shall be empowered to send for persons, papers, and records, to examine into the merits and qualifications of every student and professor, to observe with utmost exactness their several dispositions and behaviour, by which means, duly distinguishing and adapting their talents, they might produce admirable instruments for the several offices in a state, . . . civil and military, proceeding in such methods as I shall here humbly propose. And I hope the gentle reader will give some allowance to my great solicitudes in this important affair, upon account of that high esteem I have ever borne that honourable society, whereof I had some time the happiness to be an unworthy member.

Is any student tearing his straw in piecemeal, swearing and blaspheming, biting his grate, foaming at the mouth, and emptying his vessel in the spectators' faces? Let the right worshipful the

Commissioners of Inspection give him a regiment of dragoons, and send him into Flanders among the rest. Is another eternally talking, sputtering, gaping, bawling, in a sound without period or article? What wonderful talents are here mislaid! Let him be furnished immediately with a green bag and papers, and three-pence in his pocket,[1] and away with him to Westminster Hall. You will find a third gravely taking the dimensions of his kennel, a person of foresight and insight, though kept quite in the dark; for why, like Moses, *Ecce cornuta erat ejus facies.* He walks duly in one pace, entreats your penny with due gravity and ceremony, talks much of hard times, and taxes, and the whore of Babylon, bars up the wooden of his cell constantly at eight o'clock, dreams of fire, and shoplifters, and court-customers, and privileged places. Now what a figure would all these acquirements amount to if the owner were sent into the City among his brethren! Behold a fourth in much and deep conversation with himself, biting his thumbs at proper junctures, his countenance chequered with business and design; sometimes walking very fast, with his eyes nailed to a paper that he holds in his hands; a great saver of time, somewhat thick of hearing, very short of sight, but more of memory; a man ever in haste, a great hatcher and breeder of business, and excellent at the famous art of whispering nothing; a huge idolator of monosyllables and procrastination, so ready to give his word to everybody that he never keeps it; one that has forgot the common meaning of words, but an admirable retainer of the sound; extremely subject to the looseness, for his occasions are perpetually calling him away. If you approach his grate in his familiar intervals, "Sir," says he, "give me a penny and I'll sing you a song; but give me the penny first" (hence comes the common saying and commoner practice of parting with money for a song). What a complete system of court-skill is here described in every branch of it, and all utterly lost with wrong application. Accost the hole of another kennel, first stopping your nose, you will behold a surly, gloomy, nasty, slovenly mortal, raking in his own dung and dabbling in his urine. The best

---

[1] A lawyer's coach-hire.—S.

part of his diet is the reversion of his own ordure, which expiring into steams, whirls perpetually about, and at last reinfunds. His complexion is of a dirty yellow, with a thin scattered beard, exactly agreeable to that of his diet upon its first declination, like other insects, who, having their birth and education in an excrement, from thence borrow their colour and their smell. The student of this apartment is very sparing of his words, but somewhat over-liberal of his breath. He holds his hand out ready to receive your penny, and immediately upon receipt withdraws to his former occupations. Now is it not amazing to think the society of Warwick Lane[1] should have no more concern for the recovery of so useful a member, who, if one may judge from these appearances, would become the greatest ornament to that illustrious body? Another student struts up fiercely to your teeth, puffing with his lips, half squeezing out his eyes, and very graciously holds out his hand to kiss. The keeper desires you not to be afraid of this professor, for he will do you no hurt; to him alone is allowed the liberty of the ante-chamber, and the orator of the place gives you to understand that this solemn person is a tailor run mad with pride. This considerable student is adorned with many other qualities, upon which at present I shall not further enlarge. . . . Hark in your ear. . . . I am strangely mistaken if all his address, his motions, and his airs would not then be very natural and in their proper element.

I shall not descend so minutely as to insist upon the vast number of beaux, fiddlers, poets, and politicians that the world might recover by such a reformation, but what is more material, beside the clear gain redounding to the commonwealth by so large an acquisition of persons to employ, whose talents and acquirements, if I may be so bold to affirm it, are now buried or at least misapplied. It would be a mighty advantage accruing to the public from this inquiry that all these would very much excel and arrive at great perfection in their several kinds, which I think is manifest from what I have already shown, and shall enforce by this one plain instance, that even I myself, the author of these momentous

[1] The College of Physicians.

truths, am a person whose imaginations are hard-mouthed and exceedingly disposed to run away with his reason, which I have observed from long experience to be a very light rider, and easily shook off; upon which account my friends will never trust me alone without a solemn promise to vent my speculations in this or the like manner, for the universal benefit of human kind, which perhaps the gentle, courteous, and candid reader, brimful of that modern charity and tenderness usually annexed to his office, will be very hardly persuaded to believe.

SECTION X.

A FARTHER DIGRESSION.

I T is an unanswerable argument of a very refined age the wonderful civilities that have passed of late years between the nation of authors and that of readers.　There can hardly pop out a play, a pamphlet, or a poem without a preface full of acknowledgments to the world for the general reception and applause they have given it, which the Lord knows where, or when, or how, or from whom it received.　In due deference to so laudable a custom, I do here return my humble thanks to His Majesty and both Houses of Parliament, to the Lords of the King's most honourable Privy Council, to the reverend the Judges, to the Clergy, and Gentry, and Yeomanry of this land; but in a more especial manner to my worthy brethren and friends at Will's Coffee-house, and Gresham College, and Warwick Lane, and Moorfields, and Scotland Yard, and Westminster Hall, and Guildhall; in short, to all inhabitants and retainers whatsoever, either in court, or church, or camp, or city, or country, for their generosity and universal acceptance of this divine treatise.　I accept their approbation and good opinion with extreme gratitude, and to the utmost of my poor capacity shall take hold of all opportunities to return the obligation.

I am also happy that fate has flung me into so blessed an age for the mutual felicity of booksellers and authors, whom I may safely affirm to be at this day the two only satisfied parties in England.　Ask an author how his last piece has succeeded, "Why, truly he thanks his stars the world has been very favourable, and he has not the least reason to complain."　And yet he wrote it in a week at bits and starts, when he could steal an hour from his urgent affairs, as it is a hundred to one you may see further in the preface, to which he refers you, and for the rest to the bookseller. There you go as a customer, and make the same question, "He blesses his God the thing takes wonderful; he is just printing a second edition, and has but three left in his shop." You beat down the price; "sir, we shall not differ," and in hopes of your custom another time, lets you have it as reasonable as you please; "And pray send as many of your acquaintance as you will; I shall upon your account furnish them all at the same rate."

Now it is not well enough considered to what accidents and occasions the world is indebted for the greatest part of those noble writings which hourly start up to entertain it. If it were not for a rainy day, a drunken vigil, a fit of the spleen, a course of physic, a sleepy Sunday, an ill run at dice, a long tailor's bill, a beggar's purse, a factious head, a hot sun, costive diet, want of books, and a just contempt of learning,—but for these events, I say, and some others too long to recite (especially a prudent neglect of taking brimstone inwardly), I doubt the number of authors and of writings would dwindle away to a degree most woeful to behold. To confirm this opinion, hear the words of the famous troglodyte philosopher. "It is certain," said he, "some grains of folly are of course annexed as part in the composition of human nature; only the choice is left us whether we please to wear them inlaid or embossed, and we need not go very far to seek how that is usually determined, when we remember it is with human faculties as with liquors, the lightest will be ever at the top."

There is in this famous island of Britain a certain paltry scribbler, very voluminous, whose character the reader cannot wholly be a stranger to. He deals in a pernicious kind of writings called "Second Parts," and usually passes under the name of "The Author of the First." I easily foresee that as soon as I lay down my pen this nimble operator will have stole it, and treat me as inhumanly as he has already done Dr. Blackmore, Lestrange, and many others who shall here be nameless. I therefore fly for justice and relief into the hands of that great rectifier of saddles and lover of mankind, Dr. Bentley, begging he will take this enormous grievance into his most modern consideration; and if it should so happen that the furniture of an ass in the shape of a second part must for my sins be clapped, by mistake, upon my back, that he will immediately please, in the presence of the world, to lighten me of the burthen, and take it home to his own house till the true beast thinks fit to call for it.

In the meantime, I do here give this public notice that my resolutions are to circumscribe within this discourse the whole stock of matter I have been so many years providing. Since my vein is once opened, I am content to exhaust it all at a running, for the peculiar advantage of my dear country, and for the universal benefit of mankind. Therefore, hospitably considering the number of my guests, they shall have my whole entertainment at a meal, and I scorn to set up the leavings in the cupboard. What the guests cannot eat may be given to the poor, and the dogs under the table may gnaw the bones.[1] This I understand for a more generous proceeding than to turn the company's stomachs by inviting them again to-morrow to a scurvy meal of scraps.

If the reader fairly considers the strength of what I have advanced in the foregoing section, I am convinced it will produce a wonderful revolution in his notions and opinions, and he will be abundantly better prepared to receive and to relish the concluding part of this miraculous treatise. Readers may be divided into three classes—the superficial, the ignorant, and the learned, and I have with much felicity fitted my pen to the genius and advantage of each. The superficial reader will be strangely provoked to laughter, which clears the breast and the lungs, is sovereign against the spleen, and the most innocent of all diuretics. The ignorant reader (between whom and the former the distinction is extremely nice) will find himself disposed to stare, which is an admirable remedy for ill eyes, serves to raise and enliven the spirits, and wonderfully helps perspiration. But the reader truly learned, chiefly for whose benefit I wake when others sleep,

---

[1] The bad critics.

and sleep when others wake, will here find sufficient matter to employ his speculations for the rest of his life. It were much to be wished, and I do here humbly propose for an experiment, that every prince in Christendom will take seven of the deepest scholars in his dominions and shut them up close for seven years in seven chambers, with a command to write seven ample commentaries on this comprehensive discourse. I shall venture to affirm that, whatever difference may be found in their several conjectures, they will be all, without the least distortion, manifestly deducible from the text. Meantime it is my earnest request that so useful an undertaking may be entered upon (if their Majesties please) with all convenient speed, because I have a strong inclination before I leave the world to taste a blessing which we mysterious writers can seldom reach till we have got into our graves, whether it is that fame being a fruit grafted on the body, can hardly grow and much less ripen till the stock is in the earth, or whether she be a bird of prey, and is lured among the rest to pursue after the scent of a carcass, or whether she conceives her trumpet sounds best and farthest when she stands on a tomb, by the advantage of a rising ground and the echo of a hollow vault.

It is true, indeed, the republic of dark authors, after they once found out this excellent expedient of dying, have been peculiarly happy in the variety as well as extent of their reputation. For night being the universal mother of things, wise philosophers hold all writings to be fruitful in the proportion they are dark, and therefore the true illuminated (that is to say, the darkest of all) have met with such numberless commentators, whose scholiastic midwifery hath delivered them of meanings that the authors themselves perhaps never conceived, and yet may very justly be allowed the lawful parents of them, the words of such writers being like seed, which, however scattered at random, when they light upon a fruitful ground, will multiply far beyond either the hopes or imagination of the sower.

And therefore, in order to promote so useful a work, I will here take leave to glance a few innuendos that may be of great assistance to those sublime spirits who shall be appointed to labour in a universal comment upon this wonderful discourse. And first, I have couched a very profound mystery in the number of o's multiplied by seven and divided by nine. Also, if a devout brother of the Rosy Cross will pray fervently for sixty-three mornings with a lively faith, and then transpose certain letters and syllables according to prescription, in the second and fifth section they will certainly reveal into a full receipt of the *opus magnum.* Lastly, whoever will be at the pains to calculate the whole number of each letter in this treatise, and sum up the difference exactly between the several numbers, assigning the true natural cause for every such difference, the discoveries in the product will plentifully reward his labour. But then he must beware of Bythus and Sigè, and be sure not to forget the qualities of Acamoth ; *a cujus lacrymis humecta prodit substantia, à risu lucida, à tristitiâ solida, et à timore mobilis,* wherein Eugenius Philalethes[1] hath committed an unpardonable mistake.

1. A name under which Thomas Vaughan wrote. The Latin reads: "[One] from whose tears watery substance issued; from whose laugh, clear substance; from whose gloom, firm substance; and from whose fear changeable substance."

SECTION XI.

A TALE OF A TUB.

AFTER so wide a compass as I have wandered, I do now gladly overtake and close in with my subject, and shall henceforth hold on with it an even pace to the end of my journey, except some beautiful prospect appears within sight of my way, whereof, though at present I have neither warning nor expectation, yet upon such an accident, come when it will, I shall beg my reader's favour and company, allowing me to conduct him through it along with myself. For in writing it is as in travelling. If a man is in haste to be at home (which I acknowledge to be none of my case, having never so little business as when I am there), if his horse be tired with long riding and ill ways, or be naturally a jade, I advise him clearly to make the straightest and the commonest road, be it ever so dirty; but then surely we must own such a man to be a scurvy companion at best. He spatters himself and his fellow-travellers at every step. All their thoughts, and wishes, and conversation turn entirely upon the subject of their journey's end, and at every splash, and plunge, and stumble they heartily wish one another at the devil.

On the other side, when a traveller and his horse are in heart and plight, when his purse is full and the day before him, he takes the road only where it is clean or convenient, entertains his company there as agreeably as he can, but upon the first occasion carries them along with him to every delightful scene in view, whether of art, of Nature, or of both; and if they chance to refuse out of stupidity or weariness, let them jog on by themselves, and be d——n'd. He'll overtake them at the next town, at which arriving, he rides furiously through, the men, women, and children run out to gaze, a hundred noisy curs run barking after him, of which, if he honours the boldest with a lash of his whip, it is rather out of sport than revenge. But should some sourer mongrel dare too near an approach, he receives a salute on the chaps by an accidental stroke from the courser's heels, nor is any ground lost by the blow, which sends him yelping and limping home.

I now proceed to sum up the singular adventures of my renowned Jack, the state of whose dispositions and fortunes the careful reader does, no doubt, most exactly remember, as I last parted with them in the conclusion of a former section. Therefore, his next care must be from two of the foregoing to extract a scheme of notions that may best fit his understanding for a true relish of what is to ensue.

Jack had not only calculated the first revolution of his brain so prudently as to give rise to that epidemic sect of Æolists, but succeeding also into a new and strange variety of conceptions, the fruitfulness of his imagination led him into certain notions which, although in appearance very unaccountable, were not without their mysteries and their meanings, nor wanted followers to countenance and improve them. I shall therefore be extremely careful and exact in recounting such material passages of this nature as I have been able to collect, either from undoubted tradition or indefatigable reading, and shall describe them as graphically as it is possible, and as far as notions of that height and latitude can be brought within the compass of a pen. Nor do I at all question but they will furnish plenty of noble matter for such whose converting imaginations dispose them to reduce all things into types, who can make shadows—no thanks to the sun—and then mould them into substances—no thanks to philosophy—whose peculiar talent lies in fixing tropes and allegories to the letter, and refining what is literal into figure and mystery.

Jack had provided a fair copy of his father's will, engrossed in form upon a large skin of parchment, and resolving to act the part of a most dutiful son, he became the fondest creature of it imaginable. For although, as I have often told the reader, it consisted wholly in certain plain, easy directions about the management and wearing of their coats, with legacies and penalties in case of obedience or neglect, yet he began to entertain a fancy that the matter was deeper and darker, and therefore must needs have a great deal more of mystery at the bottom. "Gentlemen," said he, "I will prove this very skin of parchment to be meat, drink, and cloth, to be the philosopher's stone and the universal medicine." In consequence of which raptures he resolved to make use of it in the most necessary as well as the most paltry occasions of life. He had a way of working it into any shape he pleased, so that it served him for a nightcap when he went to bed, and for an umbrella in rainy weather. He would lap a piece of it about a sore toe; or, when he had fits, burn two inches under his nose; or, if anything lay heavy on his stomach, scrape off and swallow as much of the powder as would lie on a silver penny—they were all infallible remedies. With analogy to these refinements, his common talk and conversation ran wholly in the praise of his Will, and he circumscribed the utmost of his eloquence within that compass, not daring to let slip a syllable without authority from thence. Once at a strange house he was suddenly taken short upon an urgent juncture, whereon it may not be allowed too particularly to dilate, and being not able to call to mind, with that suddenness the occasion required, an authentic phrase for demanding the way to the back, he chose rather, as the more prudent course, to incur the penalty in such cases usually annexed; neither was it possible for the united rhetoric of mankind to prevail with him to make himself clean again, because, having consulted the will upon this emergency, he met with a passage near the bottom (whether foisted in by the transcriber is not known) which seemed to forbid it.[1]

He made .it a part of his religion never to say grace to his meat, nor could all the world persuade him, as the common phrase is, to eat his victuals like a Christian.[2]

---

[1] Revelations xxii. 11 : "He which is filthy, let him be filthy still ; " "phrase of the will," being Scripture phrase, of either Testament, applied to every occasion, and often in the most unbecoming manner.

[2] He did not kneel when he received the Sacrament.

He bore a strange kind of appetite to snap-dragon and to the livid snuffs of a burning candle,[1] which he would catch and swallow with an agility wonderful to conceive; and by this procedure maintained a perpetual flame in his belly, which issuing in a glowing steam from both his eyes, as well·as his nostrils and his mouth, made his head appear in a dark night like the skull of an ass wherein a roguish boy hath conveyed a farthing-candle, to the terror of his Majesty's liege subjects. Therefore he made use of no other expedient to light himself home, but was wont to say that a wise man was his own lanthorn.

He would shut his eyes as he walked along the streets, and if he happened to bounce his head against a post or fall into the kennel (as he seldom missed either to do one or both), he would tell the gibing apprentices who looked on that he submitted with entire resignation, as to a trip or a blow of fate, with whom he found by long experience how vain it was either to wrestle or to cuff, and whoever durst undertake to do either would be sure to come off with a swingeing fall or a bloody nose. "It was ordained," said he,[2] "some few days before the creation, that my nose and this very post should have a rencounter, and therefore Providence thought fit to send us both into the world in the same age, and to make us countrymen and fellow-citizens. Now, had my eyes been open, it is very likely the business might have been a great deal worse, for how many a confounded slip is daily got by man with all his foresight about him ! Besides, the eyes of the understanding see best when those of the senses are out of the way, and therefore blind men are observed to tread their steps with much more caution, and conduct, and judgment than those who rely with too much confidence upon the virtue of the visual nerve, which every little accident shakes out of order, and a drop or a film can wholly disconcert; like a lanthorn among a pack of roaring bullies when they scour the streets, exposing its owner and itself to outward kicks and buffets, which both might have escaped if the vanity of appearing would have suffered them to walk in the dark. But further, if we examine the conduct of

---

[1] His inward lights.　　　　　　[2] Predestination.

these boasted lights, it will prove yet a great deal worse than their fortune. It is true I have broke my nose against this post, because Providence either forgot, or did not think it convenient, to twitch me by the elbow and give me notice to avoid it. But let not this encourage either the present age of posterity to trust their noses unto the keeping of their eyes, which may prove the fairest way of losing them for good and all. For, O ye eyes, ye blind guides, miserable guardians are ye of our frail noses; ye, I say, who fasten upon the first precipice in view, and then tow our wretched willing bodies after you to the very brink of destruction. But alas! that brink is rotten, our feet slip, and we tumble down prone into a gulf, without one hospitable shrub in the way to break the fall—a fall to which not any nose of mortal make is equal, except that of the giant Laurcalco,[1] who was Lord of the Silver Bridge. Most properly, therefore, O eyes, and with great justice, may you be compared to those foolish lights which conduct men through dirt and darkness till they fall into a deep pit or a noisome bog."

This I have produced as a scantling of Jack's great eloquence and the force of his reasoning upon such abstruse matters.

He was, besides, a person of great design and improvement in affairs of devotion, having introduced a new deity, who has since met with a vast number of worshippers, by some called Babel, by others Chaos, who had an ancient temple of Gothic structure upon Salisbury plain, famous for its shrine and celebration by pilgrims.

When he had some roguish trick to play, he would down with his knees, up with his eyes, and fall to prayers though in the midst of the kennel. Then it was that those who understood his pranks would be sure to get far enough out of his way; and whenever curiosity attracted strangers to laugh or to listen, he would of a sudden bespatter them with mud.

In winter he went always loose and unbuttoned, and clad as thin as possible to let in the ambient heat, and in summer lapped himself close and thick to keep it out.[2]

---

[1] *Vide* Don Quixote.—S.

[2] Swift borrowed this from the customs of Moronia—Fool's Land—in Joseph Hall's *Mundus Alter et Idem.*

In all revolutions of government, he would make his court for the office of hangman-general, and in the exercise of that dignity, wherein he was very dexterous, would make use of no other vizard than a long prayer.

He had a tongue so musculous and subtile, that he could twist it up into his nose and deliver a strange kind of speech from thence. He was also the first in these kingdoms who began to improve the Spanish accomplishment of braying; and having large ears perpetually exposed and erected, he carried his art to such a perfection, that it was a point of great difficulty to distinguish either by the view or the sound between the original and the copy.

He was troubled with a disease the reverse to that called the stinging of the tarantula, and would run dog-mad at the noise of music, especially a pair of bagpipes.[1] But he would cure himself again by taking two or three turns in Westminster Hall, or Billingsgate, or in a boarding-school, or the Royal Exchange, or a state coffee-house.

He was a person that feared no colours, but mortally hated all, and upon that account bore a cruel aversion to painters, insomuch that in his paroxysms as he walked the streets, he would have his pockets loaded with stones to pelt at the signs.[2]

Having from his manner of living frequent occasions to wash himself, he would often leap over head and ears into the water, though it were in the midst of the winter, but was always observed to come out again much dirtier, if possible, than he went in.[3]

He was the first that ever found out the secret of contriving a soporiferous medicine to be conveyed in at the ears.[4] It was a compound of sulphur and balm of Gilead, with a little pilgrim's salve.

He wore a large plaister of artificial caustics on his stomach,

---

[1] The Presbyterians objected to church-music, and had no organs in their meeting-houses.

[2] Opposed to the decoration of church walls.

[3] Baptism by immersion.

[4] Preaching.

with the fervour of which he could set himself a groaning like the famous bóard upon application of a red-hot iron.

He would stand in the turning of a street, and calling to those who passed by, would cry to one, " Worthy sir, do me the honour of a good slap in the chaps ; " to another, " Honest friend, pray favour me with a handsome kick in the rear ; " " Madam, shall I entreat a small box in the ear from your ladyship's fair hands ? " " Noble captain, lend a reasonable thwack, for the love of God, with that cane of yours over these poor shoulders." And when he had by such earnest solicitations made a shift to procure a basting sufficient to swell up his fancy and his sides, he would return home extremely comforted, and full of terrible accounts of what he had undergone for the public good. " Observe this stroke," said he, showing his bare shoulders ; " a plaguy janissary gave it me this very morning at seven o'clock, as, with much ado, I was driving off the Great Turk. Neighbours mine, this broken head deserves a plaister ; had poor Jack been tender of his noddle, you would have seen the Pope and the French King long before this time of day among your wives and your warehouses. Dear Christians, the Great Moghul was come as far as Whitechapel, and you may thank these poor sides that he hath not—God bless us—already swallowed up man, woman, and child."

It was highly worth observing the singular effects of that aversion or antipathy which Jack and his brother Peter seemed, even to affectation, to bear towards each other. Peter had lately done some rogueries that forced him to abscond, and he seldom ventured to stir out before night for fear of bailiffs. Their lodgings were at the two most distant parts of the town from each other, and whenever their occasions or humours called them abroad, they would make choice of the oddest, unlikely times, and most uncouth rounds that they could invent, that they might be sure to avoid one another. Yet, after all this, it was their perpetual fortune to meet, the reason of which is easy enough to apprehend, for the frenzy and the spleen of both having the same foundation, we may look upon them as two pair of compasses equally extended, and the fixed foot of each remaining in the same centre, which, though moving contrary ways at first, will be sure to encounter somewhere or other in the circumference. Besides, it was among the great misfortunes of Jack to bear a huge personal resemblance with his brother Peter. Their humour and dispositions were not only the same, but there was a close analogy in their shape, their size, and their mien; insomuch as nothing was more frequent than for a bailiff to seize Jack by the shoulders and cry, "Mr. Peter, you are the king's prisoner;" or, at other times, for one of Peter's nearest friends to accost Jack with open arms: "Dear Peter, I am glad to see thee; pray send me one of your best medicines for the worms." This, we may suppose, was a mortifying return of those pains and proceedings Jack had laboured in so long, and finding how directly opposite all his endeavours had answered to the sole end and intention which he had proposed to himself, how could it avoid having terrible effects upon a head and heart so furnished as his? However, the poor remainders of his coat bore all the punishment. The orient sun never entered upon his diurnal progress without missing a piece of it. He hired a tailor to stitch up the collar so close that it was ready to choke him, and squeezed out his eyes at such a rate as one could see nothing but the white. What little was left of the main substance of the coat he rubbed every day for two hours against a rough-cast wall, in order to grind away the remnants of lace and embroidery, but at the same time went on with so much violence that he proceeded a heathen philosopher. Yet after all he could do of this kind, the success continued still to disappoint his expectation, for as it is the nature of rags to bear a kind of mock resemblance to finery, there being a sort of fluttering appearance in both, which is not to be distinguished at a distance in the dark or by short-sighted eyes, so in those junctures it fared with Jack and his tatters, that they offered to the first view a ridiculous flaunting, which, assisting the resemblance in person and air, thwarted all his projects of separation, and left so near a similitude between them as frequently deceived the very disciples and followers of both. • • • • • • • • • • •

• 　 *Desunt nonnulla.* • 　 • 　 • 　 • 　 • 　 • 　 • 　 • 　 •

The old Sclavonian proverb said well that it is with men as with asses; whoever would keep them fast must find a very good hold at their ears. Yet I think we may affirm, and it hath been verified by repeated experience, that—

"Effugiet tamen hæc sceleratus vincula Proteus."[1]

It is good, therefore, to read the maxims of our ancestors with great allowances to times and persons; for if we look into primitive records we shall find that no revolutions have been so great or so frequent as those of human ears. In former days there was a curious invention to catch and keep them, which I think we may justly reckon among the *artes perditæ;* and how can it be otherwise, when in these latter centuries the very species is not only diminished to a very lamentable degree, but the poor remainder is also degenerated so far as to mock our skilfullest tenure? For if only the slitting of one ear in a stag hath been found sufficient to propagate the defect through a whole forest, why should we wonder at the greatest consequences, from so many loppings and mutilations to which the ears of our fathers and our own have been of late so much exposed? It is true, indeed, that while this island of ours was under the dominion of grace, many endeavours were made to improve the growth of ears once more among us. The proportion of largeness was not only looked upon as an ornament of the outward man, but as a type of grace in the inward. Besides, it is held by naturalists that if there be a protuberancy of parts in the superior region of the body, as in the ears and nose, there must be a parity also in the inferior; and therefore in that truly pious age the males in every assembly, according as they were gifted, appeared very forward in exposing their ears to view, and the regions about them; because Hippocrates[2] tells us that when the vein behind the ear happens to be cut, a man becomes a eunuch, and the females were nothing backwarder in beholding and edifying by them;

---

[1] "This wicked Proteus shall escape the chain."—*Francis's Horace.*
[2] Lib. de Aëre, Locis, et Aquis.—S.

whereof those who had already used the means looked about them with great concern, in hopes of conceiving a suitable offspring by such a prospect; others, who stood candidates for benevolence, found there a plentiful choice, and were sure to fix upon such as discovered the largest ears, that the breed might not dwindle between them. Lastly, the devouter sisters, who looked upon all extraordinary dilatations of that member as protrusions of zeal or spiritual excrescences, were sure to honour every head they sat upon as if they had been cloven tongues, but especially that of the preacher, whose ears were usually of the prime magnitude, which upon that account he was very frequent and exact in exposing with all advantages to the people in his rhetorical paroxysms, turning sometimes to hold forth the one, and sometimes to hold forth the other; from which custom the whole operation of preaching is to this very day among their professors styled by the phrase of holding forth.

Such was the progress of the saints for advancing the size of that member, and it is thought the success would have been every way answerable, if in process of time a cruel king had not arose, who raised a bloody persecution against all ears above a certain standard;[1] upon which some were glad to hide their flourishing sprouts in a black border, others crept wholly under a periwig; some were slit, others cropped, and a great number sliced off to the stumps. But of this more hereafter in my general " History of Ears," which I design very speedily to bestow upon the public.

From this brief survey of the falling state of ears in the last age, and the small care had to advance their ancient growth in the present, it is manifest how little reason we can have to rely upon a hold so short, so weak, and so slippery; and that whoever desires to catch mankind fast must have recourse to some other methods. Now he that will examine human nature with circumspection enough may discover several handles, whereof the six[2]

---

[1] Charles II., by the Act of Uniformity, which drove two thousand ministers of religion, including some of the most devout, in one day out of the Church of England.

[2] " Including Scaliger's," is Swift's note in the margin. The sixth sense was the "common sense" which united and conveyed to the mind as one whole the

senses afford one apiece, beside a great number that are screwed
to the passions, and some few riveted to the intellect. Among
these last, curiosity is one, and of all others affords the firmest
grasp; curiosity, that spur in the side, that bridle in the mouth,
that ring in the nose of a lazy, an impatient, and a grunting reader.
By this handle it is that an author should seize upon his readers;
which as soon as he hath once compassed, all resistance and strug-
gling are in vain, and they become his prisoners as close as he
pleases, till weariness or dulness force him to let go his grip.

And therefore I, the author of this miraculous treatise, having
hitherto, beyond expectation, maintained by the aforesaid handle
a firm hold upon my gentle readers, it is with great reluctance
that I am at length compelled to remit my grasp, leaving them
in the perusal of what remains to that natural oscitancy inherent
in the tribe. I can only assure thee, courteous reader, for both
our comforts, that my concern is altogether equal to thine, for my
unhappiness in losing or mislaying among my papers the remaining part of these memoirs, which consisted of accidents, turns,
and adventures, both new, agreeable, and surprising, and therefore
calculated in all due points to the delicate taste of this our noble
age. But alas! with my utmost endeavours I have been able only
to retain a few of the heads. Under which there was a full
account how Peter got a protection out of the King's Bench, and
of a reconcilement between Jack and him, upon a design they had
in a certain rainy night to trepan brother Martin into a spunging-
house, and there strip him to the skin. How Martin, with much
ado, showed them both a fair pair of heels. How a new warrant
came out against Peter, upon which Jack left him in the lurch,
stole his protection, and made use of it himself. How Jack's
tatters came into fashion in court and city; how he got upon a
great horse and ate custard.[1] But the particulars of all these, with

information brought in by the other five. Common sense did not originally mean
the kind of sense common among the people generally. A person wanting in
common sense was one whose brain did not properly combine impressions brought
into it by the eye, the ear, &c.

[1] Reference here is to the exercise by James II. of a dispensing power which
illegally protected Roman Catholics, and incidentally Dissenters also; to the con-

several others which have now slid out of my memory, are lost beyond all hopes of recovery. For which misfortune, leaving my readers to condole with each other as far as they shall find it to agree with their several constitutions, but conjuring them by all the friendship that has passed between us, from the title-page to this, not to proceed so far as to injure their healths for an accident past remedy, I now go on to the ceremonial part of an accomplished writer, and therefore by a courtly modern least of all others to be omitted.

sequent growth of feeling against the Roman Catholics. "Jack on a great horse and eating custard" represents what was termed the occasional conformity of men who "blasphemed custard through the nose," but complied with the law that required them to take Sacrament in the Church of England as qualification for becoming a Lord Mayor or holding any office of public authority.

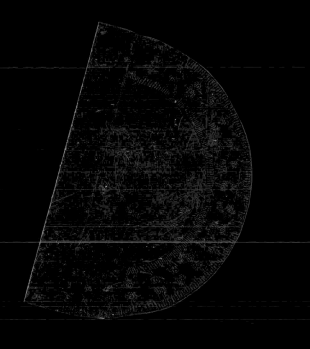

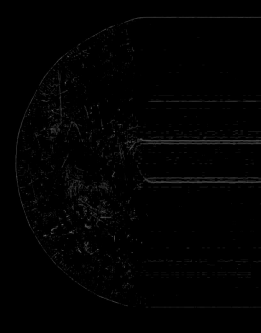

THE CONCLUSION.

GOING too long is a cause of abortion as effectual, though not so frequent, as going too short, and holds true especially in the labours of the brain. Well fare the heart of that noble Jesuit [1] who first adventured to confess in print that books must be suited to their several seasons, like dress, and diet, and diversions; and better fare our noble notion for refining upon this among other French modes. I am living fast to see the time when a book that misses its tide shall be neglected as the moon by day, or like mackerel a week after the season. No man has more nicely observed our climate than the bookseller who bought the copy of this work. He knows to a tittle what subjects will best go off in a dry year, and which it is proper to expose foremost when the weather-glass is fallen to much rain. When he had seen this treatise and consulted his almanac upon it, he gave me to understand that he had manifestly considered the two principal things, which were the bulk and the subject, and found it would never take but after a long vacation, and then only in case it should happen to be a hard year for turnips. Upon which I desired to know, considering my urgent necessities, what he thought might be acceptable this month. He looked westward and said, "I doubt we shall have a bit of bad weather. However, if you could prepare some pretty little banter (but not in verse), or a small treatise upon the ——, it would run like wildfire. But if it hold up, I have already hired an author to write something against Dr. Bentley, which I am sure will turn to account."

At length we agreed upon this expedient, that when a customer comes for one of these, and desires in confidence to know the

[1] Père d'Orleans.—S.

author, he will tell him very privately as a friend, naming whichever of the wits shall happen to be that week in the vogue, and if
Durfey's last play should be in course, I had as lieve he may be the
person as Congreve.   This I mention, because I am wonderfully
well acquainted with the present relish of courteous readers, and
have often observed, with singular pleasure, that a fly driven from
a honey-pot will immediately, with very good appetite, alight and
finish his meal on an excrement.

I have one word to say upon the subject of profound writers,
who are grown very numerous of late, and I know very well the
judicious world is resolved to list me in that number.   I conceive,
therefore, as to the business of being profound, that it is with
writers as with wells.   A person with good eyes can see to the
bottom of the deepest, provided any water be there; and that
often when there is nothing in the world at the bottom besides
dryness and dirt, though it be but a yard and half under ground,
it shall pass, however, for wondrous deep, upon no wiser a reason
than because it is wondrous dark.

I am now trying an experiment very frequent among modern
authors, which is to write upon nothing, when the subject is utterly
exhausted to let the pen still move on; by some called the ghost
of wit, delighting to walk after the death of its body.   And to say
the truth, there seems to be no part of knowledge in fewer hands
than that of discerning when to have done.   By the time that an
author has written out a book, he and his readers are become
old acquaintance, and grow very loathe to part; so that I have
sometimes known it to be in writing as in visiting, where the
ceremony of taking leave has employed more time than the whole
conversation before.   The conclusion of a treatise resembles the
conclusion of human life, which has sometimes been compared
to the end of a feast, where few are satisfied to depart *ut plenus
vitæ conviva.*   For men will sit down after the fullest meal, though
it be only to dose or to sleep out the rest of the day.   But in
this latter I differ extremely from other writers, and shall be too
proud if, by all my labours, I can have any ways contributed to
the repose of mankind in times so turbulent and unquiet as these.

Neither do I think such an employment so very alien from the office of a wit as some would suppose; for among a very polite nation in Greece [1] there were the same temples built and consecrated to Sleep and the Muses, between which two deities they believed the strictest friendship was established.

I have one concluding favour to request of my reader, that he will not expect to be equally diverted and informed by every line or every page of this discourse, but give some allowance to the author's spleen and short fits or intervals of dulness, as well as his own, and lay it seriously to his conscience whether, if he were walking the streets in dirty weather or a rainy day, he would allow it fair dealing in folks at their ease from a window, to criticise his gate and ridicule his dress at such a juncture.

In my disposure of employments of the brain, I have thought fit to make invention the master, and to give method and reason the office of its lackeys. The cause of this distribution was from observing it my peculiar case to be often under a temptation of being witty upon occasion where I could be neither wise nor sound, nor anything to the matter in hand. And I am too much a servant of the modern way to neglect any such opportunities, whatever pains or improprieties I may be at to introduce them. For I have observed that from a laborious collection of seven hundred and thirty-eight flowers and shining hints of the best modern authors, digested with great reading into my book of commonplaces, I have not been able after five years to draw, hook, or force into common conversation any more than a dozen. Of which dozen the one moiety failed of success by being dropped among unsuitable company, and the other cost me so many strains, and traps, and ambages to introduce, that I at length resolved to give it over. Now this disappointment (to discover a secret), I must own, gave me the first hint of setting up for an author, and I have since found among some particular friends that it is become a very general complaint, and has produced the same effects upon many others. For I have remarked many a towardly word to be wholly neglected or despised in discourse,

[1] Trazenii, Pausan. l. 2.—S.

which hath passed very smoothly with some consideration and esteem after its preferment and sanction in print. But now, since, by the liberty and encouragement of the press, I am grown absolute master of the occasions and opportunities to expose the talents I have acquired, I already discover that the issues of my observanda begin to grow too large for the receipts. Therefore I shall here pause awhile, till I find, by feeling the world's pulse and my own, that it will be of absolute necessity for us both to resume my pen.

A Discourse Concerning the
Mechanical Operation of the Spirit

In keeping with *A Tale of a Tub* (1704), of which it should be considered a part, *The Mechanical Operation of the Spirit* is a satire on the obscure way in which some scientists communicate with one another. By pretending that the imagination was strictly a physical-mechanical process that occurs within the body, Swift was also ridiculing the pretension of insisting that the imagination was divine in origin. None of us, Swift insisted, is capable of communicating with God.

CONCERNING THE

MECHANICAL OPERATION OF THE SPIRIT
IN A LETTER TO A FRIEND. A FRAGMENT.

THE BOOKSELLER'S ADVERTISEMENT

THE following Discourse came into my hands perfect and entire; but there being several things in it which the present age would not very well bear, I kept it by me some years, resolving it should never see the light. At length, by the advice and assistance of a judicious friend, I retrenched those parts that might give most offence, and have now ventured to publish the remainder. Concerning the author I am wholly ignorant; neither can I conjecture whether it be the same with that of the two foregoing pieces, the original having been sent me at a different time, and in a different hand. The learned reader will better determine, to whose judgment I entirely submit it.

A DISCOURSE, ETC.

For T. H., Esquire,[1] at his chambers in the
Academy of the Beaux Esprits, in New Holland.[2]

SIR,—It is now a good while since I have had in my head something, not only very material, but absolutely necessary to my

---

1. Possibly Thomas Hobbes, the object of some of Swift's satire here.
2. That part of Australia that the Dutch had been exploring.

health, that the world should be informed in; for, to tell you a secret, I am able to contain it no longer. However, I have been perplexed for some time to resolve what would be the most proper form to send it abroad in. To which end I have been three days coursing through Westminster-hall, and St. Paul's churchyard, and Fleet-street, to peruse titles; and I do not find any which holds so general a vogue as that of a Letter to a Friend; nothing is more common than to meet with long epistles addressed to persons and places where, at first thinking, one would be apt to imagine it not altogether so necessary or convenient; such as a neighbour at next door, a mortal enemy, a perfect stranger, or a person of quality in the clouds; and these upon subjects, in appearance, the least proper for conveyance by the post; as long schemes in philosophy, dark and wonderful mysteries of state, laborious dissertations in criticism and philosophy, advice to parliaments, and the like.

Now, sir, to proceed after the method in present wear; for, let me say what I will to the contrary, I am afraid you will publish this letter as soon as ever it comes to your hand. I desire you will be my witness to the world how careless and sudden a scribble it has been; that it was but yesterday when you and I began accidentally to fall into discourse on this matter; that I was not very well when we parted; that the post is in such haste I have had no manner of time to digest it into order or correct the style; and if any other modern excuses for haste and negligence shall occur to you in reading, I beg you to insert them, faithfully promising they shall be thankfully acknowledged.

Pray, sir, in your next letter to the Iroquois virtuosi,[1] do me the favour to present my humble service to that illustrious body, and assure them I shall send an account of those phenomena as soon as we can determine them at Gresham.

---

1. The "Iroquois virtuosi" and the references in subsequent paragraphs to "Gresham" and "literati of Topinambou" were probably satiric digs at the Royal Society, which met at Gresham College, and other philosophical societies. The Topinambou were Brazilian Indians.

I have not had a line from the literati of Topinambou these three last ordinaries.

And now, sir, having despatched what I had to say of form or of business, let me entreat you will suffer me to proceed upon my subject, and to pardon me if I make no further use of the epistolary style till I come to conclude.

SECTION I

It is recorded of Mahomet that, upon a visit he was going to pay in Paradise, he had an offer of several vehicles to conduct him upwards; as fiery chariots, winged horses, and celestial sedans; but he refused them all, and would be borne to heaven upon nothing but his ass. Now this inclination of Mahomet, as singular as it seems, has been since taken up by a great number of devout Christians, and doubtless with very good reason. For, since that Arabian is known to have borrowed a moiety of his religious system from the Christian faith, it is but just he should pay reprisals to such as would challenge them; wherein the good people of England, to do them all right, have not been backward; for, though there is not any other nation in the world so plentifully provided with carriages for that journey, either as to safety or ease, yet there are abundance of us who will not be satisfied with any other machine beside this of Mahomet.

For my own part, I must confess to bear a very singular respect to this animal, by whom I take human nature to be most admirably held forth in all its qualities, as well as operations; and therefore, whatever in my small reading occurs concerning this our fellow-creature, I do never fail to set it down by way of commonplace; and when I have occasion to write upon human reason, politics, eloquence, or knowledge, I lay my memorandums before me, and insert them with a wonderful facility of application. However, among all the qualifications ascribed to this distinguished brute, by ancient or modern authors, I cannot remember this talent of bearing his rider to heaven has been recorded for a part of his character, except in the two examples mentioned already; therefore I conceive the methods of this art to be a point of useful knowledge in very few hands, and which the learned world would gladly be better informed in: this is what I have undertaken to perform in the following discourse. For towards the operation already mentioned many peculiar properties are required both in the rider and the ass, which I shall endeavour to set in as clear a light as I can.

But, because I am resolved, by all means, to avoid giving offence to any party whatever, I will leave off discoursing so closely to the letter as I have hitherto done, and go on for the future by way of allegory; though in such a manner that the judicious reader may, without much straining, make his applications as often as he shall think fit. Therefore, if you please, from henceforward, instead of the term ass, we shall make use of gifted or enlightened teacher; and the word rider we will exchange for that of fanatic auditory, or any other denomination of the like import. Having settled this weighty point, the great subject of inquiry before us is to examine by what methods this teacher arrives at his gifts, or spirit, or light; and by what intercourse between him and his assembly it is cultivated and supported.

In all my writings I have had constant regard to this great end, not to suit and apply them to particular occasions and circumstances of time, of place, or of person, but to calculate them for universal nature and mankind in general. And of such catholic use I esteem this present disquisition; for I do not remember any other temper of body, or quality of mind, wherein all nations and ages of the world have so unanimously agreed as that of a fanatic strain or tincture of enthusiasm; which, improved by certain persons or societies of men, and by them practised upon the rest, has been able to produce revolutions of the greatest figure in history, as will soon appear to those who know anything of Arabia, Persia, India, or China, of

Morocco and Peru. Farther, it has possessed as great a power in the kingdom of knowledge, where it is hard to assign one art or science which has not annexed to it some fanatic branch; such are, the philosopher's stone, the grand elixir, the planetary worlds, the squaring of the circle, the *summum bonum*,[1] Utopian commonwealths, with some others of less or subordinate note, which all serve for nothing else but to employ or amuse this grain of enthusiasm dealt into every composition.

But if this plant has found a root in the fields of empire and of knowledge, it has fixed deeper amd spread yet farther upon holy ground; wherein, though it has passed under the general name of enthusiasm, and perhaps arisen from the same original, yet hath it produced certain branches of a very different nature, however often mistaken for each other. The word, in its universal acceptation, may be defined, a lifting up of the soul, or its faculties, above matter. This description will hold good in general, but I am only to understand it as applied to religion; wherein there are three general ways of ejaculating the soul, or transporting it beyond the sphere of matter. The first is the immediate act of God, and is called prophecy or inspiration. The second is the immediate act of the devil, and is termed possession. The third is the product of natural causes, the effect of strong imagination, spleen, violent anger, fear, grief, pain, and the like. These three have been abundantly treated on by authors, and therefore shall not employ my inquiry. But the fourth method of religious enthusiasm, or launching out of the soul, as it is purely an effect of artifice and mechanic operation, has been sparingly handled, or not at all, by any writer; because, though it is an art of great antiquity, yet, having been confined to few persons, it long wanted those advancements and refinements which it afterwards met with, since it has grown so epidemic, and fallen into so many cultivating hands.

It is therefore upon this mechanical operation of the spirit

---

1. The highest good.

that I mean to treat, as it is at present performed by our British workmen. I shall deliver to the reader the result of many judicious observations upon the matter; tracing, as near as I can, the whole course and method of this trade, producing parallel instances and relating certain discoveries that have luckily fallen in my way.

I have said that there is one branch of religious enthusiasm which is purely an effect of nature; whereas the part I mean to handle is wholly an effect of art, which, however, is inclined to work upon certain natures and constitutions more than others. Besides, there is many an operation which in its original was purely an artifice, but through a long succession of ages has grown to be natural. Hippocrates tells us that among our ancestors the Scythians there was a nation called Long-heads, which at first began by a custom among midwives and nurses of moulding, and squeezing, and bracing up the heads of infants; by which means nature, shut out at one passage, was forced to seek another, and, finding room above, shot upwards in the form of a sugar-loaf; and, being diverted that way for some generations, at last found it out for herself, needing no assistance from the nurse's hand. This was the original of the Scythian Long-heads, and thus did custom, from being a second nature, proceed to be a first. To all which there is something very analogous among us of this nation, who are the undoubted posterity of that refined people. For in the age of our fathers there arose a generation of men in this island called Round-heads,[1] whose race is now spread over three kingdoms; yet in its beginning was merely an operation of art produced by a pair of scissors, a squeeze of the face, and a black cap. These heads, thus formed into a perfect sphere in all assemblies, were

---

1. The fanatics in the time of Charles I, ignorantly applying the text, "Ye know that it is a shame for men to have long hair," cut theirs very short. It is said that the Queen, once seeing Pym, a celebrated patriot, thus cropped, inquired who that round-headed man was; and that from this incident the distinction became general, and the party were called the Round-heads.— *Hawkesworth.*

most exposed to the view of the female sort, which did influence their conceptions so effectually, that nature at last took the hint and did it of herself; so that a round-head has been ever since as familiar a sight among us as a long-head among the Scythians.

Upon these examples, and others easy to produce, I desire the curious reader to distinguish, first, between an effect grown from art into nature, and one that is natural from its beginning; secondly, between an effect wholly natural, and one which has only a natural foundation, but where the superstructure is entirely artificial. For the first and the last of these I understand to come within the districts of my subject. And having obtained these allowances, they will serve to remove any objections that may be raised hereafter against what I shall advance.

The practitioners of this famous art proceed, in general, upon the following fundamental; that the corruption of the senses is the generation of the spirit; because the senses in men are so many avenues to the fort of reasons, which in this operation is wholly blocked up. All endeavours must be therefore used, either to divert, bind up, stupefy, fluster, and amuse the senses, or else to justle them out of their stations; and, while they are either absent or otherwise employed, or engaged in a civil war against each other, the spirit enters and performs its part.

Now, the usual methods of managing the senses upon such conjunctures are, what I shall be very particular in delivering, as far as it is lawful for me to do; but, having had the honour to be initiated into the mysteries of every society, I desire to be excused from divulging any rites wherein the profane must have no part.

But here, before I can proceed farther, a very dangerous objection must, if possible, be removed. For it is positively denied by certain critics that the spirit can, by any means, be introduced into an assembly of modern saints; the disparity being so great in many material circumstances between the primitive way of inspiration and that which is practised in the present age. This they pretend to prove from the second chapter of the Acts,[1] where, comparing both, it appears, first, that the apostles were gathered together with one accord, in one place; by which is meant a universal agreement in opinion and form of worship; a harmony, say they, so far from being found between any two conventicles among us, that it is in vain to expect it between any two heads in the same. Secondly, the spirit instructed the apostles in the gift of speaking several languages; a knowledge so remote from our dealers in this art, that they neither understand propriety of words or phrases in their own. Lastly, say these objectors, the modern artists do utterly exclude all approaches of the spirit, and bar up its ancient way of entering, by covering themselves so close and so industriously a-top; for they will needs have it as a point clearly gained, that the cloven tongues never sat upon the apostles' heads while their hats were on.

Now, the force of these objections seems to consist in the different acceptation of the word spirit; which, if it be understood for a supernatural assistance approaching from without, the objectors have reason, and their assertions may be allowed; but the spirit we treat of here proceeding entirely from within, the argument of these adversaries is wholly eluded. And upon the same account, our modern artificers find it an expedient of absolute necessity to cover their heads as close as they can in order to prevent perspiration, than which nothing is observed to be a greater spender of mechanic light, as we may perhaps further show in a convenient place.

To proceed therefore upon the phenomenon of spiritual mechanism, it is here to be noted that in forming and working up the spirit the assembly has a considerable share as well as the preacher. The method of this arcanum is as follows: they violently strain their eyeballs inward, half closing the lids;

---

1. This refers to the Acts of the Apostles where the Holy Spirit is described as appearing in cloven tongues of fire and the Apostles are described as speaking with other tongues.

then, as they sit, they are in a perpetual motion of see-saw, making long hums at proper periods, and continuing the sound at equal height, choosing their time in those intermissions while the preacher is at ebb. Neither is this practice in any part of it so singular and improbable as not to be traced in distant regions from reading and observation. For, first, the Jauguis [Bernier, *Mem. de Megol.*], or enlightened saints of India, see all their visions by help of an acquired straining and pressure of the eyes. Secondly, the art of see-saw on a beam, and swinging by session upon a cord, in order to raise artificial ecstasies, has been derived to us from our Scythian [Guagnini, *Hist. Sarmat.*] ancestors, where it is practised at this day among the women. Lastly, the whole proceeding, as I have here related it, is performed by the natives of Ireland with a considerable improvement; and it is granted that this noble nation has, of all others, admitted fewer corruptions and degenerated least from the purity of the old Tartars. Now, it is usual for a lot of Irish men and women to abstract themselves from matter, bind up all their senses, grow visionary and spiritual, by influence of a short pipe of tobacco handed round the company, each preserving the smoke in his mouth till it comes again to his turn to take in fresh; at the same time there is a concert of a continued gentle hum, repeated and renewed by instinct as occasion requires; and they move their bodies up and down to a degree that sometimes their heads and points lie parallel to the horizon. Meanwhile you may observe their eyes turned up, in the posture of one who endeavours to keep himself awake; by which, and many other symptoms among them, it manifestly appears that the reasoning faculties are all suspended and superseded, that imagination has usurped the seat, scattering a thousand deliriums over the brain. Returning from this digression, I shall describe the methods by which the spirit approaches. The eyes being disposed according to art, at first you can see nothing; but after a short pause a small glimmering light begins to appear and dance before you: then, by frequently moving your body up and down, you perceive the vapours to ascend very fast, till you are perfectly dosed and flustered like one who drinks too much in a morning. Meanwhile the preacher is also at work; he begins a loud hum which pierces you quite through; this is immediately returned by the audience, and you find yourself prompted to imitate them by a mere spontaneous impulse, without knowing what you do. The *interstitia* are duly filled up by the preacher to prevent too long a pause, under which the spirit would soon faint and grow languid.

This is all I am allowed to discover about the progress of the spirit with relation to that part which is borne by the assembly; but in the methods of the preacher, to which I now proceed, I shall be more large and particular.

SECTION II

You will read it very gravely remarked in the books of those illustrious and right eloquent penmen, the modern travellers, that the fundamental difference in point of religion between the wild Indians and us, lies in this—that we worship God, and they worship the devil. But there are certain critics who will by no means admit of this distinction, rather believing that all nations whatsoever adore the true God, because they seem to intend their devotions to some invisible power of greatest goodness and ability to help them; which perhaps will take in the brightest attributes ascribed to the Divinity. Others again inform us that those idolators adore two principles—the principle of good, and that of evil; which indeed I am apt to look upon as the most universal notion that mankind, by the mere light of nature, ever entertained of things invisible. How this idea has been managed by the Indians and us, and with what advantage to the understandings of either, may well deserve to be examined. To me the difference appears little more than this, that they are put oftener upon their knees by their fears, and we by our desires; that the former set them a praying, and us a cursing. What I applaud them for is, their discretion in limiting their devotions and their deities to their several districts, nor ever suffering the liturgy of the white God to cross or to interfere with that of the black. Not so with us, who, pretending by the lines and measures of our reason to extend the dominion of one invisible power, and contract that of the other, have discovered a gross ignorance in the natures of good and evil, and most horribly confounded the frontiers of both. After men have lifted up the throne of their divinity to the *coelum empyroeum,* adorned with all such qualities and accomplishments as themselves seem most to value and possess—after they have sunk their principle of evil to the lowest centre, bound him with chains, loaded him with curses, furnished him with viler dispositions than any rake-hell of the town, accoutred him with tail, and horns, and huge claws, and saucer eyes—I laughed aloud to see these reasoners at the same time engaged in wise dispute, about certain walks and purlieus, whether they are in the verge of God or the devil; seriously debating whether such and such influences come into men's minds from above or below; whether certain passions and affections are guided by the evil spirit or the good—

> Dum fas atque nefas exiguo fine libidinum
> Discernunt avidi.[1]

Thus do men establish a fellowship of Christ with Belial, and such is the analogy they make between cloven tongues and cloven feet. Of the like nature is the disquisition before us: it has continued these hundred years an even debate whether the deportment and the cant of our English enthusiastic preachers were possession or inspiration; and a world of argument has been drained on either side, perhaps to little purpose. For I think it is in life as in tragedy, where it is held a conviction of great defect, both in order and invention, to interpose the

---

1. "While those eager for indulgence of their desires scarcely discriminate between the permissible and impermissible." (Horace, *Odes* 1.18.10–11)

assistance of preternatural power without an absolute and last necessity. However, it is a sketch of human vanity for every individual to imagine the whole universe is interested in his meanest concern. If he has got cleanly over a kennel, some angel unseen descended on purpose to help him by the hand; if he has knocked his head against a post, it was the devil for his sins let loose from hell on purpose to buffet him. Who that sees a little paltry mortal, droning, and dreaming, and drivelling to a multitude, can think it agreeable to common good sense that either heaven or hell should be put to the trouble of influence or inspection upon what he is about? Therefore I am resolved immediately to weed this error out of mankind, by making it clear that this mystery of vending spiritual gifts is nothing but a trade, acquired by as much instruction and mastered by equal practice and application, as others are. This will best appear by describing and deducing the whole process of the operation, as variously as it hath fallen under my knowledge or experience.

(Here the whole scheme of spiritual mechanism was deduced and explained, with an appearance of great reading and observation; but it was thought neither safe nor convenient to print it.)

Here it may not be amiss to add a few words upon the laudable practice of wearing quilted caps;[1] which is not a matter of mere custom, humour, or fashion, as some would pretend, but an institution of great sagacity and use: these, when moistened with sweat, stop all perspiration; and, by reverberating the heat, prevent the spirit from evaporating any way but at the mouth; even as a skilful housewife that covers her still with a wet clout for the same reason, and finds the same effect. For it is the opinion of choice *virtuosi* that the brain is only a crowd of little animals, but with teeth and claws extremely sharp, and therefore cling together in the contexture we behold,

---

1. Associated with the Puritans.

like the picture of Hobbes's Leviathan,[1] or like bees in perpendicular swarm upon a tree, or like a carrion corrupted into vermin, still preserving the shape and figure of the mother animal: that all invention is formed by the morsure[2] of two or more of these animals upon certain capillary nerves which proceed from thence, whereof three branches spread into the tongue, and two into the right hand. They hold also that these animals are of a constitution extremely cold; that their food is the air we attract, their excrement phlegm; and that what we vulgarly call rheums, and colds, and distillations, is nothing else but an epidemical looseness, to which that little commonwealth is very subject from the climate it lies under. Further, that nothing less than a violent heat can disentangle these creatures from their hamated station of life, or give them vigour and humour to imprint the marks of their little teeth. That if the morsure be hexagonal it produces poetry; the circular gives eloquence: if the bite hath been conical, the person whose nerve is so affected shall be disposed to write upon politics; and so of the rest.

I shall now discourse briefly by what kind of practices the voice is best governed toward the composition and improvement of the spirit; for, without a competent skill in tuning and toning each word, and syllable, and letter, to their due cadence, the whole operation is incomplete, misses entirely of its effect on the hearers, and puts the workman himself to continual pains for new supplies, without success. For it is to be understood that, in the language of the spirit, cant and droning supply the place of sense and reason in the language of men: because, in spiritual harangues, the disposition of the words according to the art of grammar has not the least use, but the skills and influence wholly lie in the choice and cadence of the syllables;

---

1. The title page of the first edition of Hobbes's *Leviathan* showed a figure wearing a crown and holding a sword, its body and arms made up of tiny figures.
2. A bite.

even as a discreet composer, who, in setting a song, changes the words and order so often, that he is forced to make it nonsense before he can make it music. For this reason it has been held by some that the art of canting is ever in greatest perfection when managed by ignorance; which is thought to be enigmatically meant by Plutarch, when he tells us that the best musical instruments were made from the bones of an ass. And the profounder critics upon that passage are of opinion, the word, in its genuine signification, means no other than a jaw-bone; though some rather think it to have been the *os sacrum*;[1] but in so nice a case I shall not take upon me to decide; the curious are at liberty to pick from it whatever they please.

The first ingredient toward the art of canting is, a competent share of inward light: that is to say, a large memory, plentifully fraught with theological polysyllables and mysterious texts from holy writ, applied and digested by those methods and mechanical operations already related: the bearers of this light resembling lanterns compact of leaves from old Geneva bibles; which invention, Sir Humphrey Edwin[2] during his mayorality, of happy memory, highly approved and advanced; affirming the Scripture to be now fulfilled, where it says, Thy word is a lantern to my feet, and a light to my paths.

Now, the art of canting consists in skilfully adapting the voice to whatever words the spirit delivers, that each may strike the ears of the audience with its most significant cadence. The force or energy of this eloquence is not to be found, as among ancient orators, in the disposition of words to a sentence, or the turning of long periods; but, agreeably to the modern refinements in music, is taken up wholly in dwelling and dilating upon syllables and letters. Thus, it is frequent for a single vowel to draw sighs from a multitude, and for a whole assembly of saints to sob to the music of one solitary liquid. But these

---

1. Sacred mouth.
2. A Presbyterian, who, when Lord Mayor of London, went in his official character to a Meeting-house.

are trifles, when even sounds inarticulate are observed to produce as forcible effects. A master workman shall blow his nose so powerfully as to pierce the hearts of his people, who were disposed to receive the excrements of his brain with the same reverence as the issue of it. Hawking, spitting, and belching, the defects of other men's rhetoric, are the flowers, and figures, and ornaments of his. For the spirit being the same in all, it is of no import through what vehicle it is conveyed.

It is a point of too much difficulty to draw the principles of this famous art within the compass of certain adequate rules. However, perhaps I may one day oblige the world with my critical essay upon the art of canting; philosophically, physically, and musically considered.

But, among all improvements of the spirit, wherein the voice has borne a part, there is none to be compared with that of conveying the sound through the nose, which, under the denomination of snuffing, has passed with so great applause in the world. The originals of this institution are very dark: but, having been initiated into the mystery of it, and leave being given me to publish it to the world, I shall deliver as direct a relation as I can.

This art, like many other famous inventions, owed its birth, or at least improvement and perfection, to an effect of chance; but was established upon solid reasons, and has flourished in this island ever since with great lustre. All agree that it first appeared upon the decay and discouragement of bagpipes, which, having long suffered under the mortal hatred of the brethren, tottered for a time, and at last fell with monarchy. The story is thus related.

As yet snuffling was not, when the following adventure happened to a Banbury[1] saint. Upon a certain day, while he was far engaged among the tabernacles of the wicked, he felt the outward man put into odd commotions, and strangely pricked forward by the inward; an effect very usual among

---

1. Banbury, in Oxfordshire, was notorious for the zealotry of its Puritans.

the modern inspired. For some think that the spirit is apt to feed on the flesh, like hungry wines upon raw beef. Others rather believe there is a perpetual game at leap-frog between both; and sometimes the flesh is uppermost, and sometimes the spirit; adding that the former, while it is in the state of a rider, wears huge Rippon[1] spurs; and, when it comes to the turn of being bearer, is wonderfully headstrong and hard-mouthed. However it came about, the saint felt his vessel full extended in every part; (a very natural effect of strong inspiration); and the place and time falling out so unluckily that he could not have the convenience of evacuating upwards, by repetition, prayer, or lecture, he was forced to open an inferior vent. In short, he wrestled with the flesh so long, that he at length subdued it, coming off with honourable wounds all before. The surgeon had now cured the parts primarily affected; but the disease, driven from its post, flew up into his head; and, as a skilful general, valiantly attacked in his trenches, and beaten from the field, by flying marches withdraws to the capital city, breaking down the bridges to prevent pursuit; so the disease, repelled from its first station, fled before the rod of Hermes to the upper region, there fortifying itself; but, finding the foe making attacks at the nose, broke down the bridge and retired to the headquarters. Now, the naturalists observe that there is in human noses an idiosyncrasy, by virtue of which, the more the passage is obstructed, the more our speech delights to go through, as the music of a flageolot is made by the stops. By this method the twang of the nose becomes perfectly to resemble the snuffle of a bagpipe, and is found to be equally attractive of British ears; whereof the saint had sudden experience, by practising his new faculty with wonderful success, in the operation of the spirit; for in a short time, no doctrine passed for sound and orthodox unless it were delivered through the nose. Straight every pastor copied after this original;

---

1. Ripon, in Yorkshire, was known for its manufacture of high-quality equestrian equipment, including fine spurs.

and those who who could not otherwise arrive to a perfection, spirited by a noble zeal, made use of the same experiment to acquire it; so that, I think, it may be truly affirmed the saints owe their empire to the snuffling of one animal, as Darius did his to the neighing of another; and both stratagems were performed by the same art; for we read how the Persian beast acquired his faculty by covering a mare the day before.

I should now have done, if I were not convinced that whatever I have yet advanced upon this subject is liable to great exception. For, allowing all I have said to be true, it may still be justly objected that there is in the commonwealth of artificial enthusiasm some real foundation for art to work upon in the temper and complexion of individuals, which other mortals seems to want. Observe but the gesture, the motion, and the countenance of some choice professors, though in their most familiar actions, you will find them of a different race from the rest of human creatures. Remark your commonest pretender to a light within, how dark, and dirty, and gloomy he is without; as lanterns, which, the more light they bear in their bodies, cast out so much the more soot, and smoke, and fuliginous matter to adhere to the sides. Listen but to their ordinary talk, and look on the mouth that delivers it, you will imagine you are hearing some ancient oracle, and your understanding will be equally informed. Upon these, and the like reasons, certain objectors pretend to put it beyond all doubt that there must be a sort of preternatural spirit possessing the heads of the modern saints; and some will have it to be the heat of zeal working upon the dregs of ignorance, as other spirits are produced from lees by the force of fire. Some again think, that when our earthly tabernacles are disordered and desolate, shaken and out of repair, the spirit delights to dwell within them; as houses are said to be haunted when they are forsaken and gone to decay.

To set this matter in as fair a light as possible, I shall here very briefly deduce the history of fanaticism from the most early ages to the present. And if we are able to fix upon any one material or fundamental point, wherein the chief professors have universally agreed, I think we may reasonably lay hold on that, and assign it for the great seed or principle of the spirit.

The most early traces we meet with of fanatics in ancient story are among the Egyptians, who instituted those rites known in Greece by the names of Orgia, Panegyres, and Dionysia; whether introduced there by Orpheus or Melampus we shall not dispute at present, nor in all likelihood at any time for the future. These feasts were celebrated to the honour of Osiris, whom the Grecians called Dionysus, and is the same with Bacchus: which has betrayed some superficial readers to imagine that the whole business was nothing more than a set of roaring, scouring companions, overcharged with wine; but this is a scandalous mistake, foisted on the world by a sort of modern authors, who have too literal an understanding; and, because antiquity is to be traced backwards, do therefore, like Jews, begin their books at the wrong end, as if learning were a sort of conjuring. These are the men who pretend to understand a book by scouring through the index; as if a traveller should go about to describe a palace, when he had seen nothing but the privy; or like certain fortune-tellers in North America, who have a way of reading a man's destiny by peeping in his breech. For, at the time of instituting these mysteries, there was not one vine in all Egypt, the natives drinking nothing but ale; which liquor seems to have been far more ancient than wine, and has the honour of owing its invention and progress, not only to the Egyptian Osiris, but to the Grecian Bacchus; who, in their famous expedition, carried the receipt of it along with them, and gave it to the nations they visited or subdued. Besides, Bacchus himself was very seldom or never drunk; for it is recorded of him that he was the first inventor of the mitre, which he wore continually on his head (as the whole company of bacchanals did), to prevent vapours and the headache after hard drinking. And for this reason, say some, the scarlet whore, when she makes the kings of the earth drunk with her cup of abomination, is always sober herself, though she never balks the glass in her turn, being, it seems, kept upon her legs by the virtue of her triple mitre. Now these feasts were instituted in imitation of the famous expedition Osiris made through the world, and of the company that attended him, whereof the bacchanalian ceremonies were so many types and symbols. From which account it is manifest that the fanatic rites of these bacchanals cannot be imputed to intoxications by wine, but must needs have had a deeper foundation. What this was, we may gather large hints from certain circumstances in the course of their mysteries. For, in the first place, there was, in their processions, an entire mixture and confusion of sexes; they affected to ramble about hills and deserts; their garlands were of ivy and vine, emblems of cleaving and clinging; or of fir, the parent of turpentine. It is added that they imitated satyrs, were attended by goats, and rode upon asses, all companions of great skill and practice in affairs of gallantry. They bore for their ensigns certain curious figures, perched upon long poles, made into the shape and size of the *virga genitalis*,[1] with its appurtenances; which were so many shadows and emblems of the whole mystery, as well as trophies set up by the female conquerors. Lastly, in a certain town in Attica, the whole solemnity, stripped of all its types, were performed *in puris naturalibus*,[2] the votaries not flying in coveys, but sorted into couples. The same may be further conjectured from the death of Orpheus, one of the institutors of these mysteries, who was torn in pieces by women, because he refused to communicate his orgies to them; which others explained by telling us he had castrated himself upon grief for the loss of his wife.

Omitting many others of less note, the next fanatics we meet with of any eminence were the numerous sects of heretics appearing in the five first centuries of the Christian era, from Simon Magus and his followers to those of Eutyches. I have

---

1. The organ of creation.
2. Quite naked.

collected their systems from infinite reading, and, comparing them with those of their successors in the several ages since, I find there are certain bounds set even to the irregularity of human thought, and those a great deal narrower than is commonly apprehended. For, as they all frequently interfere even in their wildest ravings, so there is one fundamental point wherein they are sure to meet, as lines in a centre, and that is, the community of women. Great were their solicitudes in this matter, and they never failed of certain articles, in their schemes of worship, on purpose to establish it.

The last fanatics of note were those which started up in Germany a little after the reformation of Luther, springing as mushrooms do at the end of a harvest; such were John of Leyden,[1] David George, Adam Neuster, and many others, whose visions and revelations always terminated in leading about half-a-dozen sisters a-piece, and making that practice a fundamental part of their system. For human life is a continual navigation, and if we expect our vessels to pass with safety through the waves and tempests of this flucuating world, it is necessary to make a good provision of the flesh, as seamen lay in store of beef for a long voyage.

Now, from this brief survey of some principle sects among the fanatics in all ages (having omitted the Mahometans and others, who might also help to confirm the argument I am about), to which I might add several among ourselves, such as the family of love, sweet singers of Israel, and the like; and, from reflecting upon that fundamental point in their doctrines about women wherein they have so unanimously agreed, I am apt to imagine that the seed or principle which has ever put men upon visions in things invisible is of a corporeal nature; for the profounder chemists inform us that the strongest spirits may be extracted from human flesh. Besides, the spinal marrow,

---

1. John of Leyden and David George were leaders of German and Dutch Anabaptists respectively. Adam Neuster was a German theologian who denied Christ's divinity.

being nothing else but a continuation of the brain, must needs create a very free communication between the superior faculties and those below; and thus the thorn in the flesh serves for a spur to the spirit. I think it is agreed among physicians that nothing affects the head so much as a tentiginous humour,[1] repelled and elated to the upper region, found, by daily practice, to run frequently up into madness. A very eminent member of the faculty assured me that when the Quakers first appeared he seldom was without some female patients among them for the *furor*—; persons of a visionary devotion, either men or women, are, in their complexion, of all others, the most amorous; for zeal is frequently kindled from the same spark with other fires, and, from inflaming brotherly love, will proceed to raise that of a gallant. If we inspect into the usual process of modern courtship, we shall find it to consist in a devout turn of the eyes, called ogling; an artificial form of canting and whining by rote, every interval, for want of other matter, made up with a shrug or a hum, a sigh, or a groan; the style compact of insignificant words, incoherences, and repetition. These I take to be the most accomplished rules of address to a mistress; and where are these performed with more dexterity than by the saints? Nay, to bring this argument yet closer, I have been informed by certain sanguine brethren of the first class, that in the height and orgasmus of the spiritual exercise, it has been frequent with them . . . ; immediately after which, they found the spirit to relax and flag of a sudden with the nerves, and they were forced to hasten to a conclusion. This may be further strengthened by observation, with wonder, how unaccountably all females are attracted by visionary or enthusiastic preachers, though ever so contemptible in their outward mien; which is usually supposed to be done upon considerations purely spiritual, without any carnal regards at all. But I have reason to think the sex has certain characteristics, by which they form a truer judgment of human abilities and performings

---

1. I.e., lechery.

than we ourselves can possibly do of each other. Let that be as it will, thus much is certain, that, however spiritual intrigues begin, they generally conclude like all others: they may branch upward toward heaven, but the root is in the earth. Too intense a contemplation is not the business of flesh and blood; it must, by the necessary course of things, in a little time let go its hold, and fall into matter. Lovers for the sake of celestial converse are but another sort of Platonics, who pretend to see stars and heaven in ladies' eyes, and to look or think no lower; but the same pit is provided for both; and they seem a perfect moral to the story of that philosopher,[1] who, while his thoughts and eyes were fixed upon the constellations, found himself seduced by his lower parts into a ditch.

I had somewhat more to say upon this part of the subject; but the post is just going, which forces me in great haste to conclude, Sir, yours, etc.

Pray burn this letter as soon as it comes to your hands.

---

1. Thales.

A Tritical Essay

As Swift's introductory note implies, *A Tritical Essay* (1707) is a satire on unimaginative essayists who write on "stale Topicks," make use of clichés and platitudes and treat their subjects in the most superficial way. Swift's technique here is to parody these faults by creating a pastiche of cliché and commonplace ideas. It reflects Swift's intolerance of jargon and banality.

A TRITICAL ESSAY

FACULTIES OF THE MIND.

To ———

SIR,—Being so great a lover of antiquities, it was reasonable to suppose you would be very much obliged with anything that was new. I have been of late offended with many writers of essays and moral discourses for running into stale topics and threadbare quotations, and not handling their subject fully and closely —all which errors I have carefully avoided in the following essay, which I have proposed as a pattern for young writers to imitate. The thoughts and observations being entirely new, the quotations untouched by others, the subject of mighty importance, and treated with much order and perspicuity, it has cost me a great deal of time; and I desire you will accept and consider it as the utmost effort of my genius.

THE ESSAY.

PHILOSOPHERS say that man is a microcosm or little world, resembling in miniature every part of the great; and, in my opinion, the body natural may be compared to the body politic; and if this be so, how can the Epicurean's opinion be true that the universe was formed by a fortuitous concourse of atoms, which I will no more believe than that the accidental jumbling of the letters of the alphabet could fall by chance into a most ingenious and learned treatise of philosophy. *Risum teneatis amici.*[1] This false opinion must needs create many more; it is like an error in the first concoction, which cannot be corrected in the second; the foundation is weak, and whatever superstructure you raise upon it must of necessity fall to the ground. Thus men are led from one error to another, until, with Ixion, they embrace a cloud instead of Juno, or, like the dog in the fable, lose the substance in gaping at the shadow. For such opinions cannot cohere, but, like the iron and clay in the toes of Nebuchadnezzar's image, must separate and break in pieces. I have read in a certain author that Alexander wept because he had no more worlds to conquer, which he needed not have done if the fortuitous concourse of atoms could create one; but this is an opinion fitter for that many-headed beast, the vulgar, to entertain than for so wise a man as Epicurus. The corrupt part of his sect only borrowed his name, as the monkey did the cat's claw to draw the chestnut out of the fire.

However, the first step to the cure is to know the disease, and though Truth may be difficult to find, because, as the philosopher observes, she lives in the bottom of a well, yet we need not, like blind men, grope in open daylight. I hope I may be allowed, among so many far more learned men, to offer my mite, since a stander-by may sometimes perhaps see more of the game than he that plays it. But I do not think a philosopher obliged to account for every phenomenon in Nature, or drown himself with Aristotle for not being able to solve the ebbing and flowing of the tide, in that fatal sentence he passed upon himself—*Quia te non capio, tu capies me*—wherein he was at once the judge and the criminal, the accuser and executioner. Socrates, on the other hand, who said he knew nothing, was pronounced by the oracle to be the wisest man in the world.

But to return from this digression; I think it as clear as any demonstration of Euclid that Nature does nothing in vain. If we were able to dive into her secret recesses, we should find that

[1] Swift solemnly verifies the next of his trite quotations from Horace.

the smallest blade of grass or most contemptible weed has its particular use. But she is chiefly admirable in her minutest compositions; the least and most contemptible insect most discovers the art of Nature, if I may so call it, though Nature, which delights in variety, will always triumph over art, and, as the poet observes—

"Naturam expellas furcâ licet, usque recurret."[1]

Hor. Lib. i. Epist. x. 24.

But the various opinions of philosophers have scattered through the world as many plagues of the mind as Pandora's box did those of the body, only with this difference, that they have not left hope at the bottom. And if truth be not fled with Astrea, she is certainly as hidden as the source of the Nile, and can be found only in Utopia. Not that I would reflect on those wise sages, which would be a sort of ingratitude, and he that calls a man ungrateful sums up all the evil that a man can be guilty of—

"Ingratum si dixeris, omnia dicis."

But what I blame the philosophers for (though some may think it a paradox) is chiefly their pride; nothing less than an *ipse dixit*, and you must pin your faith on their sleeve. And though Diogenes lived in a tub, there might be, for aught I know, as much pride under his rags as in the fine-spun garments of the divine Plato. It is reported of this Diogenes that when Alexander came to see him, and promised to give him whatever he would ask, the cynic only answered, "Take not from me what thou canst not give me, but stand from between me and the light;" which was almost as extravagant as the philosopher that flung his money into the sea with this remarkable saying ———

How different was this man from the usurer, who, being told his son would spend all he had got, replied, "He cannot take more pleasure in spending than I did in getting it." These men could see the faults of each other, but not their own; those they flung into the bag behind, *non videmus id manticæ quod in tergo est.*

---

[1] " For Nature, driven out with proud disdain,
All-powerful goddess, will return again.—*Francis.*

I may perhaps be censured for my free opinions by those carping Momuses whom authors worship, as the Indians do the devil—for fear. They will endeavour to give my reputation as many wounds as the man in the almanac; but I value it not; and perhaps, like flies, they may buzz so often about the candle till they burn their wings. They must pardon me if I venture to give them this advice—not to rail at what they cannot under-stand; it does but discover that self-tormenting passion of envy, than which the greatest tyrant never invented a more cruel tor-ment—

> "Invidiâ Siculi non invenere Tyranni
> Tormentum majus"—*Hor.* Lib. i. Epist. ii. 58.

I must be so bold to tell my critics and witlings that they can no more judge of this than a man that is born blind can have any true idea of colours. I have always observed that your empty vessels sound loudest: I value their lashes as little as the sea did those of Xerxes when he whipped it. The utmost favour a man can expect from them is that which Polyphemus promised Ulysses, that he would devour him the last; they think to subdue a writer, as Cæsar did his enemy, with a *Veni, vidi, vici.* I confess I value the opinion of the judicious few, a Rymer, a Dennis, or a W——k; but for the rest, to give my judgment at once, I think the long dispute among the philosophers about a vacuum may be determined in the affirmative that it is to be found in a critic's head. They are at best but the drones of the learned world, who devour the honey, and will not work themselves; and a writer need no more regard them than the moon does the barking of a little senseless cur. For, in spite of their terrible roaring, you may with half an eye discover the ass under the lion's skin.

But to return to our discourse. Demosthenes being asked what was the first part of an orator, replied, action; what was the second, action; what was the third, action; and so on *ad infini-tum.* This may be true in oratory; but contemplation in other things exceeds action. And therefore a wise man is never less alone than when he is alone: *Nunquam minus solus, quam cum solus.* And Archimedes, the famous mathematician, was so intent upon his problems that he never minded the soldiers who came to kill him. Therefore, not to detract from the just praise which belongs to orators, they ought to consider that Nature, which gave us two eyes to see and two ears to hear, has given us but one tongue to speak; wherein, however, some do so abound, that the virtuosi, who have been so long in search for the perpetual motion, may infallibly find it there.

Some men admire republics because orators flourish there most, and are the greatest enemies of tyranny; but my opinion is that one tyrant is better than a hundred. Besides, these orators inflame the people, whose anger is really but a short fit of madness—

"Ira furor brevis est."—*Hor.* Lib. i. Epist. ii. 62.

After which laws are like cobwebs, which may catch small flies, but let wasps and hornets break through; but in oratory the greatest art is to hide art : *Artis est celare artem.*

But this must be the work of time; we must lay hold on all opportunities and let slip no occasion, else we shall be forced to weave Penelope's web, unravel in the night what we spun in the day. And therefore I have observed that time is painted with a lock before, and bald behind, signifying thereby that we must take time (as we say) by the forelock, for when it is once past there is no recalling it.

The mind of man is at first (if you will pardon the expression) like a *tabula rasa*, or like wax, which, while it is soft, is capable of any impression, till time has hardened it. And at length Death, that grim tyrant, stops us in the midst of our career. The greatest conquerors have at last been conquered by Death, which spares none, from the sceptre to the spade : *Mors omnibus communis.*

All rivers go to the sea, but none return from it. Xerxes wept when he beheld his army, to consider that in less than a hundred years they would be all dead. Anacreon was choked with a grape-stone, and violent joy kills as well as violent grief. There is nothing in this world constant but inconstancy ; yet Plato thought that if virtue would appear to the world in her own native dress, all men would be enamoured with her. But now, since interest governs the world, and men neglect the golden mean, Jupiter himself, if he came to the earth, would be despised unless it were, as he did to Danaë, in a golden shower; for men now-a-days worship the rising sun, and not the setting—

" Donec eris felix multos numerabis amicos." [1]

Thus have I, in obedience to your commands, ventured to expose myself to censure in this critical age. Whether I have done right to my subject must be left to the judgment of my learned reader. However I cannot but hope that my attempting of it may be encouragement for some able pen to perform it with more success.

1. "As long as you are happy, you will have many friends."

A Meditation Upon a Broomstick

A light piece Swift wrote to amuse a friend, Lady Berkeley,
who had become enamored of a book, Robert Boyle's *Occasional
Reflections*, that Swift considered pretentious. Swift's *Meditation*
here was a parody of Boyle.

MEDITATION UPON A BROOMSTICK,

ACCORDING TO THE STYLE AND MANNER OF THE HONOURABLE ROBERT BOYLE.

(1703.)

THIS single stick, which you now behold ingloriously lying in that neglected corner, I once knew in a flourishing state in a forest; it was full of sap, full of leaves, and full of boughs; but now, in vain does the busy art of man pretend to vie with Nature by tying that withered bundle of twigs to its sapless trunk; it is now, at best, but the reverse of what it was, a tree turned upside down, the branches on the earth, and the root in the air; it is now handled by every dirty wench, condemned to do her drudgery, and, by a capricious kind of fate destined to make other things clean and be nasty itself; at length, worn to the stumps in the service of the maids, it is either thrown out of doors or condemned to the last use of kindling a fire. When I beheld this, I sighed, and said within myself: SURELY MAN IS A BROOMSTICK; Nature sent him into the world strong and lusty, in a thriving condition, wearing his own hair on his head, the proper branches of this reasoning vegetable, until the axe of intemperance has lopped off his green boughs and left him a withered trunk; he then flies to art and puts on a periwig, valuing himself upon an unnatural bundle of hairs (all covered with powder), that never grew on his head; but now, should this our broomstick pretend to enter the scene, proud of those birchen spoils it never bore, and all covered with dust, though the sweepings of the finest lady's chamber, we should be apt to ridicule and despise its vanity. Partial judges that we are of our own excellences and other men's defaults.

But a broomstick, perhaps you will say, is an emblem of a tree standing on its head; and pray what is man but a topsy-turvy creature, his animal faculties perpetually mounted on his rational, his head where his heels should be, grovelling on the earth! And yet, with all his faults, he sets up to be a universal reformer and corrector of abuses, a remover of grievances, rakes into every slut's corner of Nature, bringing hidden corruption to the light, and raises a mighty dust where there was none before; sharing deeply all the while in the very same pollutions he pretends to sweep away. His last days are spent in slavery to women, and generally the least deserving; till, worn out to the stumps, like his brother besom, he is either kicked out of doors, or made use of to kindle flames for others to warm themselves by.

Thoughts on Various Subjects

These *Thoughts* were ideals and random impressions that Swift jotted down in a commonplace book that he kept for most of his lifetime. Many are fragmentary. Some are strongly held ideas, others little more than transitory thoughts. Collectively, the *Thoughts* are more a reflection of Swift the moralist than of the humorist. Although his subjects vary, statements about human nature clearly dominate.

THOUGHTS ON VARIOUS SUBJECTS,

MORAL AND DIVERTING.

(OCTOBER, 1706.)

WE have just enough religion to make us hate, but not enough to make us love one another.

Reflect on things past, as wars, negotiations, factions, &c. We enter so little into those interests, that we wonder how men could possibly be so busy and concerned for things so transitory; look on the present times, we find the same humour, yet wonder not at all.

A wise man endeavours, by considering all circumstances, to make conjectures and form conclusions; but the smallest accident intervening (and in the course of affairs it is impossible to foresee all) does often produce such turns and changes, that at last he is just as much in doubt of events as the most ignorant and unexperienced person.

Positiveness is a good quality for preachers and orators, because he that would obtrude his thoughts and reasons upon a multitude will convince others the more as he appears convinced himself.

How is it possible to expect that mankind will take advice when they will not so much as take warning?

I forget whether advice be among the lost things which Ariosto says are to be found in the moon; that and Time ought to have been there.

No preacher is listened to but Time, which gives us the same train and turn of thought that elder people have tried in vain to put into our heads before.

When we desire or solicit anything, our minds run wholly on the good side or circumstances of it; when it is obtained, our minds run wholly on the bad ones.

In a glasshouse, the workmen often fling in a small quantity of fresh coals, which seems to disturb the fire, but very much enlivens it. This seems to allude to a gentle stirring of the passions, that the mind may not languish.

Religion seems to have grown an infant with age, and requires miracles to nurse it, as it had in its infancy.

All fits of pleasure are balanced by an equal degree of pain or languor; it is like spending this year part of the next year's revenue.

The latter part of a wise man's life is taken up in curing the follies, prejudices, and false opinions he had contracted in the former.

Would a writer know how to behave himself with relation to posterity, let him consider in old books what he finds that he is glad to know, and what omissions he most laments.

Whatever the poets pretend, it is plain they give immortality to none but themselves; it is Homer and Virgil we reverence and admire, not Achilles or Æneas. With historians it is quite the contrary; our thoughts are taken up with the actions, persons, and events we read, and we little regard the authors.

When a true genius appears in the world, you may know him by this sign, that the dunces are all in confederacy against him.

Men who possess all the advantages of life are in a state where there are many accidents to disorder and discompose, but few to please them.

It is unwise to punish cowards with ignominy; for if they had regarded that, they would not have been cowards: death is their proper punishment, because they fear it most.

The greatest inventions were produced in the times of ignorance; as the use of the compass, gunpowder, and printing; and by the dullest nation, as the Germans.

One argument to prove that the common relations of ghosts and spectres are generally false may be drawn from the opinion held, that spirits are never seen by more than one person at a time; that is to say, it seldom happens to above one person in a company to be possessed with any high degree of spleen or melancholy.

I am apt to think that, in the day of judgment, there will be small allowance given to the wise for their want of morals, and to the ignorant for their want of faith, because both are without excuse. This renders the advantages equal of ignorance and knowledge. But some scruples in the wise and some vices in the ignorant will perhaps be forgiven upon the strength of temptation to each.

The value of several circumstances in story lessens very much by distance of time, though some minute circumstances are very valuable, and it requires great judgment in a writer to distinguish.

It is grown a word of course for writers to say, "This critical age," as divines say, "This sinful age."

It is pleasant to observe how free the present age is in laying taxes on the next: future ages shall talk of this; this shall be famous to all posterity: whereas their time and thoughts will be taken up about present things, as ours are now.

The chameleon, who is said to feed upon nothing but air, has of all animals the nimblest tongue.

When a man is made a spiritual peer, he loses his surname; when a temporal, his Christian name.

It is in disputes as in armies, where the weaker side sets up false lights and makes a great noise, to make the enemy believe them more numerous and strong than they really are.

Some men, under the notion of weeding out prejudices, eradicate virtue, honesty, and religion.

In all well-instituted commonwealths, care has been taken to limit men's possessions; which is done for many reasons, and among the rest, for one which perhaps is not often considered: that when bounds are set to men's desires, after they have acquired as much as the laws will permit them, their private interest is at an end, and they have nothing to do but to take care of the public.

There are but three ways for a man to revenge himself of the censure of the world; to despise it, to return the like, or to endeavour to live so as to avoid it: the first of these is usually pretended, the last is almost impossible, the universal practice is for the second.

Herodotus tells us that in cold countries beasts very seldom have horns, but in hot they have very large ones. This might bear a pleasant application.

I never heard a finer piece of satire against lawyers than that of astrologers, when they pretend, by rules of art, to tell when a suit will end, and whether to the advantage of the plaintiff or defendant, thus making the matter depend entirely upon the influence of the stars, without the least regard to the merits of the cause.

The expression in Apocrypha about Tobit and his dog following him I have often heard ridiculed; yet Homer has the same words of Telemachus more than once, and Virgil says something like it of Evander; and I take the Book of Tobit to be partly poetical.

I have known some men possessed of good qualities, which were very serviceable to others but useless to themselves; like a sundial on the front of a house, to inform the neighbours and passengers, but not the owner within.

If a man would register all his opinions upon love, politics, religion, learning, &c., beginning from his youth, and so go on to old age, what a bundle of inconsistencies and contradictions would appear at last!

What they do in heaven we are ignorant of; what they do not we are told expressly, that they neither marry nor are given in marriage.

When a man observes the choice of ladies now-a-days in the dispensing of their favours, can he forbear paying some veneration to the memory of those mares mentioned by Xenophon, who, while their manes were on, that is, while they were in their beauty, would never admit the embraces of an ass?

It is a miserable thing to live in suspense; it is the life of a spider.

> " Vive quidem, pende tamen, improba, dixit."
> —*Ovid. Metam.*

The stoical scheme of supplying our wants by lopping off our desires is like cutting off our feet when we want shoes.

Physicians ought not to give their judgment of religion, for the same reason that butchers are not admitted to be jurors upon life and death.

The reason why so few marriages are happy is because young ladies spend their time in making nets, not in making cages.

If a man will observe as he walks the streets, I believe he will find the merriest countenances in mourning-coaches.

Nothing more unqualifies a man to act with prudence than a misfortune that is attended with shame and guilt.

The power of fortune is confessed only by the miserable; for the happy impute all their success to prudence and merit.

Ambition often puts men upon doing the meanest offices; so climbing is performed in the same posture with creeping.

Ill company is like a dog, who dirts those most whom he loves best.

Censure is the tax a man pays to the public for being eminent.

Although men are accused for not knowing their own weakness, yet perhaps as few know their own strength. It is in men as in soils, where sometimes there is a vein of gold which the owner knows not of.

Satire is reckoned the easiest of all wit; but I take it to be otherwise in very bad times : for it is as hard to satirise well a man of distinguished vices as to praise well a man of distinguished virtues. It is easy enough to do either to people of moderate characters.

Invention is the talent of youth, and judgment of age, so that our judgment grows harder to please when we have fewer things to offer it : this goes through the whole commerce of life. When we are old, our friends find it difficult to please us, and are less concerned whether we be pleased or not.

No wise man ever wished to be younger.

An idle reason lessens the weight of the good ones you gave before.

The motives of the best actions will not bear too strict an inquiry. It is allowed that the cause of most actions, good or bad, may be resolved into the love of ourselves; but the self-love of some men inclines them to please others, and the self-love of others is wholly employed in pleasing themselves. This makes the great distinction between virtue and vice. Religion is the best motive of all actions, yet religion is allowed to be the highest instance of self-love.

When the world has once begun to use us ill, it afterward continues the same treatment with less scruple or ceremony.

Old men view best at a distance with the eyes of their understanding, as well as with those of Nature.

Some people take more care to hide their wisdom than their folly.

Arbitrary power is the natural object of temptation to a prince, as wine or women to a young fellow, or a bribe to a judge, or avarice to old age, or vanity to a woman.

Anthony Henley's farmer dying of an asthma, said, "Well, if I can get this breath once out, I'll take care it shall never get in again."

The humour of exploding many things under the name of trifles, fopperies, and only imaginary goods, is a very false proof either of wisdom or magnanimity, and a great check to virtuous actions. For instance, with regard to fame, there is in most people a reluctance and unwillingness to be forgotten. We observe even among the vulgar how fond they are to have an inscription over their grave. It requires but little philosophy to discover and observe that there is no intrinsic value in all this; however, if it be founded in our nature as an incitement to virtue, it ought not to be ridiculed.

Complaint is the largest tribute Heaven receives, and the sincerest part of our devotion.

The common fluency of speech in many men and most women

is owing to a scarcity of matter and a scarcity of words; for whoever is a master of language, and has a mind full of ideas, will be apt in speaking to hesitate upon the choice of both; whereas common speakers have only one set of ideas, and one set of words to clothe them in, and these are always ready at the mouth; so people come faster out of a church when it is almost empty than when a crowd is at the door.

Few are qualified to shine in company, but it is in most men's power to be agreeable. The reason, therefore, why conversation runs so low at present is not the defect of understanding, but pride, vanity, ill-nature, affectation, singularity, positiveness, or some other vice, the effect of a wrong education.

To be vain is rather a mark of humility than pride. Vain men delight in telling what honours have been done them, what great company they have kept, and the like, by which they plainly confess that these honours were more than their due, and such as their friends would not believe if they had not been told; whereas a man truly proud thinks the greatest honours below his merit, and consequently scorns to boast. I therefore deliver it as a maxim, that whoever desires the character of a proud man ought to conceal his vanity.

Law in a free country is, or ought to be, the determination of the majority of those who have property in land.

One argument used to the disadvantage of Providence I take to be a very strong one in its defence. It is objected that storms and tempests, unfruitful seasons, serpents, spiders, flies, and other noxious or troublesome animals, with many more instances of the like kind, discover an imperfection in Nature, because human life would be much easier without them, but the design of Providence may clearly be perceived in this proceeding. The motions of the sun and moon, in short, the whole system of the universe, as far as philosophers have been able to discover and observe, are in the utmost degree of regularity and perfection; but wherever God has left to man the power of interposing a remedy by thought or labour, there he has placed things in a state of imperfection on purpose to stir up human industry, without which life would stagnate, or indeed rather could not subsist at all. *Curis acuunt mortalia corda.*

Praise is the daughter of present power.

How inconsistent is man with himself.

I have known several persons of great fame for wisdom in public affairs and councils governed by foolish servants.

I have known great ministers, distinguished for wit and learning, who preferred none but dunces.

I have known men of great valour cowards to their wives.

I have known men of the greatest cunning perpetually cheated.

I knew three great ministers who could exactly compute and settle the accounts of a kingdom, but were wholly ignorant of their own economy.

The preaching of divines helps to preserve well-inclined men in the course of virtue, but seldom or never reclaims the vicious.

Princes usually make wiser choices than the servants whom they trust for the disposal of places. I have known a prince more than once choose an able minister, but I never observed that minister to use his credit in the disposal of an employment to a person whom he thought the fittest for it. One of the greatest in this age owned and excused the matter from the violence of parties and the unreasonableness of friends.

Small causes are sufficient to make a man uneasy when great ones are not in the way ; for want of a block he will stumble at a straw.

Dignity, high station, or great riches are in some sort necessary to old men in order to keep the younger at a distance, who are otherwise too apt to insult them upon the score of their age.

Every man desires to live long, but no man would be old.

Love of flattery in most men proceeds from the mean opinion they have of themselves; in women, from the contrary.

If books and laws continue to increase as they have done for fifty years past, I am in some concern for future ages how any man will be learned or any man a lawyer.

Kings are commonly said to have long hands; I wish they had as long ears.

Princes in their infancy, childhood, and youth are said to discover prodigious parts and wit, to speak things that surprise and astonish; strange so many hopeful princes and so many shameful kings. If they happen to die young, they would have been prodigies of wisdom and virtue; if they live, they are often prodigies indeed, but of another sort.

Politics, as the word is commonly understood, are nothing but corruptions, and consequently of no use to a good king or a good ministry, for which reason all courts are so full of politics.

Silenus, the foster-father of Bacchus, is always carried by an ass, and has horns on his head. The moral is, that drunkards are led by fools, and have a great chance to be cuckolds.

Venus, a beautiful good-natured lady, was the goddess of love; Juno, a terrible shrew, the goddess of marriage, and they were always mortal enemies.

Those who are against religion must needs be fools; and therefore we read that, of all animals, God refused the first-born of an ass.

A very little wit is valued in a woman, as we are pleased with a few words spoken plain by a parrot.

A nice man is a man of nasty ideas.

Apollo was held the god of physic and sender of diseases. Both were originally the same trade, and still continue.

Old men and comets have been reverenced for the same reason, their long beards and pretences to foretell events.

A person was asked at court what he thought of an ambassador and his train, who were all embroidery and lace, full of bows, cringes, and gestures. He said, "It was Solomon's importation, gold and apes."

There is a story in Pausanias of a plot for betraying a city discovered by the braying of an ass; the cackling of geese saved the Capitol, and Catiline's conspiracy was discovered by a whore. These are the only three animals, as far as I remember, famous in history as evidences and informers.

Most sorts of diversion in men, children, and other animals are in imitation of fighting.

Augustus meeting an ass with a lucky name, foretold himself good fortune. I meet many asses, but none of them have lucky names.

If a man makes me keep my distance, the comfort is he keeps his at the same time.

Who can deny that all men are violent lovers of truth when we see them so positive in their errors, which they will maintain out of their zeal to truth, although they contradict themselves every day of their lives.

That was excellently observed, say I, when I read a passage in an author where his opinion agrees with mine. When we differ, there I pronounce him to be mistaken.

As universal a practice as lying is, and as easy a one as it seems, I do not remember to have heard three good lies in all my conversation, even from those who were most celebrated in that faculty.

Very few men, properly speaking, live at present, but are providing to live another time.

An Argument Against Abolishing
Christianity in England

ARGUMENT

TO PROVE THAT THE ABOLISHING OF

CHRISTIANITY IN ENGLAND

MAY, AS THINGS NOW STAND, BE ATTENDED WITH
SOME INCONVENIENCES, AND PERHAPS NOT PRO-
DUCE THOSE MANY GOOD EFFECTS
PROPOSED THEREBY.

(WRITTEN IN 1708.)

I AM very sensible what a weakness and presumption it is to
reason against the general humour and disposition of the
world. I remember it was, with great justice and a due regard
to the freedom both of the public and the press, forbidden, upon
several penalties, to write or discourse or lay wagers against the
union, even before it was confirmed by Parliament, because that
was looked upon as a design to oppose the current of the people,
which, beside the folly of it, is a manifest breach of the fundamental law that makes this majority of opinion the voice of God.
In like manner, and for the very same reason, it may perhaps be
neither safe nor prudent to argue against the abolishing of Christianity at a juncture when all parties appear so unanimously
determined upon the point, as we cannot but allow from their
actions, their discourses, and their writings. However, I know
not how, whether from the affectation of singularity or the per-
verseness of human nature, but so it unhappily falls out that I

cannot be entirely of this opinion. Nay, though I were sure an order were issued for my immediate prosecution by the attorney-general, I should still confess that in the present posture of our affairs at home or abroad I do not yet see the absolute necessity of extirpating the Christian religion from among us.

This perhaps may appear too great a paradox, even for our wise and paradoxical age to endure ; therefore I shall handle it with all tenderness, and with the utmost deference to that great and profound majority, which is of another sentiment.

And yet the curious may please to observe how much the genius of a nation is liable to alter in half an age : I have heard it affirmed for certain by some very old people that the contrary opinion was, even in their memories, as much in vogue as the other is now, and that a project for the abolishing of Christianity would then have appeared as singular and been thought as absurd as it would be at this time to write or discourse in its defence.

Therefore I freely own that all appearances are against me. The system of the gospel, after the fate of other systems, is generally antiquated and exploded, and the mass or body of the common people, among whom it seems to have had its latest credit, are now grown as much ashamed of it as their betters ; opinions, like fashions, always descending from those of quality to the middle sort, and thence to the vulgar, where at length they are dropped and vanish.

But here I would not be mistaken, and must therefore be so bold as to borrow a distinction from the writers on the other side, when they make a difference between nominal and real Trinitarians. I hope no reader imagines me so weak to stand up in the defence of real Christianity, such as used, in primitive times (if we may believe the authors of those ages), to have an influence upon men's belief and actions ; to offer at the restoring of that would indeed be a wild project ; it would be to dig up foundations—to destroy at one blow all the wit and half the learning of the kingdom, to break the entire frame and constitution of things, to ruin trade, extinguish arts and sciences with the professors of them ; in short, to turn our courts, exchanges, and shops into deserts, and would be full as absurd as the proposal of Horace where he advises the Romans all in a body to leave their city, and seek a new seat in some remote part of the world, by way of cure for the corruption of their manners.

Therefore I think this caution was in itself altogether unnecessary (which I have inserted only to prevent all possibility of cavilling), since every candid reader will easily understand my discourse to be intended only in defence of nominal Christianity, the other having been for some time wholly laid aside by general consent as utterly inconsistent with our present schemes of wealth and power.

But why we should therefore cast off the name and title of Christians, although the general opinion and resolution be so violent for it, I confess I cannot (with submission) apprehend, nor is the consequence necessary. However, since the undertakers propose such wonderful advantages to the nation by this project, and advance many plausible objections against the system of Christianity, I shall briefly consider the strength of both, fairly allow them their greatest weight, and offer such answers as I think most reasonable; after which I will beg leave to show what inconveniences may possibly happen by such an innovation in the present posture of our affairs.

First, one great advantage proposed by the abolishing of Christianity is, that it would very much enlarge and establish liberty of conscience, that great bulwark of our nation, and of the Protestant religion, which is still too much limited by priestcraft, notwithstanding all the good intentions of the Legislature, as we have lately found by a severe instance. For it is confidently reported that two young gentlemen of real hopes, bright wit, and profound judgment, who, upon a thorough examination of causes and effects, and by the mere force of natural abilities, without the least tincture of learning, having made a discovery that there was no God, and generously communicating their thoughts for the good of the public, were some time ago by an unparalleled severity, and upon I know not what obsolete law, broke for blasphemy. And, as it has been wisely observed, if persecution once begins, no man alive knows how far it may reach, or where it will end.

In answer to all which, with deference to wiser judgments, I think this rather shows the necessity of a nominal religion among us. Great wits love to be free with the highest objects, and if they cannot be allowed a God to revile or renounce, they will speak evil of dignities, abuse the Government, and reflect upon the Ministry, which I am sure few will deny to be of much more pernicious consequence, according to the saying of Tiberius, *Deorum offensa diis curæ.* As to the particular fact related, I think it is not fair to argue from one instance; perhaps another cannot be produced; yet (to the comfort of all those who may be apprehensive of persecution) blasphemy we know is freely spoken a million of times in every coffee-house and tavern, or wherever else good company meet. It must be allowed, indeed, that to break an English free-born officer only for blasphemy was, to speak the gentlest of such an action, a very high strain of absolute power. Little can be said in excuse for the general; perhaps he was afraid it might give offence to the allies, among whom, for aught we know, it may be the custom of the country to believe a God. But if he argued, as some have done, upon a mistaken principle, that an officer, who is guilty of speaking blasphemy, may some time or other proceed so far as to raise a mutiny, the consequence is by no means to be admitted, for surely the commander of an English army is likely to be but ill obeyed whose soldiers fear and reverence him as little as they do a deity.

It is further objected against the gospel system that it obliges men to the belief of things too difficult for freethinkers, and such who have shaken off the prejudices that usually cling to a confined education. To which I answer that men should be cautious how they raise objections which reflect upon the wisdom of the nation. Is not everybody freely allowed to believe whatever he pleases, and to publish his belief to the world whenever he thinks fit, especially if it serves to strengthen the party which is in the right? Would any indifferent foreigner

who should read the trumpery lately written by Asgyll,[1] Tindal,
Toland, Coward,[2] and forty more imagine the gospel to be our
rule of faith, and confirmed by Parliaments? Does any man
either believe, or say he believes, or desire to have it thought
that he says he believes, one syllable of the matter? And is any
man worse received upon that score, or does he find his want of
nominal faith a disadvantage to him in the pursuit of any civil or
military employment? What if there be an old dormant statute
or two against him? Are they not now obsolete to a degree, that
Epsom and Dudley themselves, if they were now alive, would
find it impossible to put them in execution?

It is likewise urged that there are, by computation, in this
kingdom above ten thousand parsons, whose revenues, added to
those of my lords the bishops, would suffice to maintain at least
two hundred young gentlemen of wit and pleasure and freethinking, enemies to priestcraft, narrow principles, pedantry, and prejudices, who might be an ornament to the court and town ; and
then, again, so great a number of able-bodied divines might be a
recruit to our fleet and armies. This indeed appears to be a
consideration of some weight ; but then, on the other side, several
things deserve to be considered likewise, as first, whether it may
not be thought necessary that, in certain tracts of country, like
what we call parishes, there shall be one man at least of abilities
to read and write. Then it seems a wrong computation that the
revenues of the Church throughout this island would be large
enough to maintain two hundred young gentlemen, or even half

[1] John Asgyll, an ingenious writer and eminent lawyer, died November 10, 1738,
aged upwards of fourscore. In 1698 he wrote a treatise entitled, "An Argument
proving that, according to the Covenant of Eternal Life revealed in the Scriptures,
Man may be translated from hence into that Eternal Life without passing through
Death, although the Human Nature of Christ could not thus be translated till He
had passed through Death." This publication was the alleged cause of his being
expelled the House of Commons in 1707, though it is more probable that the des-
perate state of his affairs was the real motive. After his expulsion he became more
embarrassed in his circumstances, and spent the last thirty years of his life in prison.
During this time he published a multitude of small tracts, most of which were well
received.—*John Nichols.*

[2] Coward asserted the mortality of the soul, and alleged the seat of it to be in the
blood.—*Hawkesworth.*

that number, after the present refined way of living; that is, to allow each of them such a rent as, in the modern form of speech, would make them easy. But still there is in this project a greater mischief behind; and we ought to beware of the woman's folly who killed the hen that every morning laid her a golden egg. For pray, what would become of the race of men in the next age if we had nothing to trust to beside the scrofulous, consumptive productions furnished by our men of wit and pleasure, when, having squandered away their vigour, health, and estates, they are forced, by some disagreeable marriage, to piece up their broken fortunes, and entail rottenness and politeness on their posterity? Now here are ten thousand persons reduced, by the wise regulations of Henry the Eighth, to the necessity of a low diet and moderate exercise, who are the only great restorers of our breed, without which the nation would, in an age or two, become one great hospital.

Another advantage proposed by the abolishing of Christianity is the clear gain of one day in seven, which is now entirely lost, and consequently the kingdom one-seventh less considerable in trade, business, and pleasure; beside the loss to the public of so many stately structures now in the hands of the clergy, which might be converted into play-houses, market-houses, exchanges, common dormitories, and other public edifices.

I hope I shall be forgiven a hard word if I call this a perfect *cavil*. I readily own there has been an old custom, time out of mind, for people to assemble in the churches every Sunday, and that shops are still frequently shut, in order, as it is conceived, to preserve the memory of that ancient practice; but how this can prove a hindrance to business or pleasure is hard to imagine. What if the men of pleasure are forced, one day in the week, to game at home instead of the chocolate-houses? Are not the taverns and coffee-houses open? Can there be a more convenient season for taking a dose of physic? Are fewer claps got upon Sundays than other days? Is not that the chief day for traders to sum up the accounts of the week, and for lawyers to prepare their briefs? But I would fain know how it can be pretended that the churches are misapplied. Where are more appointments and rendezvouses of gallantry? Where more care to appear in the foremost box with greater advantage of dress? Where more meetings for business? Where more bargains driven of all sorts? And where so many conveniences or incitements to sleep?

There is one advantage greater than any of the foregoing proposed by the abolishing of Christianity, that it will utterly extinguish parties among us by removing those factious distinctions of High and Low Church, of Whig and Tory, Presbyterian and Church of England, which are now so many grievous clogs upon public proceedings, and are apt to dispose men to prefer the gratifying of themselves or depressing of their adversaries before the most important interest of the state.

I confess, if it were certain that so great an advantage would redound to the nation by this expedient, I would submit and be silent; but will any man say that if the words *drinking, cheating, lying, stealing*, were by Act of Parliament ejected out of the English tongue and dictionaries, we should all awake next morning temperate, honest and just, and lovers of truth? Is this a fair consequence? Or if the physicians should forbid us to pronounce the words *gout, rheumatism*, and *stone*, would that expedient serve, like so many talismans, to destroy the diseases themselves? Are *party* and *faction* rooted in men's hearts no deeper than phrases borrowed from religion or founded upon no firmer principles, and is our language so poor that we cannot find other terms to express them? Are *envy, pride, avarice*, and *ambition* such ill nomenclators, that they cannot furnish appellations for their owners? Will not *heydukes* and *mamelukes, mandarins* and *patshaws*, or any other words formed at pleasure, serve to distinguish those who are in the ministry from others who would be in it if they could? What, for instance, is easier than to vary the form of speech, and instead of the word *church*, make it a question in politics whether the Monument be in danger? Because religion was nearest at hand to furnish a few convenient phrases, is our invention so barren we can find no other? Suppose for argument-sake that the Tories favoured Margarita,[1] the Whigs Mrs. Tofts, and the Trimmers Valentini; would not Margaritians, Toftians, and Valentinians be very tolerable marks of distinction? The Prasini and Veniti, two most virulent factions in Italy, began (if I remember right) by a distinction of colours in ribands, and we might contend with as good a grace about the dignity of the *blue* and the *green*, which would serve as properly to divide the court, the Parliament, and the kingdom between them as any terms of art whatsoever borrowed from religion. And therefore I think there is little force in this objection against Christianity, or prospect of so great an advantage as is proposed in the abolishing of it.

It is again objected as a very absurd, ridiculous custom, that a set of men should be suffered, much less employed and hired, to bawl one day in seven against the lawfulness of those methods most in use toward the pursuit of greatness, riches, and pleasure, which are the constant practice of all men alive on the other six. But this objection is, I think, a little unworthy of so refined an age as ours. Let us argue this matter calmly. I appeal to the breast of any polite freethinker whether, in the pursuit of gratifying a predominant passion, he has not always felt a wonderful incitement by reflecting it was a thing forbidden, and therefore we see, in order to cultivate this taste, the wisdom of the nation has taken special care that the ladies should be furnished with prohibited silks and the men with prohibited wine. And indeed it were to be wished that some other prohibitions were promoted in order to improve the pleasures of the town, which, for want of such expedients, begin already, as I am told, to flag and grow languid, giving way daily to cruel inroads from the spleen.

It is likewise proposed, as a great advantage to the public, that if we once discard the system of the gospel, all religion will of course be banished for ever, and consequently, along with it, those grievous prejudices of education which, under the names of *virtue, conscience, honour, justice,* and the like, are so apt to dis-

---

[1] Italian singers then in vogue. Margarita was afterwards married to Dr. Pepusch.—*Hawkesworth.*

turb the peace of human minds, and the notions whereof are so hard to be eradicated by right reason or freethinking sometimes during the whole course of our lives.

Here I first observe how difficult it is to get rid of a phrase which the world is once grown fond of, though the occasion that first produced it be entirely taken away. For several years past, if a man had but an ill-favoured nose, the deep thinkers of the age would, some way or other, contrive to impute the cause to the prejudice of his education. From this fountain were said to be derived all our foolish notions of justice, piety, love of our country, all our opinions of God or a future state, heaven, hell, and the like, and there might formerly perhaps have been some pretence for this charge. But so effectual care has been since taken to remove those prejudices by an entire change in the methods of education, that (with honour I mention it to our polite innovators) the young gentlemen who are now on the scene seem to have not the least tincture of those infusions or string of those weeds, and, by consequence, the reason for abolishing nominal Christianity upon that pretext is wholly ceased.

For the rest, it may perhaps admit a controversy whether the banishing of all notions of religion whatsoever would be convenient for the vulgar. Not that I am in the least of opinion with those who hold religion to have been the invention of politicians to keep the lower part of the world in awe by the fear of invisible powers, unless mankind were then very different to what it is now, for I look upon the mass or body of our people here in England to be as freethinkers, that is to say, as staunch unbelievers, as about any of the highest rank. But I conceive some scattered notions of a superior power to be of singular use for the common people, as furnishing excellent materials to keep children quiet when they grow peevish, and providing topics of amusement on a tedious winter night.

Lastly, it is proposed, as a singular advantage, that the abolishing of Christianity will very much contribute to the uniting of Protestants by enlarging the terms of communion, so as to take in all sorts of Dissenters who are now shut out of the pale upon account of a few ceremonies which all sides confess to be things indifferent; that this alone will effectually answer the great ends of a scheme for comprehension by opening a large noble gate at which all bodies may enter, whereas the chaffering with Dissenters, and dodging about this or the other ceremony, is but like opening a few wickets and leaving them ajar, by which no more than one can get in at a time, and that not without stooping and sidling and squeezing his body.

To all this I answer that there is one darling inclination of mankind which usually affects to be a retainer to religion, though she be neither its parent, its godmother, or its friend; I mean the spirit of opposition, that lived long before Christianity, and can easily subsist without it. Let us, for instance, examine wherein the opposition of sectaries among us consists; we shall find Christianity to have no share in it at all. Does the gospel anywhere prescribe a starched, squeezed countenance, a stiff, formal gait, a singularity of manners and habit, or any affected modes of speech different from the reasonable part of mankind? Yet if Christianity did not lend its name to stand in the gap and to employ or divert these humours, they must of necessity be spent in contraventions to the laws of the land and disturbance of the public peace. There is a portion of enthusiasm assigned to every nation, which, if it has not proper objects to work on, will burst out and set all in a flame. If the quiet of a state can be bought by only flinging men a few ceremonies to devour, it is a purchase no wise man would refuse. Let the mastiffs amuse themselves about a sheep's skin stuffed with hay, provided it will keep them from worrying the flock. The institution of convents abroad seems, in one point, a strain of great wisdom, there being few irregularities in human passions that may not have recourse to vent themselves in some of those orders, which are so many retreats for the speculative, the melancholy, the proud, the silent, the politic, and the morose, to spend themselves and evaporate the noxious particles, for each of whom we, in this island, are forced to provide a several sect of religion to keep them quiet;

and whenever Christianity shall be abolished, the Legislature must find some other expedient to employ and entertain them. For what imports it how large a gate you open, if there will be always left a number who place a pride and a merit in refusing to enter?

Having thus considered the most important objections against Christianity, and the chief advantages proposed by the abolishing thereof, I shall now, with equal deference and submission to wiser judgments as before, proceed to mention a few inconveniences that may happen if the gospel should be repealed, which perhaps the projectors may not have sufficiently considered.

And first I am very sensible how much the gentlemen of wit and pleasure are apt to murmur and be shocked at the sight of so many draggle-tail parsons who happen to fall in their way and offend their eyes; but at the same time these wise reformers do not consider what an advantage and felicity it is for great wits to be always provided with objects of scorn and contempt in order to exercise and improve their talents, and divert their spleen from falling on each other or on themselves, especially when all this may be done without the least imaginable danger to their persons.

And to urge another argument of a parallel nature; if Christianity were once abolished, how could the freethinkers, the strong reasoners, and the men of profound learning be able to find another subject so calculated in all points whereon to display their abilities? What wonderful productions of wit should we be deprived of from those whose genius by continual practice has been wholly turned upon raillery and invectives against religion, and would therefore never be able to shine or distinguish themselves upon any other subject! We are daily complaining of the great decline of wit among us, and would we take away the greatest, perhaps the only, topic we have left? Who would ever have suspected Asgyll for a wit or Toland for a philosopher, if the inexhaustible stock of Christianity had not been at hand to provide them with materials? What other subject through all art or nature could have produced Tindal for a profound author or furnished him with readers? It is the wise choice of the subject that alone adorns and distinguishes the writer.[1]   For had a hundred such pens as these been employed on the side of religion, they would have immediately sunk into silence and oblivion.

Nor do I think it wholly groundless, or my fears altogether imaginary, that the abolishing Christianity may perhaps bring the Church into danger, or at least put the Senate to the trouble of another securing vote.   I desire I may not be mistaken.   I am far from presuming to affirm or think that the Church is in danger at present, or as things now stand, but we know not how soon it may be so, when the Christian religion is repealed.   As plausible as this project seems, there may be a dangerous design lurking under it.   Nothing can be more notorious than that the Atheists, Deists, Socinians, Antitrinitarians, and other subdivisions of freethinkers, are persons of little zeal for the present ecclesiastical establishment; their declared opinion is for repealing the sacramental test; they are very indifferent with regard to ceremonies, nor do they hold the *jus divinum* of episcopacy; therefore this may be intended as one politic step towards altering the constitution of the Church established, and setting up Presbytery in the stead, which I leave to be further considered by those at the helm.

In the last place, I think nothing can be more plain than that, by this expedient, we shall run into the evil we chiefly pretend to avoid, and that the abolishment of the Christian religion will be the readiest course we can take to introduce Popery.   And I am the more inclined to this opinion, because we know it has been the constant practice of the Jesuits to send over emissaries, with instructions to personate themselves members of the several prevailing sects among us.   So it is recorded that they have at sundry times appeared in the disguise of Presbyterians, Anabaptists, Independents, and Quakers, according as any of these were most in credit; so, since the fashion has been taken up of exploding religion, the Popish missionaries have not been wanting to

---

[1] "This passage," says Dr. Johnson, "deserves to be selected," and he has accordingly given it at full length in his Life of Swift, adding, "the reasonableness of a test is not hard to be proved, but perhaps it must be allowed that the proper test has not been chosen,"—*Nichols.*

mix with the freethinkers, among whom Toland, the great oracle of the Antichristians, is an Irish priest, the son of an Irish priest. And the most learned and ingenious author of a book called "The Rights of the Christian Church" was in a proper juncture reconciled to the Romish faith, whose true son, as appears by a hundred passages in his treatise, he still continues. Perhaps I could add some others to the number; but the fact is beyond dispute, and the reasoning they proceed by is right; for supposing Christianity to be extinguished, the people will never be at ease till they find out some other method of worship, which will as infallibly produce superstition as superstition will end in Popery.

And therefore if, notwithstanding all I have said, it still be thought necessary to have a bill brought in for repealing Christianity, I would humbly offer an amendment that, instead of the word *Christianity*, may be put *religion in general*, which, I conceive, will much better answer all the good ends proposed by the projectors of it. For as long as we leave in being a God and His providence, with all the necessary consequences which curious and inquisitive men will be apt to draw from such premises, we do not strike at the root of the evil, though we should ever so effectually annihilate the present scheme of the gospel; for of what use is freedom of thought if it will not produce freedom of action? which is the sole end, how remote soever in appearance, of all objections against Christianity; and therefore the freethinkers consider it as a sort of edifice, wherein all the parts have such a mutual dependence on each other, that if you happen to pull out one single nail, the whole fabric must fall to the ground. This was happily expressed by him who had heard of a text brought for proof of the Trinity, which in an ancient manuscript was differently read. He thereupon immediately took the hint, and, by a sudden deduction of a long *sorites*, most logically concluded, "Why, if it be as you say, I may safely whore and drink on, and defy the parson." From which, and many the like instances easy to be produced, I think nothing can be more manifest than that the quarrel is not against any particular points of hard digestion in the Christian system, but against religion in general, which, by laying restraints on human nature, is supposed the great enemy to the freedom of thought and action.

Upon the whole, if it shall still be thought for the benefit of Church and State that Christianity be abolished, I conceive, however, it may be more convenient to defer the execution to a time of peace, and not venture, in this conjuncture, to disoblige our allies, who, as it falls out, are all Christians, and many of them, by the prejudices of their education, so bigoted as to place a sort of pride in the appellation.   If, upon being rejected by them, we are to trust to an alliance with the Turk, we shall find ourselves much deceived, for, as he is too remote, and generally engaged in war with the Persian emperor, so his people would be more scandalised at our infidelity than our Christian neighbours.   For the Turks are not only strict observers of religious worship, but, what is worse, believe a God, which is more than is required of us, even while we preserve the name of Christians.

To conclude, whatever some may think of the great advantages to trade by this favourite scheme, I do very much apprehend that in six months time after the Act is passed for the extirpation of the gospel, the Bank and East India stock may fall at least one per cent.   And since that is fifty times more than ever the wisdom of our age thought fit to venture for the preservation of Christianity, there is no reason we should be at so great a loss merely for the sake of destroying it.

On Political Lying

ON POLITICAL LYING

The Examiner, No. 14

November 9, 1710.

E quibus hi vacuas implent sermonibus aures,
Hi narrata ferunt alio: mensuraque ficti
Crescit, et auditis aliquid novus adjicit auctor.
Illic Credulitas, illic temerarius Error,
Vanaque Laetitia est, consternatique Timores,
Seditioque recens, dubioque auctore Susurri.

With idle tales this fills our empty ears;
The next reports what from the first he hears.
The rolling fictions grow in strength and size,
Each author adding to the former lies.
Here vain credulity, with new desires,
Leads us astray, and groundless joy inspires;
The dubious whispers, tumults fresh design'd,
And chilling fears astound the anxious mind.

Ovid, *Metamorphoses* 12.56–61

I AM prevailed on, through the importunity of friends, to interrupt the scheme I had begun in my last paper, by an "Essay upon the Art of Political Lying." We are told the devil is the father of lies, and was a liar from the beginning; so that, beyond contradiction, the invention is old; and, which is more, his first Essay of it was purely political, employed in undermining the authority of his prince, and seducing a third part of the subjects from their obedience: for which he was driven down from heaven, where (as Milton expresses it) he had been viceroy of a great western province;[1] and forced to exercise his talent in inferior regions among other fallen spirits, poor or deluded men, whom he still daily tempts to his own sin, and will ever do so, till he be chained in the bottomless pit.

But although the devil be the father of lies, he seems, like the great inventors, to have lost much of his reputation by the continual improvements that have been made upon him.

Who first reduced lying into an art, and adapted it to politics, is not so clear from history, although I have made some diligent inquiries. I shall, therefore, consider it only according to the modern system, as it has been cultivated these twenty years past in the southern part of our own island.

The poets tell us that, after the giants were overthrown by the gods, the Earth in revenge produced her last offspring, which was Fame. And the fable is thus interpreted: that when tumults and seditions are quieted, rumours and false reports are plentifully spread through a nation. So that, by this account, lying is the last relief of a routed, earth-born, rebellious party in a state. But here the moderns have made great additions, applying their art to the gaining of power and preserving it, as well as revenging themselves after they have lost it; as the same instruments are made use of by animals to feed themselves when they are hungry, and to bite those that tread upon them.

But the same genealogy cannot always be admitted for political lying; I shall therefore desire to refine upon it, by adding some circumstances of its birth and parents. A political lie is sometimes born out of a discarded stateman's head, and thence delivered to be nursed and dandled by a rabble. Sometimes it is pronounced a monster, and licked into shape: at other times it comes into the world completely formed, and is spoiled in the licking. It is often born an infant in the regular way, and requires time to mature it; and often it sees the light in its full growth, but dwindles away by degrees. Sometimes it

---

1. An allusion to the Earl of Wharton, Lord Lieutenant of Ireland at this time and the object of Swift's satire here.

is of noble birth, and sometimes the spawn of a stock-jobber.
Here it screams aloud at the opening of the womb, and there
it is delivered with a whisper. I know a lie that now disturbs
half the kingdom with its noise, which, although too proud
and great at present to own its parents, I can remember its
whisperhood. To conclude the nativity of this monster; when
it comes into the world without a sting it is still-born; and
whenever it loses its sting it dies.

No wonder if an infant so miraculous in its birth should
be destined for great adventures; and accordingly we see it
has been the guardian spirit of a prevailing party[1] for almost
twenty years. It can conquer kingdoms without fighting, and
sometimes with the loss of battle. It gives and resumes employments; can sink a mountain to a mole-hill, and raise a mole-
hill to a mountain: has presided for many years at committees
of elections; can wash a blackmoor white; make a saint of an
atheist, and a patriot of a profligate; can furnish foreign ministers with intelligence, and raise or let fall the credit of the
nation. This goddess flies with a huge looking-glass in her hands,
to dazzle the crowd, and make them see, according as she turns
it, their ruin in their interest, and their interest in their ruin.
In this glass you will behold your best friends, clad in coats
powdered with *fleurs de lis* and triple crowns;[2] their girdles hung
round with chains, and beads, and wooden shoes; and your
worst enemies adorned with the ensigns of liberty, property,
indulgence, moderation, and a cornucopia in their hands. Her
large wings, like those of a flying-fish, are of no use but while
they were moist; she therefore dips them in mud, and, soaring
aloft, scatters it in the eyes of the multitude, flying with great
swiftness; but at every turn is forced to stoop in dirty ways
for new supplies.

I have been sometimes thinking, if a man had the art of
the second sight for seeing lies, as they have in Scotland for

---

1. I.e., the Whigs.
2. Emblems of France, a major defender of Catholicism and papal power.

seeing spirits, how admirably he might entertain himself in this town, by observing the different shapes, sizes, and colours of those swarms of lies which buzz about the heads of some people, like flies about a horse's ears in summer; or those legions hovering every afternoon in Exchange-alley,[1] enough to darken the air; or over a club of discontented grandees, and thence sent down in cargoes to be scattered at elections.

There is one essential point wherein a political liar differs from others of the faculty, that he ought to have but a short memory, which is necessary, according to the various occasions he meets with every hour of differing from himself, and swearing to both sides of a contradiction, as he finds the persons disposed with whom he has to deal. In describing the virtues and vices of mankind, it is convenient, upon every article, to have some eminent person in our eye, from whom we copy our description. I have strictly observed this rule, and my imagination this minute represents before me a certain great man[2] famous for this talent, to the constant practice of which he owes his twenty years' reputation of the most skillful head in England for the management of nice affairs. The superiority of his genius consists in nothing else but an inexhaustible fund of political lies, which he plentifully distributes every minute he speaks, and by an unparalleled generosity forgets, and consequently contradicts, the next half hour. He never yet considered whether any proposition were true or false, but whether it were convenient for the present minute or company to affirm or deny it; so that, if you think fit to refine upon him, by interpreting everything he says, as we do dreams, by the contrary, you are still to seek, and will find yourself equally deceived whether you believe or not: the only remedy is to suppose that you have heard some inarticulate sounds, without any meaning at all; and besides, that will take off the horror you might be apt to conceive at the oaths wherewith he

---

1. The center of commerce in London.
2. Wharton.

perpetually tags both ends of every proposition: although, at the same time, I think he cannot with any justice be taxed with perjury when he invokes God and Christ, because he has often fairly given public notice to the world that he believes in neither.

Some people may think that such an accomplishment as this can be of no great use to the owner, or his party, after it has been often practised and is become notorious; but they are widely mistaken. Few lies carry the inventor's mark, and the most prostitute enemy to truth may spread a thousand without being known for the author: besides, as the vilest writer has his readers, so the greatest liar has his believers: and it often happens that, if a lie be believed only for an hour, it has done its work, and there is no further occasion for it. Falsehood flies, and truth comes limping after it, so that when men come to be undeceived it is too late; the jest is over, and the tale has had its effect: like a man who has thought of a good repartee when the discourse is changed or the company parted; or like a physician who has found out an infallible medicine after the patient is dead.

Considering that natural disposition in many men to lie, and in multitudes to believe, I have been perplexed what to do with that maxim so frequent in everybody's mouth, that truth will at last prevail. Here has this island of ours, for the greatest part of twenty years, lain under the influence of such counsels and persons, whose principle and interest it was to corrupt our manners, blind our understanding, drain our wealth, and in time destroy our constitution both in church and state, and we at last were brought to the very brink of ruin; yet by the means of perpetual misrepresentations, have never been able to distinguish between our enemies and friends. We have seen a great part of the nation's money got into the hands of those who, by their birth, education, and merit, could pretend no higher than to wear our liveries; while others, who, by their credit, quality, and fortune, were only able to give reputation and success to the Revolution, were not only laid aside as dangerous and useless, but loaded with the scandal of Jacobites, men of arbitrary principles, and pensioners to France; while truth, who is said to lie in a well, seemed now to be buried there under a heap of stones. But I remember it was a usual complaint among the Whigs, that the bulk of landed men was not in their interests, which some of the wisest looked on as an ill omen; and we saw it was with the utmost difficulty that they could preserve a majority, while the court and ministry were on their side, till they had learned those admirable expedients for deciding elections and influencing distant boroughs by powerful motives[1] from the city. But all this was mere force and constraint, however upheld by most dexterous artifice and management, until the people began to apprehend their properties, their religion, and the monarchy itself in danger; when we saw them greedily laying hold on the first occasion to interpose. But of this mighty change in the dispositions of the people I shall discourse more at large in some following paper: wherein I shall endeavour to undeceive or discover those deluded or deluding persons who hope or pretend it is only a short madness in the vulgar, from which they may soon recover; whereas, I believe it will appear to be very different in its causes, its symptoms, and its consequences; and prove a great example to illustrate the maxim I lately mentioned, that truth (however sometimes late) will at last prevail.

---

1. I.e., bribery.

The Drapier Letters

DRAPIER LETTER, NO. 1

TO THE TRADESMEN, SHOPKEEPERS, FARMERS, AND COUNTRY PEOPLE IN GENERAL, OF THE KINGDOM OF IRELAND

CONCERNING THE BRASS HALFPENCE COINED BY ONE WILLIAM WOOD, HARDWAREMAN, WITH A DESIGN TO HAVE THEM PASS IN THIS KINGDOM:

Wherein is shown the power of his Patent, the value of his Halfpence, and how far every person may be obliged to take the same in payments, and how to behave himself, in case such an attempt should be made by Wood, or any other person.

(VERY PROPER TO BE KEPT IN EVERY FAMILY.)

BY M. B. DRAPIER. 1724.[1]

BRETHREN, FRIENDS, COUNTRYMEN,
AND FELLOW-SUBJECTS,

WHAT I intended now to say to you is, next to your duty to God and the care of your salvation, of the greatest concern to yourselves and your children: your bread and clothing, and every common necessary of life, entirely depend upon it. Therefore I do most earnestly exhort you as men, as Christians, as parents, and as lovers of your country, to read this paper with the utmost attention, or get it read to you by others; which that you may do at the less expense, I have ordered the printer to sell it at the lowest rate.

---

1. We do not know the significance of the initials "M. B." or why Swift chose "Drapier" in place of the more common "Draper."

It is a great fault among you, that when a person writes with no other intention than to do you good, you will not be at the pains to read his advices. One copy of this paper may serve a dozen of you, which will be less than a farthing a-piece. It is your folly that you have no common or general interest in your view, not even the wisest among you; neither do you know, or inquire, or care, who are your friends, or who are your enemies.

About four years ago a little book[1] was written, to advise all people to wear the manufactures of this our own dear country. It had no other design, said nothing against the king or parliament, or any person whatsoever; yet the poor printer was prosecuted two years with the utmost violence, and even some weavers themselves (for whose sake it was written), being upon the JURY, found him guilty. This would be enough to discourage any man from endeavouring to do you good, when you will either neglect him or fly in his face for his pains, and when he must expect only danger to himself, and to be fined and imprisoned, perhaps to his ruin.

However, I cannot but warn you once more of the manifest destruction before your eyes, if you do not behave yourselves as you ought.

I will therefore first tell you the plain story of the fact; and then I will lay before you how you ought to act, in common prudence, according to the laws of your country.

The fact is this: It having been many years since COPPER HALFPENCE OR FARTHINGS were last coined in this kingdom, they have been for some time very scarce, and many counterfeits passed about under the name of *raps:* several applications were made to England that we might have liberty to coin new ones, as in former times we did; but they did not succeed. At last, one Mr. Wood, a mean ordinary man, a hardware-dealer, procured a patent under His Majesty's broad seal to coin 108,000*l.* in copper for this kingdom; which patent, however, did not

---

1. Swift's *Proposal for the Universal Use of Irish Manufacture* (1720).

oblige any one here to take them, unless they pleased. Now you must know that the halfpence and farthings in England pass for very little more than they are worth; and if you should beat them to pieces, and sell them to the brazier, you would not lose much above a penny in a shilling. But Mr. Wood made his halfpence of such base metal, and so much smaller than the English ones, that the brazier would hardly give you above a penny of good money for a shilling of his; so that this sum of 108,000*l.* in good gold and silver, must be given for trash that will not be worth eight or nine thousand pounds real value. But this is not the worst; for Mr. Wood, when he pleases, may by stealth send over another 108,000*l.*, and buy all our goods for eleven parts in twelve under the value. For example, if a hatter sells a dozen of hats for 5*s.* a-piece, which amounts to 3*l.*, and receives the payment in Wood's coin, he really receives only the value of 5*s.*

Perhaps you will wonder how such an ordinary fellow as this Mr. Wood could have so much interest as to get His Majesty's broad seal for so great a sum of bad money to be sent to this poor country; and that all the nobility and gentry here could not obtain the same favour, and let us make our own halfpence as we used to do. Now I will make that matter very plain: we are at a great distance from the King's court, and have nobody there to solicit for us, although a great number of lords and squires whose estates are here, and are our countrymen, spend all their lives and fortunes there; but this same Mr. Wood was able to attend constantly for his own interest; he is an Englishman, and had great friends;[1] and, it seems, knew very well where to give money to those that would speak to others, that could speak to the King and would tell a fair story. And His Majesty, and perhaps the great lord or lords who advise him, might think it was for our country's good; and so, as the lawyers express it, "the King was deceived

---

1. A reference to the rumor that Wood might have purchased the patent from a royal mistress, the Duchess of Kendal.

in his grant," which often happens in all reigns. And I am sure if His Majesty knew that such a patent, if it should take effect according to the desire of Mr. Wood, would utterly ruin this kingdom, which has given such great proofs of its loyalty, he would immediately recall it, and perhaps show his displeasure to somebody or other, but a word to the wise is enough. Most of you must have heard with what anger our honourable House of Commons received an account of this Wood's patent. There were several fine speeches made upon upon it, and plain proofs that it was all a wicked cheat from the bottom to the top; and several smart votes were printed, which that same Wood had the assurance to answer likewise in print; and in so confident a way, as if he were a better man than our whole Parliament put together.

This Wood, as soon as his patent was passed, or soon after, sends over a great many barrels of those halfpence to Cork and other sea-port towns; and to get them off, offered a hundred pounds in his coin for seventy or eighty in silver; but the collectors of the King's customs very honestly refused to take them, and so did almost everybody else. And since the Parliament has condemned them, and desired the King that they might be stopped, all the kingdom do abominate them.

But Wood is still working underhand to force his halfpence upon us; and if he can, by the help of his friends in England, prevail so far as to get an order that the commissioners and collectors of the King's money shall receive them, and that the army is to be paid with them, then he thinks his work shall be done. And this is the difficulty you will be under in such a case; for the common soldier, when he goes to the market or alehouse, will offer this money; and if it be refused, perhaps he will swagger and hector and threaten to beat the butcher or alewife, or take the goods by force, and throw them the bad halfpence. In this and the like cases, the shopkeeper or victualler, or any other tradesman, has no more to do than to demand ten times the price of his goods, if it is to be paid in Wood's money; for example, 20*d.* of that money for a quart of ale, and so in all things else, and not part with his goods till he gets the money.

For, suppose you go to an alehouse with that base money, and the landlord gives you a quart for four of these halfpence, what must the victualler do? His brewer will not be paid in that coin; or, if the brewer should be such a fool, the farmers will not take it from them for their bere,[1] because they are bound by their leases to pay their rent in good and lawful money of England; which this is not, nor of Ireland neither; and the 'squire their landlord, will never be so bewitched to take such trash for his land; so that it must certainly stop somewhere or other; and wherever it stops, it is the same thing, and we are all undone.

The common weight of these halfpence is between four and five to an ounce—suppose five; then 3s. 4d. will weigh a pound, and consequently 20s. will weight six pounds butter weight.[2] Now there are many hundred farmers who pay 200l. a-year rent; therefore, when one of these farmers comes with his half-year's rent, which is 100l., it will be at least 600 pounds weight, which is three horses' load.

If a 'squire has a mind to come to town to buy clothes, and wine, and spices, for himself and family, or perhaps to pass the winter here, he must bring with him five or six horses loaden with sacks, as the farmers bring their corn; and when his lady comes in her coach to our shops, it must be followed by a car loaden with Mr. Wood's money. And I hope we shall have the grace to take it for no more than it is worth.

They say 'Squire Conolly[3] has 16,000l. a-year; now, if he sends for his rent to town, as it is likely he does, he must have 250 horses to bring up his half-year's rent, and two or three great cellars in his house for stowage. But what the

---

1. A sort of barley in Ireland.
2. Eighteen or more ounces to the pound.
3. William Conolly, Speaker of the Irish House of Commons, who supported Wood's patent.

bankers will do I cannot tell; for I am assured that some great bankers keep by them 40,000*l.* in ready cash, to answer all payments; which sum, in Mr. Wood's money, would require 1200 horses to carry it.

For my own part, I am already resolved what to do: I have a pretty good shop of Irish stuffs and silks; and instead of taking Mr. Wood's bad copper, I intend to truck with my neighbours the butchers and bakers and brewers, and the rest, goods for goods; and the little gold and silver I have I will keep by me, like my heart's blood, til better times, or until I am just ready to starve; and then I will buy Mr. Wood's money, as my father did the brass money in King James's time,[1] who could buy 10*l.* of it with a guinea; and I hope to get as much for a pistole, and so purchase bread from those who will be such fools as to sell it to me.

These halfpence, if they once pass, will soon be counterfeited, because it may be cheaply done, the stuff is so base. The Dutch likewise will probably do the same thing; and send them over to us to pay for our goods; and Mr. Wood will never be at rest, but coin on: so that in some years we shall have at least five times 108,000*l.* of this lumber. Now the current money of this kingdom is not reckoned to be above 400,000*l.* in all; and while there is a silver sixpence left, these bloodsuckers will never be quiet.

When once the kingdom is reduced to such a condition, I will tell you what must be the end: the gentlemen of estates will all turn off their tenants for want of payments, because, as I told you before, the tenants are obliged by their leases to pay sterling, which is lawful current money of England; then they will turn their own farmers, as too many of them do already, run all into sheep where they can, keeping only such other cattle as are necessary; then they will be their own merchants, and send their wool, and butter, and hides, and

---

1. While in Ireland in 1689-90, James II paid his army in brass coins which he promised to redeem eventually in silver and gold.

linen, beyond sea, for ready money, and wine, and spices, and silks. They will keep only a few miserable cottagers: the farmers must rob, or beg, or leave their country; the shopkeepers in this and every other town must break and starve; for it is the landed man that maintains the merchant, and shopkeeper, and handicraftsman.

But when the 'squire turns farmer and merchant himself, all the good money he gets from abroad he will hoard up to send for England, and keep some poor tailor or weaver, and the like, in his own house, who will be glad to get bread at any rate.

I should never have done if I were to tell you all the miseries that we shall undergo if we be so foolish and wicked as to take this cursed coin. It would be very hard if all Ireland should be put into one scale, and this sorry fellow Wood into the other; and Mr. Wood should weigh down this whole kingdom, by which England gets above a million of good money every year clear into their pockets; and that is more than the English do by all the world besides.

But your great comfort is, that as His Majesty's patent does not oblige you to take this money, so the laws have not given the crown a power of forcing the subject to take what money the King pleases; for then, by the same reason, we might be bound to take pebble-stones, or cockle-shells, or stamped leather, for current coin, if ever we should happen to live under an ill prince; who might likewise, by the same power, make a guinea pass for ten pounds, a shilling for twenty shillings, and so on; by which he would, in a short time, get all the silver and gold of the kingdom into his own hands, and leave us nothing but brass or leather, or what he pleased. Neither is anything reckoned more cruel and oppressive in the French government than their common practice of calling in all their money, after they have sunk it very low, and then coining it anew at a much higher value; which, however, is not the thousandth part so wicked as this abominable project of Mr. Wood. For the French give their subjects silver for silver, and gold for gold; but this fellow will not so much as give us good brass or copper for our gold and silver, not even a twelfth part of their worth.

Having said thus much, I will now go on to tell you the judgment of some great lawyers in this matter, whom I fee'd on purpose for your sakes, and got their opinions under their hands, that I might be sure I went upon good grounds.

A famous law-book, called "The Mirror of Justice,"[1] discoursing of the charters (or laws) ordained by our ancient kings, declares the law to be as follows: "It was ordained that no king of this realm should change or impair the money, or make any other money than gold or silver, without the assent of all the counties;" that is, as my Lord Coke[2] says, without the assent of Parliament.

This book is very ancient, and of great authority for the time in which it was wrote, and with that character is often quoted by that great lawyer my Lord Coke. By the law of England, the several metals are divided into lawful or true metal, and unlawful or false metal; the former comprehends silver and gold, the latter all baser metals. That the former is only to pass in payments appears by an act of Parliament made the 20th year of Edward I, called the 'Statute Concerning the Passing of Pence'; which I give you here as I got it translated into English; for some of our laws at that time were, as I am told, written in Latin: "Whoever, in buying or selling, presumes to refuse a halfpenny or farthing of lawful money, bearing the stamp which it ought to have, let him be seized on as a contemner of the King's majesty, and cast into prison."

By this statute, no person is to be reckoned a contemner of the King's majesty, and for that crime to be committed to prison, but he who refuses to accept the King's coin made of lawful metal; by which, as I observed before, silver and gold only are intended.

---

1. A thirteenth-century collection of laws compiled by Andrew Horn.
2. Sir Edward Coke (1552-1634), the famous juror who insisted that parliamentary prerogatives superseded the King's.

That this is the true construction of the act appears not only from the plain meaning of the words, but from my Lord Coke's observation upon it. "By this act," says he, "it appears that no subject can be forced to take, in buying, or selling, or other payment, any money made but of lawful metal; that is of silver or gold."

The law of England gives the King all mines of gold and silver, but not the mines of other metals; the reason of which prerogative or power, as it is given by my Lord Coke, is, because money can be made of gold and silver, but not of other metals.

Pursuant to this opinion, halfpence and farthings were anciently made of silver, which is evident from the act of Parliament of Henry IV, ch. 4, whereby it is enacted as follows: "Item, for the great scarcity that is at present within the realm of England of halfpence and farthings of silver, it is ordained and established that the third part of all money of silver plate which shall be brought to the bullion shall be made into halfpence and farthings." This shows that by the words "halfpence and farthing of lawful money," in that statute concerning the passing of pence, is meant a small coin in halfpence and farthings of silver.

This is further manifest from the statute of the 9th Edward III, ch. 3, which enacts "that no sterling halfpenny or farthing be molten for to make vessels, or any other thing, by the goldsmiths or others, upon forfeiture of the money so molten" (or melted).

By another act in this king's reign, black money[1] was not to be current in England. And by an act in the 11th year of his reign, ch. 5, galley halfpence were not to pass. What kind of coin these were I do not know, but I presume they were made of base metal. And these acts were no new laws, but further declarations of the old laws relative to the coin.

Thus the law stands in relation to coin. Nor is there any example to the contrary, except one in Davis's Reports,[2] who

---

1. Money made of inferior metal.
2. *Le Primer Report* (1615) by Sir John Davis, Attorney General for Ireland.

tells us "that in the time of Tyrone's rebellion,[1] Queen Elizabeth ordered money of mixed metal to be coined in the Tower of London, and sent over hither for the payment of the army, obliging all people to receive it; and commanding that all silver money should be taken only as bullion;" that is, for as much as it weighed. Davis tells us several particulars in this matter, too long here to trouble you with, and "that the privy-council of this kingdom obliged a merchant in England to receive this mixed money for goods transmitted hither."

But this proceeding is rejected by all the best lawyers, as contrary to law, the privy-council here having no such legal power. And besides, it is to be considered that the Queen was then under great difficulties by a rebellion in this kingdom, assisted from Spain; and whatever is done in great exigencies and dangerous times should never be an example to proceed by in seasons of peace and quietness.

I will now, my dear friends, to save you the trouble, set before you, in short, what the law obliges you to do, and what it does not oblige you to.

1st. You are obliged to take all money in payments which is coined by the King, and is of the English standard or weight, provided it be of gold or silver.

2dly. You are not obliged to take any money which is not of gold or silver; not only the halfpence or farthings of England, but of any other country. And it is merely for convenience or ease that you are content to take them; because the custom of coining silver halfpence and farthings has long been left off, I suppose on account of their being subject to be lost.

3dly. Much less are you obliged to take those vile halfpence of the same Wood, by which you must lose almost eleven pence in every shilling.

Therefore, my friends, stand to it one and all; refuse this filthy trash. It is no treason to rebel against Mr. Wood. His Majesty, in his patent, obliges nobody to take these halfpence:

---

1. A rebellion in Ireland, led by the Earl of Tyrone (1598–1603).

our gracious prince has no such ill advisers about him: or, if he had, yet you see the laws have not left it in the King's power to force us to take any coin but what is lawful, of right standard gold and silver. Therefore you have nothing to fear.

And let me in the next place apply myself particularly to you who are the poorer sort of tradesmen. Perhaps you may think you will not be so great losers as the rich if these halfpence should pass; because you seldom see any silver, and your customers come to your shops or stalls with nothing but brass, which you likewise find hard to be got. But you may take my word, whenever this money gains footing among you you will be utterly undone. If you carry the halfpence to a shop for tobacco or brandy, or any other thing that you want, the shopkeeper will advance his goods accordingly, or else he must break, and leave the key under the door. "Do you think I will sell you a yard of ten-penny stuff for twenty of Mr. Wood's halfpence? No, not under 200 at least; neither will I be at the trouble of counting but weigh them in a lump." I will tell you one thing further, that if Mr. Wood's project should take, it would ruin even our beggars; for when I give a beggar a halfpenny, it will quench his thirst, or go a good way to fill his belly; but the twelfth part of a half-penny will do him no more service than if I should give him three pins out of my sleeve.

In short, these halfpence are like the "accursed thing, which," as the Scripture tells us, "the children of Israel were forbidden to touch." They will run about like the plague, and destroy every one who lays his hands upon them. I have heard scholars talk of a man who told the King that he had invented a way to torment people, by putting them into a bull of brass with fire under it; but the prince put the projector first into his brazen bull, to make the experiment. This very much resembles the project of Mr. Wood; and the like of this may possibly be Mr. Wood's fate; that the brass he contrived to torment this kingdom with may prove his own torment and his destruction at last.

N.B. The author of this paper is informed, by persons who have made it their business to be exact in their observations on the true value of these halfpence that any person may expect to get a quart of two-penny ale for thirty-six of them.

I desire that all families may keep this paper carefully by them, to refresh their memories whenever they shall have further notice of Mr. Wood's halfpence, or any other like imposture.

DRAPIER LETTER, NO. 4

TO THE WHOLE PEOPLE OF IRELAND

MY DEAR COUNTRYMEN,

HAVING already written three letters upon so disagreeable a subject as Mr. Wood and his halfpence, I conceived my task was at an end; but I find that cordials must be frequently applied to weak constitutions, political as well as natural. A people long used to hardships lose by degree the very notions of liberty. They look upon themselves as creatures at mercy, and that all impositions laid on them by a stronger hand are, in the phrase of the Report, legal and obligatory. Hence proceed that poverty and lowness of spirit to which a kingdom may be subject, as well as a particular person. And when Esau came fainting from the field at the point to die, it is no wonder that he sold his birthright for a mess of pottage.

I thought I had sufficiently shown to all who could want instruction by what methods they might safely proceed, whenever this coin should be offered to them; and I believe there has not been for many ages an example of any kingdom so firmly united in a point of great importance, as this of ours is at present against that detestable fraud. But however it so happens that some weak people begin to be alarmed anew by rumours industriously spread. Wood prescribes to the news-mongers in London what they are to write. In one of their papers, published here by some obscure printer, (and certainly with a bad design) we are told that the papists in Ireland have entered into an association against his coin, although it be notoriously known that they never once offered to stir in the matter; so that the two houses of Parliament, the privy-council, the great number of corporations, the lord mayor and alderman of Dublin, the grand juries and principal gentlemen of several counties, are stigmatized in a lump under the name of "papists."

This impostor and his crew do likewise give out, that by refusing to receive his dross for sterling we "dispute the King's prerogative, are grown ripe for rebellion, and ready to shake off the dependency of Ireland upon the crown of England." To countenance which reports he has published a paragraph in another newspaper, to let us know that the "lord lieutenant is ordered to come over immediately to settle his halfpence."

I entreat you, my dear countrymen, not to be under the least concern upon these and the like rumours, which are no more than the last howls of a dog dissected alive, as I hope he has sufficiently been. These calumnies are the only reserve that is left him. For surely our continued and (almost) un-exampled loyalty will never be called in question, for not suffering ourselves to be robbed of all that we have by one obscure iron-monger.

As to disputing the King's prerogative, give me leave to explain to those who are ignorant what the meaning of that word *prerogative* is.

The kings of these realms enjoy several powers, wherein the laws have not interposed. So they can make war and peace without the consent of Parliament—and this is a very great prerogative: but if the Parliament does not approve of the war, the King must bear the charge of it out of his own purse—and this is a great check on the crown. So the King has a prerogative to coin money without consent of Parliament; but he cannot compel the subject to take that money except it be sterling, gold or silver, because herein he is limited by law.

Some princes have, indeed, extended their prerogative further than the law allowed them; wherein, however, the lawyers of succeeding ages, as fond as they are of precedents, have never dared to justify them. But to say the truth, it is only of late times that prerogative has been fixed and ascertained;

for whoever reads the history of England will find that some former kings, and those none of the worst, have upon several occasions ventured to control the laws, with very little ceremony or scruple, even later than the days of Queen Elizabeth. In her reign, that pernicious counsel of sending base money hither very narrowly failed of losing the kingdom—being complained of by the lord-deputy, the council, and the whole body of the English here; so that soon after her death it was recalled by her successor, and lawful money paid in exchange.

Having thus given you some notion of what is meant by "the King's prerogative," as far as a tradesman can be thought capable of explaining it, I will only add the opinion of the great Lord Bacon: "That, as God governs the world by the settled laws of nature, which he has made, and never transcends those laws but upon high and important occasions, so among earthly princes those are the wisest and the best who govern by the known laws of the country, and seldomest make use of their prerogative."

Now here you may see that the vile accusation of Wood and his accomplices, charging us with disputing the King's prerogative by refusing his brass, can have no place—because compelling the subject to take any coin which is not sterling is no part of the King's prerogative, and I am very confident if it were so we should be the last of his people to dispute it; as well from that inviolable loyalty we have always paid to His Majesty as from the treatment we might, in such a case, justly expect from some who seem to think we have neither common sense nor common senses. But God be thanked, the best of them are only our fellow-subjects and not our masters. One great merit I am sure we have, which those of English birth can have no pretence to—that our ancestors reduced this kingdom to the obedience of England; for which we have been rewarded with a worse climate,—the privilege of being governed by laws to which we do not consent,—a ruined trade,—a house of peers without jurisdiction,—almost an incapacity for all employments,—and the dread of Wood's halfpence.

But we are so far from disputing the King's prerogative in coining, that we own he has power to give a patent to any man for setting his royal image and superscription upon whatever materials he pleases, and liberty to the patentee to offer them in any country from England to Japan; only attended with one small limitation—that nobody alive is obliged to take them.

Upon these considerations, I was ever against all recourse to England for a remedy against the present impending evil; especially when I observed that the addresses of both houses, after long expectance, produced nothing but a REPORT, altogether in favour of Wood; upon which I made some observations in a former letter,[1] and might at least have made as many more, for it is a paper of as singular a nature as I ever behold.

But I mistake; for before this Report was made, His Majesty's most gracious answer to the House of Lords was sent over, and printed; wherein are these words, granting the patent for coining halfpence and farthings, AGREEABLE TO THE PRACTICE OF HIS ROYAL PREDECESSORS, &c. That King Charles II and King James II (AND THEY ONLY) did grant patents for this purpose is indisputable, and I have shown it at large.[2] Their patents were passed under the great seal of Ireland, by references to Ireland; the copper to be coined in Ireland; the patentee was bound, on demand, to receive his coin back in Ireland and pay silver and gold in return. Wood's patent was made under the great seal of England; the brass coined in England; not the least reference made to Ireland; the sum immense, and the patentee under no obligation to receive it again and give good money for it. This I only mention, because in my private thoughts I have sometimes made a query whether the penner of those words in His Majesty's most gracious answer, "agreeable to the practice of his royal predecessors," had maturely considered the several circumstances which, in my poor opinion, seem to make a difference.

---

1. The first Drapier letter.
2. In the third Drapier letter.

Let me now say something concerning the other great cause of some people's fear, as Wood has taught the London newswriter to express it, that His Excellency the Lord Lieutenant is coming over to settle Wood's halfpence.

We know very well, that the lords lieutenants, for several years past, have not thought this kingdom worthy the honour of their residence longer than was absolutely necessary for the King's business, which consequently wanted no speed in the dispatch. And therefore it naturally fell into most men's thoughts that a new governor, coming at an unusual time, must portend some unusual business to be done; especially if the common report be true that the Parliament, prorogued to I know not when, is by a new summons revoking that prorogation to assemble soon after the arrival; for which extraordinary proceeding the lawyers on the other side the water have, by great good fortune, found two precedents.

All this being granted, it can never enter into my head, that so little a creature as Wood could find credit enough with the King and his ministers, to have the Lord Lieutenant of Ireland sent hither in a hurry upon his errand.

For let us take the whole matter nakedly as it lies before us, without the refinements of some people, with which we have nothing to do. Here is a patent granted under the great seal of England, upon false suggestions, to one William Wood, for coining copper halfpence for Ireland. The Parliament here, upon apprehensions of the worst consequences from the said patent, address the King to have it recalled. This is refused; and a committee of the privy council report to His Majesty that Wood has performed the conditions of his patent. He then is left to do the best he can with his halfpence, no man being obliged to receive them; the people here, being likewise left to themselves, unite as one man, resolving they will have nothing to do with his ware.

By this plain account of the fact it is manifest, that the King and his ministry are wholly out of the case, and the matter is left to be disputed between him and us. Will any man, therefore, attempt to persuade me that a lord lieutenant is to be dispatched over in great haste before the ordinary time, and a Parliament summoned by anticipating a prorogation, merely to put a hundred thousand pounds into the pocket of a sharper, by the ruin of a most loyal kingdom?

But supposing all this to be true, by what arguments could a lord lieutenant prevail on the same Parliament, which addressed with so much zeal and earnestness against this evil, to pass it into a law? I am sure their opinion of Wood and his project is not mended since their last prorogation; and supposing those methods should be used which detractors tell us have been sometimes put in practice for gaining votes, it is well known that in this kingdom there are few employments to be given; and if there were more it is as well known to whose share they must fall.

But, because great numbers of you are altogether ignorant of the affairs of your country, I will tell you some reasons why there are so few employments to be disposed of in this kingdom.

All considerable offices for life are here possessed by those to whom the reversions were granted; and these have been generally followers of the chief governors, or persons who had interest in the court of England. So the Lord Berkeley of Stratton holds that great office of master of the rolls; the Lord Palmerstown is first remembrancer, worth near 2000*l.* per annum. One Dodington, secretary to the Earl of Pembroke, begged the reversion of clerk of the pells, worth 2500*l.* a-year, which he now enjoys by the death of the Lord Newtown. Mr. Southwell is secretary of state, and the Earl of Burlington lord high treasurer of Ireland by inheritance. These are only a few among many others which I have been told of, but cannot remember. Nay, the reversion of several employments during pleasure[1] are granted the same way. This, among many others, is a circumstance whereby the kingdom of Ireland is distinguished

---

1. The right to succeed to an office by the pleasure of the King.

from all other nations upon earth, and makes it so difficult
an affair to get into a civil employ that Mr. Addison was forced
to purchase an old obscure place, called keeper of the records
in Bermingham's tower, of 10*l.* a-year, and to get a salary of
400*l.* annexed to it, though all the records there are not worth
half-a-crown either for curiosity or use. And we lately saw
a favourite secretary[1] descend to be master of the revels, which
by his credit and extortion he has made pretty considerable.
I say nothing of the under-treasurership, worth about 9000*l.*
a-year, nor of the commissioners of the revenue, four of whom
generally live in England, for I think none of these are granted
in reversion. But the jest is, that I have known upon occasion
some of these absent officers as keen against the interest of
Ireland as if they had never been indebted to her for a single
groat.

I confess I have been sometimes tempted to wish that this
project of Wood's might succeed; because I reflected with some
pleasure what a jolly crew it would bring over among us of
lords and squires and pensioners of both sexes, and officers
civil and military, where we should live together as merry and
sociable as beggars, only with this one abatement, that we should
neither have meat to feed nor manufactures to clothe us, unless
we could be content to prance about in coats of mail or eat
brass as ostriches do iron.

I return from this digression to that which gave me the
occasion of making it. And I believe you are now convinced
that if the Parliament of Ireland were as temptable as any other
assembly within a mile of Christendom (which God forbid!),
yet the managers must of necessity fail for want of tools to
work with. But I will yet go one step further, by supposing
that a hundred new employments were erected on purpose
to gratify compliers; yet still an insuperable difficulty would
remain. For it happens, I know not how, that money is neither

---

1. Edward Hopkins, English MP and secretary to the Duke of Grafton,
then Lord Lieutenant of Ireland.

Whig nor Tory, neither of town nor country party; and it is not improbable, that a gentleman would rather choose to live upon his own estate, which brings gold and silver, than with the addition of an employment, when his rents and salary must both be paid in Wood's brass at above 80 per cent. discount.

For these and many other reasons I am confident you need not be under the least apprehension from the sudden expectation of the Lord Lieutenant,[1] while we continue in our present hearty disposition, to alter which no suitable temptation can possibly be offered. And if, as I have often asserted from the best authority, the law has not left a power in the Crown to force any money, except sterling, upon the subject, much less can the crown devolve such a power upon another.

This I speak with the utmost respect to the person and dignity of His Excellency the Lord Carteret, whose character was lately given me by a gentleman that has known him from his first appearance in the world. That gentleman describes him as a young man of great accomplishments, excellent learning, regular in his life, and of much spirit and vivacity. He has since, as I have heard, been employed abroad; was principal secretary of state; and is now, about the thirty-seventh year of his age, appointed Lord Lieutenant of Ireland. From such a governor this kingdom may reasonably hope for as much prosperity as, under so many discouragements, it can be capable of receiving.

It is true, indeed, that within the memory of man there have been governors of so much dexterity as to carry points of terrible consequence to this kingdom by their power with those who are in office; and by their arts in managing or deluding others with oaths, affability, and even with dinners. If Wood's brass had in those times been upon the anvil, it is obvious enough to conceive what methods would have been taken. Depending persons would have been told in plain terms, "that

---

1. Lord Carteret, afterwards Earl Granville, in some respects a favorite of the dean.

it was a service expected from them, under the pain of the public business being put into more complying hands." Others would be allured by promises. To the country gentlemen, beside good words, burgundy, and closeting,[1] it might perhaps have been hinted, "how kindly it would be taken to comply with a royal patent, although it were not compulsory; that if any inconveniencies ensued, it might be made up with other graces or favours hereafter; that gentlemen ought to consider whether it were prudent or safe to disgust England. They would be desired to think of some good bills for encouraging of trade and setting the poor to work; some further acts against popery, and for uniting Protestants." There would be solemn engagements, "that we should never be troubled with above 40,000*l.* in his coin, and all of the best and weightiest sort, for which we should only give our manufactures in exchange, and keep our gold and silver at home." Perhaps a seasonable report of some invasion would have been spread in the most proper juncture; which is a great smoother of rubs in public proceedings; and we should have been told "that this was no time to create differences when the kingdom was in danger."

These, I say, and the like methods would, in corrupt times, have been taken to let in this deluge of brass among us; and I am confident, even then would not have succeeded; much less under the administration of so excellent a person as the Lord Carteret, and in a country where the people of all ranks, parties and denominations, are convinced to a man that the utter undoing of themselves and their posterity for ever will be dated from the admission of that execrable coin; that if it once enters, it can be no more confined to a small or moderate quantity than a plague can be confined to a few families; and that no equivalent can be given by any earthly power, any more than a dead carcass can be recovered to life by a cordial.

There is one confortable circumstance in this universal opposition to Mr. Wood, that the people sent over hither from

---

1. The act of intimidating someone during a private discussion.

England, to fill up our vacancies, ecclesiastical, civil and military, are all on our side. Money, the great divider of the world, has, by a strange revolution, been a great uniter of a most divided people. Who would leave 100*l*. a-year in England (a country of freedom) to be paid 1000*l*. in Ireland out of Wood's exchequer? The gentleman they have lately made a primate[1] would never quit his seat in an English House of Lords, and his preferments at Oxford and Bristol, worth 1200*l*. a-year, for four times the denomination here but not half the value; therefore, I expect to hear he will be as good an Irishman, at least upon this one article, as any of his brethren, or even of us who have had the misfortune to be born in this island. For those who in the common phrase do not come hither to learn the language would never change a better country for a worse, to receive brass instead of gold.

Another slander spread by Wood and his emissaries is "that by opposing him we discover an inclination to throw off our dependence upon the crown of England." Pray observe how important a person is this same William Wood, and how the public weal of two kingdoms is involved in his private interest. First, all those who refuse to take his coin are papists; for he tells us, "that none but papists are associated against him." Secondly, "they dispute the King's prerogative." Thirdly, "they are ripe for rebellion." And fourthly, "they are going to shake off their dependence upon the crown of England;" that is to say, they are going to choose another king; for there can be no other meaning in this expression, however some may pretend to strain it.

And this gives me an opportunity of explaining, to those who are ignorant, another point, which has often swelled in my breast. Those who come over hither to us from England, and some weak people among ourselves, whenever in discourse we make mention of liberty and property, shake their heads,

---

1. Hugh Boulter, Primate of England, a man Swift regarded as a tool of the English.

and tell us that "Ireland is a depending kingdom;"[1] as if they would seem by this phrase to intend that the people of Ireland are in some state of slavery or dependence different from those of England; whereas a depending kingdom is a modern term of art, unknown, as I have heard, to all ancient civilians and writers upon government, and Ireland is, on the contrary, called in some statutes "an imperial crown," as held only from God; which is as high a style as any kingdom is capable of receiving. Therefore, by this expression, "a depending kingdom," there is no more to be understood than that by a statute made here in the 33rd year of Henry VIII,[2] the King and his successors are to be kings imperial of this realm, as united and knit to the imperial crown of England. I have looked over all the English and Irish statutes without finding any law that makes Ireland depend upon England, any more than England does upon Ireland. We have indeed obliged ourselves to have the same king with them; and consequently they are obliged to have the same king with us. For the law was made by our own Parliament; and our ancestors then were not such fools (whatever they were in the preceeding reign) to bring themselves under I know not what dependence, which is now talked of without any ground of law, reason, or common sense.

Let whoever thinks otherwise, I, M. B., drapier, desire to be excepted; for I declare, next under God, I depend only on the King my sovereign and on the laws of my own country. And I am so far from depending upon the people of England, that if they should ever rebel against my sovereign (which God forbid!) I would be ready, at the first command from His Majesty, to take arms against them, as some of my countrymen did

---

1. This passage was one of those selected for prosecution by the government.

2. In 1541, Henry VIII had the Irish Parliament change his title from "Lord of Ireland" to "King of his land of Ireland as united, annexed, and knit forever to the imperial crown of the realm of England."

against theirs at Preston.[1] And if such a rebellion should prove so successful as to fix the Pretender on the throne of England, I would venture to trangress that statute so far as to lose every drop of my blood to hinder him from being King of Ireland.[2]

It is true, indeed, that within the memory of man the parliaments of England have sometimes assumed the power of binding this kingdom by laws enacted there,[3] wherein they were at first openly opposed (as far as truth, reason, and justice, are capable of opposing) by the famous Mr. Molyneux,[4] an English gentleman born here, as well as by several of the greatest patriots and best Whigs in England; but the love and torrent of power prevailed. Indeed the arguments on both sides were invincible. For in reason, all government without the consent of the governed is the very definition of slavery; but in fact, eleven men well armed will certainly subdue one single man in his shirt. But I have done; for those who have used power to cramp liberty, have gone so far as to resent even the liberty of complaining; although a man upon the rack was never known to be refused the liberty of roaring as loud as he thought fit.

And as we are apt to sink too much under unreasonable fears, so we are too soon inclined to be raised by groundless hopes, according to the nature of all consumptive bodies like ours. Thus it has been given about for several days past that somebody[5] in England empowered a second somebody to write a third somebody here to assure us that we should no more be troubled with these halfpence. And this is reported to have

---

1. In 1715, an English army, including loyalist Irish troops, defeated a rebel army attempting to reinstate the Stuarts on the English throne. The decisive battle took place at Preston in Lancashire.

2. This paragraph gave great offense.

3. During the reigns of Charles II and William III, Parliament passed severely protectionist laws, especially against Irish trade.

4. William Molyneux, the friend of Swift who was a philosopher, a scholar, patriot, and author of a book defending Ireland.

5. Sir Robert Walpole, afterwards Earl of Oxford and Prime Minister of England.

been done by the same person[1] who is said to have sworn some months ago "that he would ram them down our throats," though I doubt they would stick in our stomachs; but whichever of these reports be true or false, it is no concern of ours. For in this point we have nothing to do with English ministers, and I should be sorry to leave it in their power to redress this grievance or to enforce it, for the report of the committee has given me a surfeit. The remedy is wholly in your own hands, and therefore I have digressed a little in order to refresh and continue that spirit so seasonably raised among you, and to let you see that, by the laws of GOD, of NATURE, of NATIONS, and of your COUNTRY, you ARE and OUGHT to be as FREE a people as your brethen in England.

If the pamphlets published at London by Wood and his journeymen, in defence of his cause, were reprinted here, and our countrymen could be persuaded to read them, they would convince you of his wicked design more than all I shall ever be able to say. In short, I make him a perfect saint in comparison of what he appears to be from the writings of those whom he hires to justify his project. But he is so far master of the field (let others guess the reason) that no London printer dare publish any paper written in favour of Ireland; and here, nobody as yet has been so bold as to publish anything in favour of him.

There was a few days ago a pamphlet sent me of near fifty pages,[2] written in favour of Mr. Wood and his coinage, printed in London; it is not worth answering because probably it will never be published here. But it gave me occasion to reflect upon an unhappiness we lie under, that the people of England are utterly ignorant of our case; which however is no wonder, since it is a point they do not in the least concern

---

1. Walpole
2. This was an anonymous pamphlet entitled *Some Farther Account of the Original Disputes in Ireland About Farthings and Half-pence. In A Discourse with a Quaker of Dublin.*

themselves about, further than perhaps as a subject of discourse in a coffeehouse when they have nothing else to talk of. For I have reason to believe that no minister ever gave himself the trouble of reading any papers written in our defence, because I suppose their opinions are already determined, and are formed wholly upon the reports of Wood and his accomplices; else it would be impossible that any man could have the impudence to write such a pamphlet as I have mentioned.

Our neighbours, whose understandings are just upon a level with ours (which perhaps are none of the brightest), have a strong contempt for most nations, but especially for Ireland. They look upon us as a sort of savage Irish whom our ancestors conquered several hundred years ago. And if I should describe the Britons to you as they were in Caesar's time, when they painted their bodies or clothed themselves with the skins of beasts, I should act full as reasonably as they do. However, they are so far to be excused in relation to the present subject, that hearing only one side of the cause, and having neither opportunity nor curiosity to examine the other, they believe a lie merely for their ease; and conclude, because Mr. Wood pretends to power, he has also reason on his side.

Therefore, to let you see how this case is represented in England by Wood and his adherents, I have thought it proper to extract out of that pamphlet a few of those notorious falsehoods, in point of fact and reasoning, contained therein; the knowledge whereof will confirm my countrymen in their own right sentiments, when they will see, by comparing both, how much their enemies are in the wrong.

1st. The writer positively asserts, "that Wood's halfpence were current among us for several months, with the universal approbation of all people, without one single gainsayer; and we all to a man thought ourselves happy in having them."

2dly. He affirms, "that we were drawn into dislike of them only by some cunning, evil-designing men among us, who opposed this patent of Wood to get another for themselves."

3dly. "That those who most declared at first against Wood's

patent were the very men who intend to get another for themselves."

4thly. "That our Parliament and privy council, the lord
mayor and aldermen of Dublin, the grand juries and merchants,
and in short the whole kingdom, nay the very dogs," as he
expresses it, "were fond of those halfpence, till they they were
inflamed by those few designing persons aforesaid."

5thly. He says directly, "that all those who opposed the
halfpence were papists, and enemies to King George."

Thus far, I am confident, the most ignorant among you
can safely swear from your own knowledge that the author
is a most notorious liar in every article; the direct contrary
being so manifest to the whole kingdom that, if occasion
required, might get it confirmed under 500,000 hands.

6thly. He would persuade us, "that if we sell 5s. worth
of our goods or manufacturers for 2s. 4d. worth of copper,
although the copper were melted down, and that we could
get 5s. in gold and silver for the said goods; yet to take the
said 2s. 4d. in copper would be greatly for our advantage."

And, lastly he makes us a very fair offer, as empowered
by Wood, "that if we will take off two hundred thousand pounds
in his halfpence for our goods, and likewise pay him three per
cent. interest for thirty years for a hundred and twenty thousand pounds (at which he computes the coinage above the
intrinsic value of the copper) for the loan of his coin, he will
after that time give us good money for what halfpence will
be then left."

Let me place this offer in as clear a light as I can, to show
the insupportable villany and impudence of that incorrigible
wretch. "First," says he, "I will send two hundred thousand
pounds of my coin into your country; the copper I compute
to be, in real value, eighty thousand pounds, and I charge you
with a hundred and twenty thousand pounds for the coinage;
so that, you see, I lend you a hundred and twenty thousand
pounds for thirty years; for which you shall pay me three per
cent., that is to say, three thousand six hundred pounds per

annum, which in thirty years will amount to a hundred and eight thousand pounds. And when these thirty years are expired return me my copper, and I will give you good money for it."

This is the proposal made to us by Wood in that pamphlet, written by one of his commissioners: and the author is supposed to be the same infamous Coleby, one of his under-swearers at the committee of council, who was tried for robbing the treasury here, where he was an under-clerk.

By this proposal he will, first, receive two hundred thousand pounds in goods or sterling, for as much copper as he values at eighty thousand pounds, but in reality not worth thirty thousand pounds. Secondly, he will receive for interest a hundred and eight thousand pounds: and when our children come thirty years hence to return his halfpence upon his executors (for before that time he will be probably gone to his own place), those executors will very reasonably reject them as raps and counterfeits, which they will be, and millions of them of his own coinage.

Methinks I am fond of such a dealer as this, who mends every day upon our hands, like a Dutch reckoning;[1] wherein if you dispute the unreasonableness and exorbitance of the bill, the landlord shall bring it up every time with new additions.

Although these, and the like pamphlets published by Wood in London, are altogether unknown here, where nobody could read them without as much indignation as contempt would allow, yet I thought it proper to give you a specimen how the man employs his time, where he rides alone without any creature to contradict him; while our FEW FRIENDS there wonder at our silence: and the English in general, if they think of this matter at all, impute our refusal to wilfulness or disaffection, just as Wood and his hirelings are pleased to represent.

But although our arguments are not suffered to be printed in England, yet the consequence will be of little moment. Let Wood endeavour to persuade the people there, that we ought

---

1. A bill that is not itemized and shows only the total that is owed.

to receive his coin; and let me convince our people here, that they ought to reject it, under pain of our utter undoing; and then let him do his best and his worst.

Before I conclude, I must beg leave in all humility to tell Mr. Wood, that he is guilty of great indiscretion, by causing so honourable a name as that of Mr. Walpole to be mentioned so often and in such a manner upon this occasion. A short paper printed at Bristol,[1] and reprinted here, reports Mr. Wood to say, "that he wonders at the impudence and insolence of the Irish in refusing his coin, and what he will do when Mr. Walpole comes to town." Where, by the way, he is mistaken; for it is the true English people of Ireland who refuse it, although we take it for granted that the Irish will do so too whenever they are asked. In another printed paper of his contriving, it is roundly expressed, "that Mr. Walpole will cram his brass down our throats." Sometimes it is given out "that we must either take those halfpence or eat our brogues": and in another newsletter, but of yesterday, we read, "that the same great man has sworn to make us swallow his coin in fireballs."

This brings to my mind the known story of a Scotchman, who, receiving the sentence of death with all the circumstances of hanging, beheading, quartering, embowelling, and the like, cried out, "What need all this COOKERY?" And I think we have reason to ask the same question; for if we believe Wood, here is a dinner getting ready for us; and you see the bill of fare; and I am sorry the drink was forgot, which might easily be supplied with melted lead and flaming pitch.

What vile words are these to put into the mouth of a great counsellor, in high trust with His Majesty and looked upon as a prime minister! If Mr. Wood has no better a manner of representing his patrons, when I come to be a great man, he shall never be suffered to attend at my levee. This is not the

---

1. Another anonymous pamphlet that appeared in 1724, *A Short Defence of the people of Ireland Occasioned by the View of a Letter from Mr. Wood to one of the managers of his Copper Half-pence in Bristol.*

style of a great minister; it savours too much of the kettle and the furnace, and came entirely out of Wood's forge.

As for the threat of making us eat our brogues, we need not be in pain; for if his coin should pass, that unpolite covering for the feet would no longer be a national reproach; because then we should have neither shoe nor brogue left in the kingdom. But here the falsehood of Mr. Wood is fairly detected; for I am confident Mr. Walpole never heard of a brogue in his whole life.

As to "swallowing these halfpence in fire-balls," it is a story equally improbable. For to execute this operation, the whole stock of Mr. Wood's coin and metal must be melted down, and moulded into hollow balls with wild-fire, no bigger than a reasonable throat may be able to swallow. Now, the metal he has prepared, and already coined, will amount to at least fifty millions of halfpence, to be swallowed by a million and half of people: so that, allowing two halfpence to each ball, there will be about seventeen balls of wild-fire a-piece to be swallowed by every person in the kingdom; and to administer this dose, there cannot be conveniently fewer than fifty thousand operators, allowing one operator to every thirty; which, considering the squeamishness of some stomachs, and the peevishness of young children, is but reasonable. Now, under correction of better judgments, I think the trouble and charge of such an experiment would exceed the profit; and therefore I take this report to be spurious, or at least only a new scheme of Mr. Wood himself; which, to make it pass the better in Ireland, he would father upon a minister of state.

But I will now demonstrate beyond all contradiction, that Mr. Walpole is against this project of Mr. Wood and is an entire friend to Ireland, only by this one invincible argument; that he has the universal opinion of being a wise man, an able minister, and in all his proceedings pursuing the true interest of the King his master; and that as his integrity is above all corruption, so is his fortune above all temptation. I reckon, therefore, we are perfectly safe from that corner, and shall never be under the necessity of contending with so formidable a power, but be left to possess our brogues and potatoes in peace, as remote from thunder as we are from Jupiter.[1]

I am, my dear countrymen, your loving fellow-subject, fellow-sufferer, and humble servant, M. B.

Oct. 13, 1724.

---

1. "Procul à Jove, procul à fulmine."

A Modest Proposal

A MODEST PROPOSAL

FOR PREVENTING THE CHILDREN OF POOR PEOPLE IN IRELAND
FROM BEING A BURDEN TO THEIR PARENTS OR THE COUNTRY,
AND FOR MAKING THEM BENEFICIAL TO THE PUBLIC. 1729.

IT is a melancholy object to those who walk through this
great town[1] or travel in the country, when they see the streets,
the roads, and cabin doors, crowded with beggars of the female
sex, followed by three, four, or six children, all in rags and
importuning every passenger for an alms. These mothers, instead
of being able to work for their honest livelihood, are forced
to employ all their time in strolling to beg sustenance for their
helpless infants: who as they grow up either turn thieves for
want of work, or leave their dear native country to fight for
the pretender in Spain,[2] or sell themselves to the Barbadoes.[3]

I think it is agreed by all parties that this prodigious number
of children in the arms, or on the backs, or at the heels of
their mothers, and frequently of their fathers, is in the present
deplorable state of the kingdom a very great additional grievance; and, therefore, whoever could find out a fair, cheap, and
easy method of making these children sound, useful members
of the commonwealth, would deserve so well of the public as
to have his statue set up for a preserver of the nation.

---

1. Dublin.
2. A reference to the fact that many Irish were recruited to fight in
the Spanish and French armies against England. "The Pretender" is the son
of James II who had been forced from the English throne in the Glorious
Revolution of 1688.
3. Many Irish emigrated to the Barbadoes to improve their lot.

But my intention is very far from being confined to provide only for the children of professed beggars; it is of a much greater extent, and shall take in the whole number of infants at a certain age who are born of parents in effect as little able to suport them as those who demand our charity in the streets.

As to my own part, having turned my thoughts for many years upon this important subject, and maturely weighed the several schemes of our projectors,[1] I have always found them grossly mistaken in their computation. It is true, a child just dropped from its dam may be supported by her milk for a solar year, with little other nourishment; at most not above the value of 2*s.*, which the mother may certainly get, or the value in scraps, by her lawful occupation of begging; and it is exactly at one year old that I propose to provide for them in such a manner as instead of being a charge upon their parents or the parish, or wanting food and raiment for the rest of their lives, they shall on the contrary contribute to the feeding, and partly to the clothing, of many thousands.

There is likewise another great advantage in my scheme, that it will prevent those voluntary abortions, and the horrid practice of women murdering their bastard children, alas! too frequent among us! sacrificing the poor innocent babes, I doubt, more to avoid the expense than the shame, which would move tears and pity in the most savage and inhuman breast.

The number of souls in this kingdom being usually reckoned one million and a half, of these I calculate there may be about 200,000 couples whose wives are breeders; from which number I subtract 30,000 couples who are able to maintain their own children (although I apprehend there cannot be so many, under the present distresses of the kingdom); but this being granted, there will remain 170,000 breeders. I again subtract 50,000 for those women who miscarry, or whose children die by accident or disease within the year. There only remains 120,000 children

---

1. In the eighteenth century, the world "projector" meant more than simply "planner." It also referred to someone who proposed foolish projects.

of poor parents annually born. The question therefore is, how this number shall be reared and provided for? which, as I have already said, under the present situation of affairs, is utterly impossible by all the methods hitherto proposed. For we can neither employ them in handicraft or agriculture; we neither build houses (I mean in the country) nor cultivate land; they can very seldom pick up a livelihood by stealing, till they arrive at six years old, except where they are of towardly parts; although I confess they learn the rudiments much earlier; during which time, they can however be properly looked upon only as probationers; as I have been informed by a principal gentleman in the county of Cavan, who protested to me that he never knew above one or two instances under the age of six, even in a part of the kingdom so renowned for the quickest proficiency in that art.

I am assured by our merchants, that a boy or a girl before twelve years old is no saleable commodity; and even when they come to this age they will not yield above 3*l*. or 3*l*. 2*s*. 6*d*. at most on the exchange; which cannot turn to account either to the parents or kingdom, the charge of nutriment and rags having been at least four times that value.

I shall now therefore humbly propose my own thoughts, which I hope will not be liable to the least objection.

I have been assured by a very knowing American of my acquaintance in London, that a young healthy child well nursed is at a year old a most delicious, nourishing, and wholesome food, whether stewed, roasted, baked, or boiled; and I make no doubt that it will equally serve in a fricassee or a ragout.

I do therefore humbly offer it to public consideration that of the 120,000 children already computed, 20,000 may be reserved for breed, whereof only one-fourth part to be males; which is more than we allow to sheep, black cattle or swine; and my reason is, that these children are seldom the fruits of marriage, a circumstance not much regarded by our savages,[1] therefore one male will be sufficient to serve four females.

---

1. I.e., the Irish.

That the remaining 100,000 may, at a year old, be offered in sale to the persons of quality and fortune through the kingdom; always advising the mother to let them suck plentifully in the last month, so as to render them plump and fat for a good table. A child will make two dishes at an entertainment for friends; and when the family dines alone, the fore or hind quarter will make a reasonable dish, and seasoned with a little pepper or salt will be very good boiled on the fourth day, especially in winter.

I have reckoned upon a medium that a child just born will weight 12 pounds, and in a solar year, if tolerably nursed, will increase to 28 pounds.

I grant this food will be somewhat dear, and therefore very proper for landlords, who, as they have already devoured most of the parents, seem to have the best title to the children.

Infant's flesh will be in season throughout the year, but more plentifully in March, and a little before and after; for we are told by a grave author, an eminent French physician, that fish being a prolific diet, there are more children born in Roman Catholic countries about nine months after Lent than at any other season; therefore, reckoning a year after Lent, the markets will be more glutted than usual, because the number of popish infants is at least three to one in this kingdom: and therefore it will have one other collateral advantage, by lessening the number of papists among us.

I have already computed the charge of nursing a beggar's child (in which list I reckon all cottagers, labourers, and four-fifths of the farmers) to be about 2s. per annum, rags included; and I believe no gentleman would repine to give 10s. for the carcass of a good fat child, which, as I have said, will make four dishes of excellent nutritive meat, when he has only some particular friend or his own family to dine with him. Thus the squire will learn to be a good landlord, and grow popular among the tenants; the mother will have 8s. net profit, and be fit for work till she produces another child.

Those who are more thrifty (as I must confess the times

require) may flay the carcass; the skin of which artificially dressed will make admirable gloves for ladies, and summer boots for fine gentlemen.

As to our city of Dublin, shambles[1] may be appointed for this purpose in the most convenient parts of it, and butchers we may be assured will not be wanting; although I rather recommend buying the children alive than dressing them hot from the knife as we do roasting pigs.

A very worthy person, a true lover of his country, and whose virtues I highly esteem, was lately pleased in discoursing on this matter to offer a refinement upon my scheme. He said that many gentlemen of this kingdom, having of late destroyed their deer, he conceived that the want of venison might be well supplied by the bodies of young lads and maidens, not exceeding fourteen years of age nor under twelve; so great a number of both sexes in every country being now ready to starve for want of work and service; and these to be disposed of by their parents, if alive, or otherwise by their nearest relations. But with due deference to so excellent a friend and so deserving a patriot, I cannot be altogether in his sentiments; for as to the males, my American acquaintance assured me, from frequent experience, that their flesh was generally tough and lean, like that of our school-boys by continual exercise, and their taste disagreeable; and to fatten them would not answer the charge. Then as to the females, it would, I think, with humble submission, be a loss to the public, because they soon would become breeders themselves: and besides, it is not improbable that some scrupulous people might be apt to censure such a practice (although indeed very unjustly), as a little bordering upon cruelty; which, I confess, has always been with me the strongest objection against any project, howsoever well intended.

But in order to justify my friend, he confessed that this

---

1. A slaughterhouse, a butcher shop.

expedient was put into his head by the famous Psalmanazar,[1] a native of the island Formosa, who came from thence to London above twenty years ago: and in conversation told my friend, that in his country when any young person happened to be put to death, the executioner sold the carcass to persons of quality as a prime dainty; and that in his time the body of a plump girl of fifteen, who was crucified for an attempt to poison the emperor, was sold to His Imperial Majesty's prime minister of state, and other great mandarins of the court, in joints from the gibbet, at 400 crowns. Neither indeed can I deny, that if the same use were made of several plump girls in this town, who without one single groat to their fortunes cannot stir abroad without a chair, and appear at playhouse and assemblies in foreign fineries which they never will pay for, the kingdom would not be the worse.

Some persons of a desponding spirit are in great concern about that vast number of poor people, who are aged, diseased, or maimed, and I have been desired to employ my thoughts what course may be taken to ease the nation of so grievous an encumbrance. But I am not in the least pain upon that matter, because it is very well known that they are every day dying and rotting by cold and famine, and filth and vermin, as fast as can be reasonably expected. And as to the young labourers, they are now in as hopeful a condition; they cannot get work, and consequently pine away for want of nourishment, to a degree that if at any time they are accidentally hired to common labour, they have not strength to perform it; and thus the country and themselves are happily delivered from the evils to come.

I have too long digressed, and therefore shall return to my subject. I think the advantages by the proposal which I have made are obvious and many, as well as of the highest importance.

---

1. George Psalmanazar, a pseudonym for a French contemporary of Swift who became notorious for a series of impostures. In 1704, he published a "description" of Formosa where he claimed, falsely, that he had been born.

For first, as I have already observed, it would greatly lessen the number of papists, with whom we are yearly overrun, being the principal breeders of the nation as well as our most dangerous enemies; and who stay at home on purpose to deliver the kingdom to the Pretender, hoping to take their advantage by the absence of so many good Protestants, who have chosen rather to leave their country than stay at home and pay tithes against their conscience to an Episcopal curate.

Secondly, The poor tenants will have something valuable of their own, which by law may be made liable to distress and help to pay their landlord's rent, their corn and cattle being already seized, and money a thing unknown.

Thirdly, Whereas the maintenance of 100,000 children, from two years old and upward, cannot be computed at less than 10s. a-piece per annum, the nation's stock will be thereby increased £50,000 per annum, beside the profit of a new dish introduced to the tables of all gentlemen of fortune in the kingdom who have any refinement in taste. And the money will circulate among ourselves, the goods being entirely of our own growth and manufacture.

Fourthly, The constant breeders, beside the gain of 8s. sterling per annum by the sale of their children, will be rid of the charge of maintaining them after the first year.

Fifthly, This food would likewise bring great custom to taverns; where the vintners will certainly be so prudent as to procure the best receipts for dressing it to perfection, and consequently have their houses frequented by all the fine gentlemen, who justly value themselves upon their knowledge in good eating; and a skilful cook, who understands how to oblige his guests, will contrive to make it as expensive as they please.

Sixthly, This would be a great inducement to marriage, which all wise nations have either encouraged by rewards or enforced by laws and penalties. It would increase the care and tenderness of mothers toward their children, when they were sure of a settlement for life to the poor babes, provided in some sort by the public, to their annual profit or expense. We should see an honest emulation among the married women, which of them could bring the fattest child to the market. Men would become as fond of their wives during the time of their pregnancy as they are now of their mares in foal, their cows in calf, their sows when they are ready to farrow; nor offer to beat or kick them (as is too frequent a practice) for fear of a miscarriage.

Many other advantages might be enumerated. For instance, the addition of some thousand carcasses in our exportation of barrelled beef, the propagation of swine's flesh, and improvement in the art of making good bacon, so much wanted among us by the great destruction of pigs, too frequent at our table; which are no way comparable in taste or magnificence to a well-grown, fat, yearling child, which roasted whole will make a considerable figure at a lord mayor's feast or any other public entertainment. But this and many others I omit, being studious of brevity.

Supposing that 1000 familes in this city would be constant customers for infants' flesh, beside others who might have it at merry-meetings, particularly at weddings and christenings, I compute that Dublin would take off annually about 20,000 carcasses; and the rest of the kingdom (where probably they will be sold somewhat cheaper) the remaining 80,000.

I can think of no one objection that will possibly be raised against this proposal, unless it should be urged that the number of people will be thereby much lessened in the kingdom. This I freely own, and it was indeed one principal design in offering it to the world. I desire the reader will observe, that I calculate my remedy for this one individual kingdom of Ireland and for no other that ever was, is, or I think ever can be upon earth. Therefore let no man talk to me of other expedients:[1] *of taxing our absentees at 5s. a pound: of using neither clothes nor household furniture except what is of our own growth and manufacture: of utterly rejecting*

---

1. These expedients were, in fact, measures that Swift had seriously proposed in earlier pieces he had written.

the materials and instruments that promote foreign luxury: of curing the expensiveness of pride, vanity, idleness, and gaming in our women: of introducing a vein of parsimony, prudence, and temperance: of learning to love our country, in the want of which we differ even from LAPLANDERS and the inhabitants of TOPINAMBOO: of quitting our animosities and factions, nor acting any longer like the Jews, who were murdering one another at the very moment their city was taken: of being a little cautious not to sell our country and conscience for nothing: of teaching landlords to have at least one degree of mercy toward their tenants: lastly, of putting a spirit of honesty, industry, and skill into our shopkeepers; who, if a resolution could now be taken to buy only our negative goods, would immediately unite to cheat and exact upon us in the price, the measure, and the goodness, nor could ever yet be brought to make one fair proposal of just dealing, though often and earnestly invited to it.

Therefore I repeat, let no man talk to me of these and the like expedients, till he hath at least some glimpse of hope that there will be ever some hearty and sincere attempt to put them in practice.

But as to myself, having been wearied out for many years with offering vain, idle, visionary thoughts, and at length utterly despairing of success, I fortunately fell upon this proposal; which, as it is wholly new, so it has something solid and real, of no expense and little trouble, full in our own power, and whereby we can incur no danger in disobliging ENGLAND. For this kind of commodity will not bear exportation, the flesh being of too tender a consistence to admit a long continuance in salt, although perhaps I could name a country[1] which would be glad to eat up our whole nation without it.

After all, I am not so violently bent upon my own opinion as to reject any offer proposed by wise men, which shall be found equally innocent, cheap, easy, and effectual. But before something of that kind shall be advanced in contradiction to my scheme, and offering a better, I desire the author or authors will be pleased maturely to consider two points. First, as things

---

1. England, obviously.

now stand, how they will be able to find food and raiment for 100,000 useless mouths and backs. And secondly, there being a round million of creatures in human figure throughout this kingdom, whose whole subsistence put into a common stock would leave them in debt 2,000,000*l.* sterling, adding those who are beggars by profession to the bulk of farmers, cottagers, and labourers, with the wives and children who are beggars in effect; I desire those politicians who dislike my overture, and may perhaps be so bold as to attempt an answer, that they will first ask the parents of these mortals, whether they would not at this day think it a great happiness to have been sold for food at a year old in the manner I prescribe, and thereby have avoided such a perpetual scene of misfortunes as they have since gone through by the oppression of landlords, the impossibility of paying rent without money or trade, the want of common sustenance, with neither house nor clothes to cover them from the inclemencies of the weather, and the most inevitable prospect of entailing the like or greater miseries upon their breed for ever.

I profess, in the sincerity of my heart, that I have not the least personal interest in endeavouring to promote this necessary work, having no other motive than the *public good of my country, by advancing our trade, providing for infants, relieving the poor, and giving some pleasure to the rich.* I have no children by which I can propose to get a single penny; the youngest being nine years old, and my wife past child-bearing.

A Character, Panegyric, and Description of the Legion Club

A CHARACTER, PANEGYRIC, AND DESCRIPTION OF THE LEGION CLUB.[1]
1736.

AS I stroll the city, oft I
See a building large and lofty,
Not a bow-shot from the college;
Half the globe from sense and knowledge:
By the prudent architect
Placed against the church direct,
Making good my grandam's jest,
"Near the church"—you know the rest.[2]
    Tell us what the pile contains?
Many a head that holds no brains.   10
These demoniacs let me dub
With the name of Legion Club.
Such assemblies you might swear
Meet when butchers bait a bear:
Such a noise, and such haranguing,
When a brother thief is hanging:
Such a rout and such a rabble

---

1. Swift took his title from Scriptures, Mark 5: When Jesus asks the "unclean spirit" possessing the man who is "out of the tombs" to identify itself, the response is: "My name is Legion: for we are many." When Jesus subsequently frees the man from his possessing spirit, all "the devils" enter the bodies of a herd of nearby swine. By implication, the Irish Parliament is a legion of hellish spirits and swine, holding forth in their building, which is a kind of asylum for the damned and the mad.
2. I.e., the proverbial "The nearer the Church, the farther from God."

Run to hear Jackpudding[1] gabble:
Such a crowd their ordure throws
On a far less villain's nose.[2]   20
  Could I from the building's top
Hear the rattling thunder drop,
While the devil upon the roof
(If the devil be thunder-proof)
Should, with poker fiery red,
Crack the stones and melt the lead;
Drive them down on every skull,
When the den of thieves is full;
Quite destroy that harpies' nest;
How might then our isle be blest!   30
For divines allow that God
Sometimes makes the devil his rod!
And the gospel will inform us
He can punish sins enormous.
  Yet should Swift endow the schools
For his lunatics and fools
With a rood or two of land,
I allow the pile may stand.
You perhaps will ask me, Why so?
But it is with this proviso.   40
Since the house is like to last,
Let the royal grant be pass'd
That the club have right to dwell
Each within his proper cell,
With a passage left to creep in,
And a hole above for peeping.
  Let them, when they once get in,
Sell the nation for a pin;
While they sit a-picking straws,
Let them rave at making laws;   50

---

1. A buffoon who gathers a crown for a quack-doctor.
2. I.e., the nose of a villain in a pillory.

While they never hold their tongue,
Let them dabble in their dung:
Let them form a grand committee,
How to plague and starve the city;
Let them stare, and storm, and frown,
When they see a clergy gown;
Let them, ere they crack a louse,
Call for th' orders of the house;
Let them, with their gosling-quills,
Scribble senseless heads of bills;   60
We may, while they strain their throats,
Wipe our arses with their votes.[1]

    Let Sir Tom,[2] that rampant ass,
Stuff his guts with flax and grass;
But before the priest he fleeces,
Tear the Bible all to pieces:
At the parsons, Tom, halloo, boy,
Worthy offspring of a shoeboy,
Footman, traitor, vile seducer,
Perjured rebel, bribed accuser,   70
Lay thy paltry privilege aside,
Sprung from papists, and a regicide;
Fall a-working like a mole,
Raise the dirt about your hole.

    Come, assist me, Muse obedient;
Let us try some new expedient;
Shift the scene for half an hour,
Time and place are in thy power.
Thither, gentle Muse, conduct me;
I shall ask, and you instruct me.   80
    See, the Muse unbars the gate;

---

1. I.e., with printed lists of how the MPs voted.
2. Sir Thomas Prendergrast, MP, Postmaster General for Ireland, and hated by Swift for his antagonism toward the Church of Ireland and his opposition to the Church's claims for tithing.

Hark, the monkeys, how they prate!
    All ye gods who rule the soul:
Styx, through hell whose waters roll!
Let me be allow'd to tell
What I heard in yonder hell.
    Near the door an entrance gapes,
Crowded round with antic shapes,
Poverty, and Grief, and Care,   90
Causeless Joy, and true Despair;
Discord periwigg'd with snakes,
See the dreadful strides she takes!
    By this odious crew beset,
I began to rage and fret,
And resolved to break their pates,
Ere we enter'd at the gates;
Had not Clio in the nick
Whisper'd me, "Lay down your stick;"
What! said I, is this the mad-house?   100
These, she answer'd, are but shadows,
Phantoms bodiless and vain,
Empty visions of the brain.
In the porch Briareus[1] stands,
Shows a bribe in all his hands;
Briareus the secretary,
But we mortals call him Carey.[2]
When the rogues their country fleece,
They may hope for pence a-piece.
    Clio, who had been so wise   110
To put on a fool's disguise,
To bespeak some approbation,
And be thought a near relation,

---

1. One of the hundred-handed giants, son of Earth and Sky.
2. Walter Carey, Secretary to the Duke of Dorset, Lord Lieutenant of Ireland, 1730-37. The Secretary was the chief executive of the government in Ireland.

When she saw three hundred brutes[1]
All involved in wild disputes,
Roaring till their lungs were spent,
PRIVILEGE OF PARLIAMENT,
Now a new misfortune feels,
Dreading to be laid by th' heels.
Never durst a Muse before   120
Enter that infernal door;
Clio, stifled with the smell,
Into spleen and vapours fell,
By the Stygian streams that flew
From the dire infectious crew.
Not the stench of Lake Avernus[2]
Could have more offended her nose;
Had she flown but o'er the top,
She had felt her pinions drop,
And by exhalations dire,   130
Though a goddess, must expire.
In a fright she crept away,
Bravely I resolved to stay.
When I saw the keeper frown,
Tipping him with half-a-crown,
Now, said I, we are alone,
Name your heroes one by one,
　　Who is that hell-featured brawler?
Is it Satan? No; 'tis Waller.[3]
In what figure can a bard dress   140
Jack, the grandson of Sir Hardress?
Honest keeper, drive him further,
In his looks are hell and murther;
See his scowling visage drop,

---

1. There were three hundred members in the Irish House of Commons.
2. The lake near Naples whose waters gives off poisonous fumes.
3. John Waller, MP, grandson of one of the regicides, Hardness Waller, who condemned Charles I to death in 1649.

Just as when he murder'd Throp.[1]
    Keeper, show me where to fix
On the puppy pair of Dicks:[2]
By their lantern jaws and leathern,
You might swear they both are brethren:
Dick Fitzbaker, Dick the player,   150
Old acquaintance, are you there?
Dear companions, hug and kiss,
Toast Old Glorious[3] in your piss;
Tie them, keeper, in a tether,
Let them starve and sink together;
Both are apt to be unruly,
Lash them daily, lash them duly;
Though 'tis hopeless to reclaim them,
Scorpion rods, perhaps, may tame them.
    Keeper, yon old dotard smoke,   160
Sweetly snoring in his cloak:
Who is he? 'Tis humdrum Wynne,[4]
Half encompass'd by his kin:
There observe the tribe of Bingham,
For he never fails to bring 'em;
While he sleeps the whole debate,
They submissive round him wait;
Yet would gladly see the hunks
In his grave, and search his trunks:
See, they gently twitch his coat,   170
Just to yawn and give his vote,

---

1. An Irish clergyman, the Reverend Roger Throp, who was persecuted by his patron, John Waller, and who, according to popular belief, was driven to his death by Waller's treatment of him.

2. Richard Tighe, Irish MP and Privy Councillor—also called "Fitzbaker" by Swift. Richard Bettesworth, Irish MP and subject of numerous lampoons. At one point, he threatened to cut off Swift's ears. A subsequent confrontation produced nothing.

3. William III.

4. John Wynne, Irish MP.

Always firm in his vocation,
For the court against the nation.
    Those are Allens, Jack and Bob,[1]
First in every wicked job,
Son and brother to a queer
Brain-sick brute, they call a peer.
We must give them better quarter,
For their ancestor trod mortar,
And at Howth, to boast his fame,   180
On a chimney cut his name.
    There sit Clements, Dilks, and Harrison.[2]
How they swagger from their garrison!
Such a triplet could you tell
Where to find on this side hell?
Harrison, and Dilks, and Clements,
Keeper, see they have their payments,
Every mischief's in their hearts;
If they fail, 'tis want of parts.
    Bless us! Morgan,[3] art thou there, man?   190
Bless mine eyes! art thou the chairman?
Chairman to yon damn'd committee!
Yet I look on thee with pity.
Dreadful sight! what learned Morgan
Metamorphosed to a Gorgon?
For thy horrid looks, I own,
Half convert me to a stone.
Hast thou been so long at school
Now to turn a factious tool?
Alma Mater was thy mother,   200

---

1. John and Robert Allen, brothers, were Irish MPs. Robert had accused Swift of being a liar and a Jacobite supporter of the Stuart Pretender to the English throne. Their great-grandfather ("their ancestor") was a builder.

2. Irish MPs.

3. Marcus Antonius Morgan, Irish MP, chairman of the parliamentary committee that decided against the Irish Church on the tax issue. It was this that prompted Swift to write the poem.

Every young divine thy brother.
Thou, a disobedient varlet
Treat thy mother like a harlot!
Thou ungrateful to thy teachers,
Who are all grown rev'rend preachers?
Morgan, would it not surprise one?
Turn thy nourishment to poison!
When you walk among your books,
They reproach you with their looks;
Bind them fast, or from their shelves   210
They will come and right themselves:
Homer, Plutarch, Virgil, Flaccus,
All in arms, prepare to back us:
Soon repent, or put to slaughter
Every Greek and Roman author.
Will you, in your factious phrase,
Send the clergy all to graze?
And to make your project pass,
Leave them not a blade of grass?

    How I want thee, humorous Hogarth!   220
Thou, I hear, a pleasant rogue art.
Were but you and I acquainted,
Every monster should be painted:
You should try your graving tools
On this odious group of fools;
Draw the beasts as I describe them:
Form their features while I gibe them;
Draw them like; for I assure you,
You will need no *car'catura;*
Draw them so that we may trace   230
All the soul in every face.

    Keeper, I must now retire,
You have done what I desire:
But I feel my spirits spent
With the noise, the sight, the scent.
"Pray, be patient; you shall find

Half the best are still behind!
You have hardly seen a score;
I can show two hundred more."
    Keeper, I have seen enough.   240
Taking then a pinch of snuff,
I concluded looking round them,
"May their god, the devil, confound them!"